God Bless You

周祐明　Jack
2007.12

耶穌愛妳

D1649283

FROM FAR FORMOSA

The Island, its People and Missions

BY

GEORGE LESLIE MACKAY, D.D.

TWENTY-THREE YEARS A MISSIONARY IN FORMOSA

EDITED BY THE

REV. J. A. MACDONALD

WITH PORTRAITS, ILLUSTRATIONS AND MAPS

THIRD EDITION

SMC PUBLISHING INC.
Taipei

Original edition published by
Oliphant Anderson and Ferrier
Edinburgh and London, 1896

Reprinted by SMC Publishing Inc. 2002, 1998 & 1991

SMC PUBLISHING INC.
P.O. Box 13-342, Taipei 106,
Taiwan, Republic of China
☎ (886-2) 2362-0190
Fax (886-2) 2362-3834
http://www.smcbook.com.tw
e-mail:weitw@smcbook.com.tw

ISBN 957-638-072-3

PRINTED IN TAIWAN, R.O.C.

EDITORIAL PREFACE

FORMOSA, at one time far off, has been brought near to the Western world. All eyes were turned upon it when it became the storm-center of the China-Japan War. But there were those who had been looking across the seas to the Beautiful Isle for more than twenty years before the war-cloud darkened the sky. They were interested in its fortunes because of one who had given himself, with Pauline faith and self-renunciation, that it might be redeemed from error and sin. George Leslie MacKay has long been the missionary hero of the Presbyterian Church in Canada.

During his second furlough, which closed when he sailed from Vancouver on October 16, 1895, Dr. MacKay was elected moderator of the General Assembly of his church, and visited many points throughout the Dominion, in the United States, and in Scotland, addressing congregations and conventions. Everywhere and on all occasions the impression made was that of a great man and a hero. The demand for a fuller record of his life and work became increasingly urgent. Friends who knew that his information about Formosa was more extensive and more reliable than that of any other living man, and who believed that an account of his experiences and work would stimulate the faith and zeal of the church, but who feared lest, amid the uncertainties and perils to which his life is constantly exposed, his career should be cut short before any record that might be given to the public had been prepared, impressed upon him the duty of meeting this reasonable demand. To a man of his ardent temperament and active habits prolonged literary work is the most irksome drudgery. He would rather face a heathen mob than write a chapter for a book. But convinced of its importance, he undertook the task, receiving valuable assistance from the Rev. W. S. McTavish, B.D. For weeks together he did little else than ransack note-books and journals, and explore the stores of his capacious memory.

A few months ago Dr. MacKay put into my hands a mass of literary material—notes, observations, extracts from diaries and reports, studies in science, fragments of description, sketches of character—and laid upon me the responsibility of organizing this material into form and life. This responsibility was increased rather than diminished by the very full editorial powers allowed me. I knew how easy it was to be " worlds away " ; for, as Macaulay says about the writing of history, the details might all be true and the total impression inadequate and misleading. Every scrap of material was read and studied under the author's eye, annotations were made at his dictation, and the plan of classification and arrangement received his cordial approval. As the work progressed and the gaps in the story became apparent, additional matter was obtained, and nearly all of the manuscript in its final form was revised by him. The aim in editing has been to preserve in its integrity not only the substance but the literary style of the author—to retain something of the vigor, the boldness, the Celtic enthusiasm, so characteristic of Dr. MacKay's public speech.

It is believed that the intelligent public will appreciate solid information as well as moving incident; and it was Dr. Mac-Kay's desire that prominence should be given to what may be least romantic, but is most instructive. The chapters in the second division of the book, " The Island," are of necessity brief and fragmentary, the exigencies of space preventing the author's supplying fuller information about Formosa, its resources and people. The editor is responsible for much of the personal element found throughout the book, Dr. MacKay reluctantly consenting to the introduction, necessary to an understanding of a foreign missionary's life and work, of many incidents and personal experiences elicited in the course of conversation. While the book was being prepared the political relations of Formosa were being changed; these changes are referred to as likely to affect mission work materially, though not injuriously, but the Chinese view-point is retained.

For several months I was in constant and intimate association with Dr. MacKay, coming into closest touch with him, coming to know him as one is known only to the nearest and most sympathetic friends. To see the man of indomitable energy, unflinching courage, and iron will shrink from anything like self-assertion, and yield without dispute to another's judgment, would be a revelation for which they are not prepared who know him only as a man of speech and action. To see his modest self-effacement, and to know how real his faith is, how personal God is to him, is to grasp the secret of his success. Few men in any age of the church have had a vivider sense of the divine nearness. The God he serves is a pavilioning presence and a prevailing power in his soul. Such a prophet is Christ's greatest gift to his church. To him there can come no failure; whatever ought to be can be.

The publishers have spared no pains in the production of this book. Maps have been specially prepared, the three of North Formosa being reproduced from sketches made by Dr. MacKay, that of the island from the British Admiralty chart; illustrations have been made from photographs taken in Formosa by Koa Kau, Dr. MacKay's Chinese student; the cover design represents the flower of the rice-plant, the rice in the ear, and the method of rice harvesting described in Chapter XXII.; and the greatest care has been taken to avoid mechanical errors, to which a book dealing with life in a foreign country is liable.

It remains only to acknowledge my indebtedness to the Rev. R. P. MacKay, B.A., Toronto, secretary of the Foreign Mission Committee of the Presbyterian Church in Canada, without whose counsel and assistance the editor's work would have been less satisfactory, if, indeed, it could have been done at all in the press of other duties.

"From Far Formosa" is sent out with the prayer that it may be used of God in stimulating intelligent interest in the cause of world-wide missions.

J. A. MACDONALD.

ST. THOMAS, ONTARIO,
November, 1895.

DR. MACKAY, MRS. MACKAY AND FAMILY.

WATER BUFFALOES DRAWING SUGAR CANE.

FORMOSA ABORIGINES EATING RICE.

A VILLAGE IN EASTERN FORMOSA.

Dr. MacKay and Students on the March.

Burden Bearer   A Centurea.   Koa Kau.   Thien-leng.   Sun-a.   A Hoa.   Dr. MacKay.

Dr. MacKay and Students Descending a Mountain.

Chapel at Sin-tiam, Built of Stone.

WINNOWING RICE WITH A FANNING MILL.

212

BOUND FOR THE KI-LAI PLAIN.

ARMED PE-PO-HOAN NEAR SAVAGE TERRITORY.

Lᴀᴍ-ꜱɪ-ʜᴏᴀɴ Cʜɪᴇꜰ ᴀɴᴅ Pᴀʀᴛʏ.

IN A LAM-SI-HOAN VILLAGE.

248

Unsubdued Aborigines Living in the Mountains.

ARMED HEAD HUNTERS,

OXFORD COLLEGE, TAMSUI.

A Pe-po-hoan Weaver—The Matron of the Girls' School.

A Dental Operation—Dr. MacKay, A Hoa and Koa Kau.

CONTENTS

The Conquered Aborigines

The Mountain Savages

At Headquarters

LIST OF ILLUSTRATIONS

INTRODUCTORY

FROM FAR FORMOSA

CHAPTER I

EARLY YEARS OF THE AUTHOR

Point of view—Ancestors—Life in Zorra—William C. Burns—Home-
missionary service

FAR Formosa is dear to my heart. On that island the best
of my years have been spent. There the interest of my
life has been centered. I love to look up to its lofty peaks,
down into its yawning chasms, and away out on its surging
sea. I love its dark-skinned people—Chinese, Pepohoan, and
savage—among whom I have gone these twenty-three years,
preaching the gospel of Jesus. To serve them in the gospel
I would gladly, a thousand times over, give up my life. Before what I now write has been read I will have set my face
once more westward toward the far East, and by God's good
hand will have reached again my beloved Formosan home
beyond the Pacific Sea. There I hope to spend what remains
of my life, and when my day of service is over I should like
to find a resting-place within sound of its surf and under the
shade of its waving bamboo.

I love my island home, but not once in all these years have
I forgotten the land of my childhood or ceased to be proud

of it. Many a time in those first friendless days, when tongues were strange and hearts were hard and the mob howled loudest in the street; many a time among cruel savages in the mountains, when their orgies rose wildest into the night; many a time alone in the awful silence of primeval forests, in solitudes never before disturbed by a white man's tread— many, many a time during these three and twenty years have I looked back from far Formosa, in fancy gazed on my Zorra home, and joined in the morning or evening psalm. Memories of Canada were sweet to me then; and now, when I come to tell something of life in that far-off isle, the view-point I take is life in the land of my birth.

My father, George MacKay, a Scottish Highlander, with his wife, Helen Sutherland, emigrated from Sutherlandshire to Canada in 1830. There had been dark days in Scotland— the dark and gloomy days of the "Sutherlandshire Clearances," when hundreds of tenant-farmers, whose fathers were born on the estate and shed their blood for its duke, were with their wives and families evicted, the wild notes of their pibroch among the hills and the solemn strains of their Gaelic psalms in the glens giving place to the bleating of the sheep and the hallo of the huntsman. Ruined cottages, deserted churches, and desecrated graves were the "gloomy memories" they carried with them from Scotland, and they crossed the sea in time to face the dark and stormy days of the Canadian rebellion. They made their home in what was then the wilds of Upper Canada, and on their farm in the township of Zorra reared their family of six children, of whom I was the youngest; and in the burying-ground beside the "old log church" their weary bodies rest.

Peace to the honored dust of those brave pioneers! They were cast in nature's sternest mold, but were men of heroic soul. Little of this world's goods did they possess. All day long their axes rang in the forests, and at night the smoke of burning log-heaps hung over their humble homes. But they overcame. The wilderness and the solitary place have indeed been made glad. And more. They did more than hew down forests, construct roads, erect homes, and transform sluggish swamps into fields of brown and gold. They worshiped and served the eternal God, taught their children to read the Bible and believe it, listen to conscience and obey it, observe the Sabbath and love it, and to honor and reverence the office of the gospel ministry. Their theology may have been narrow, but it was deep and high. They left a heritage of truth, and their memory is still an inspiration. Their children have risen up to bless them in the gates. From the homes of the congregation that worshiped in the "old log church" at least thirty-eight young men have gone forth to be heralds of the cross in the ministry of the Presbyterian Church.

In such a home and amid such surroundings I was born on the 21st of March, 1844. That was the year of the disruption in Canada, and the Zorra congregation, with the Rev. Donald McKenzie, its minister, joined the Free Church. The type of religious life was distinctly Highland. Men believed and felt, but seldom spoke about their own deeper personal spiritual experiences. There were no Sabbath-schools or Christian Endeavor Societies in Zorra fifty years ago. Children were taught the Bible and the Shorter Catechism in the home, and on the Sabbath in the church the great doctrines of grace were preached with faithfulness and power. Men may talk slightingly to-day about that "stern old Calvinism." They would do well to pause and ask about its fruits. What other creed has so swept the whole field of life with the dread artillery of truth, and made men unflinchingly loyal to conscience and tremorless save in the presence of God? The iron of Calvinism is needed to-day in the blood of the church. It may be we heard much about sin and law in those olden days, but love and grace were not obscured. It may be the children were reticent and backward in the church, but they knew what secret sorrow for sin meant, and they found comfort at the cross. Before I reached the age of ten the ever-blessed Name was sweet and sacred in my ear. The paraphrase beginning with the words

" While humble shepherds watched their flocks
  In Bethlehem's plains by night,"

repeated at my mother's knee in the quiet of the Sabbath evening, early made a deep impression on my soul. It was then that the thought of being a missionary first came. William C. Burns had visited Woodstock and Zorra on his tours through Canada, and poured a new stream into the current of religious life. His name was cherished in the home, and something of his spirit touched my boyish heart. My grandfather fought at Waterloo; his martial soul went into my blood; and when once I owned the Saviour King, the command, " Go ye into all the world, and preach the gospel to every creature," made me a soldier of the cross. To be a missionary became the passion of my life. That was the dominant idea through all the years during which I served as school-teacher at Maplewood and Maitlandville, as scholar at Woodstock and Omemee grammar-schools, as student of arts in Toronto, and as student-missionary during the summer vacations at Blue Mountain, Port Burwell and Vienna, Lucan and Biddulph, Forest and MacKay.

A quarter of a century has passed since I served the church in those struggling home mission fields. The greater part of that time I have been far hence among the heathen, and am called a foreign missionary. But not now—not once in all these years—have I thought the foreign claims superior to the home, or honored the foreign missionary above his equally heroic and equally faithful brother who toils in the obscurity of a broken-down village, in the darkness of ultramontane

Quebec, or amid the pioneer hardships of the newer settlements in Canada.   It is not for me—it is not for any foreign missionary—to look loftily on the ministry at home, or think of them as less loyal, unselfish, and true.   We are all missionaries, the *sent* ones of the King, and not our fields, but our faithfulness, matters.   Many of the church's first may be last when the Master comes.

CHAPTER II

At Princeton Seminary—Offer for foreign service—Under Dr. Duff in Edinburgh—In the Scottish Highlands—Accepted by the General Assembly—Visiting the churches

HAVING completed my preparatory studies in Toronto, I went to Princeton early in September, 1867, and was enrolled as a student in the Theological Seminary there. The three years spent in that historic institution were full of interest and inspiration. All the professors were able, zealous, and devoted men. Dr. Green, the Hebraist, was vigorous and penetrating. Dr. James McCosh, of the college, lectured every Lord's day on the life of Christ, with characteristic energy and power. But it was Dr. Charles Hodge who most deeply impressed himself on my heart and life. Princeton men all loved him. No others knew his real worth. Not in his monumental work on systematic theology can Charles Hodge be best seen; but in the class-room, or in the oratory at the Sabbath afternoon conference. There you saw the real man and felt his power. Can any Princeton man forget those sacred hours? How that charming face would brighten and those large luminous eyes grow soft and tender with the light of love! How awed we sometimes were when that trembling hand came down on the desk and those lips quivered with a strange and holy speech! To look in on a Princeton class in those days would be to see what a well-founded reverence meant.

On Tuesday, April 26, 1870, I was graduated, having completed the full curriculum of the seminary. It was a memorable day. According to the old Princeton custom, the professors and the graduating class met on the campus. The graduates threw their prized diplomas on the ground, and with the professors formed a ring, joining crossed hands. We sang " From Greenland's icy mountains " and " Blest be the tie that binds." Dr. Charles Hodge stepped into the circle. There was a tremor in his voice as he prayed for us all and lifted his hands in benediction. What a benediction! His eyes were moist as he said good-by. We parted in tears. The class of '70 was soon scattered. That night I was on my way to Canada.

The summer of 1870 I spent within the Presbytery of Toronto, laboring in the mission stations of Newmarket and Mount Albert. The Rev. Professor MacLaren, D.D., at that time minister in Ottawa, was convener of the Foreign Mission Committee. To him I stated my desire to go abroad as a missionary. He encouraged me, and invited me to meet the committee early in October. I have never forgotten that meeting. It was not very hopeful or enthusiastic. It was a new experience for the committee. They scarcely knew what to do with a candidate for foreign work. When I formally offered my services to the Presbyterian Church, and asked to be sent as a missionary to the heathen, one member looked me in the face and said, " Mr. MacKay, you had better wait a few years." Another argued for delay: " As he is going to Scotland, let him go, and on his return we can think over the matter for a year or two." A third suggested Madagascar as a field for future consideration. The convener pleaded for immediate acceptance and appointment. I was told, however, that the subject would be considered and the decision made known to me in due time.

A fortnight later I found myself on board the steamship " Austrian," of the Allan line, *en route* from Quebec to Liverpool. Money was scarce, and I was content with steerage passage. It was dismal enough at best, but I was a novice and unprovided for. The dreariness of the voyage was somewhat relieved by a burly Englishman who entertained his fellows in the steerage and found expression for his loyal soul in a song about King George, which he sang regularly every night, and danced his own accompaniment. From Liverpool to Glasgow was a sickening run, on a coaster called " Penguin," with a drunken crew and carousing passengers. In Glasgow I spent a delightful hour with the great Dr. Patrick Fairbairn. Two days later, November 4th, I arrived in Edinburgh. That was my destination, and to meet one man there I had crossed the Atlantic. That man was the venerable missionary hero, Dr. Alexander Duff. The story of his life had already fired my soul, and when I met him I was not disappointed. I was a young man, unknown and poor; but when he learned the purpose of my life, and that I had crossed the sea to sit at his feet, his welcome was that of a warm-hearted, godly Highlander.

While in Edinburgh I took a postgraduate course, hearing lectures from Professor John Stuart Blackie in the university, and from Drs. Smeaton, Blaikie, Rainy, and Duff, in New College. Dr. Duff was professor of evangelistic theology, and under his supervision I studied Brahmanism and Buddhism, and learned Hindustani with Mr. Johnston of the Edinburgh Institution, having in view the India mission field. Dr. Duff's lectures were rich in matter and glowing with holy fire. At times he grew animated, threw off his gown, and gave his Celtic nature vent. He was specially kind to me. I spent many hours with him in his private room and at his home. I well remember the evening he showed me the Bible recovered after his shipwreck off the coast of Africa. It was doubly holy in my eyes. I saw him for the last time on March 13, 1871. He had gone to Aberdeen to deliver a course of lectures to the students in the Free Church College. Early in March I followed, and the first day occupied a seat in his class near the door. His unfailing kindness again was shown, and his cordial words of introduction to the students secured for me a hearty welcome: " Gentlemen, here is my friend from Canada, bound for a heathen land. Show him that there are loving hearts in the ' Granite City.' " A few days afterward, at the close of his lecture, he walked down Union Street with me. When near the Queen's Monument he stood still, looked me in the face, grasped my hand tightly in both of his, spoke words too kind and sacred to be repeated, wheeled about, and was gone. Heroic Duff! Let Scotland and India and the churches of Christendom bear testimony to the loftiness of thy spirit, the consuming energy of thy zeal, the noble heroism of thy service.

There were great preachers in Edinburgh, under whom it was a delight to sit. Who could forget Candlish or Guthrie? Arnot was there then, and Lindsay Alexander, Cairns, Mac-Gregor, and Alexander Whyte. With Candlish and Guthrie I became personally acquainted—both truly great men, but how very different! At Candlish's home I sat with him for well-nigh two hours, until the bell rang for dinner. He paced the floor all the while. Sometimes he would turn sharply and ask about something in Canada. Then, running his left hand through his long, unkempt hair, he would take a few more rapid rounds. It was not altogether reassuring to a backward young man. Guthrie, again, was the soul of geniality. His family was with him in the room, and at his side his favorite little dog. He sat in an easy-chair with his long legs stretched out, bubbling over with humor.

That winter in Edinburgh gave me experience in city mission work, and with other students I labored among the submerged outcasts in the Cowgate and Grassmarket. Like every man who claims to have Scottish blood, I came to love the famous old city, with its castle, cathedral, and palace, its historic scenes and thousand cherished memories. I was proud then of being in Edinburgh, and although I have since twice circled the globe, not in Orient or Occident have I seen a city to compare with "Scotia's darling seat."

After the close of the colleges in March, I went north to Sutherlandshire, the land of my forefathers, spending the time chiefly at Dornoch, Tain, Golspie, and Rogart. The question of my life-work now became pressing. No word had come from Canada, and I began to despair of service in connection with the Canadian church. But on Friday evening, April 14th, while I was considering seriously the advisability of offering my services to one of the Scottish or American churches, a letter came from Dr. MacLaren stating that the Foreign Mission Committee had decided to recommend the General Assembly that I be accepted as their first missionary to the heathen world. It sent a thrill of joy to my heart. Accepted, and by my own beloved church!

The next day I left the heathery hills, and three days later was on board the "Caledonia," bound from Glasgow to New York. I was again a steerage passenger, but for my companions had over seven hundred Irish Roman Catholic emigrants. I have seen something of the under-side of life since then, I have looked upon human beings in all stages of degradation and in all conditions of filth; but nothing has been able to blot out of my memory the impression made by the sights and sounds of that homeward voyage. Right glad I was, after nearly three long weeks, to breathe once more the pure air of heaven, and refresh my eyes with scenes that were wholesome and clean.

The General Assembly of the Canada Presbyterian Church was called to meet in the city of Quebec on the second Wednesday of June. I was invited by the Foreign Mission Committee to be present at that Assembly. That venerable court was opened by the retiring moderator, the late Principal Michael Willis. The Rev. John Scott, D.D., then minister of St. Andrew's Church, London, was elected moderator. There were "burning questions" before that Assembly. The "Organ" was beginning to make itself heard in the church, and the question of union with the "Old Kirk" in Canada was quite to the front. But to me all interest centered around the report of the Foreign Mission Committee. Would the Assembly adopt the committee's recommendation? If so, to what field would I be sent? The committee's report was presented on Wednesday, June 14th. It urged the Assembly "to favor mission work among the heathen." It stated: "A man has offered, and the church seems prepared to meet the liability. Mr. MacKay, a student of the church, having passed the winter under Dr. Duff, is now in this city, ready to undertake the work which the church may appoint." Three fields were suggested—India, the New Hebrides, and China. The report preferred China. The Assembly decided:

"That the offer of Mr. George L. MacKay's services as a missionary to the heathen be cordially welcomed, and that he be, as he is hereby, called by this Assembly to go forth as a missionary of the Canada Presbyterian Church to the foreign field;

"That China be chosen as the field to which Mr. MacKay shall be sent;

"That the Presbytery of Toronto be authorized to ordain Mr. MacKay to the holy ministry, and to make arrangements, in accordance with the Foreign Mission Committee, for his designation to the work whereunto he has been called."

That evening I was introduced to the General Assembly

as "the first foreign missionary of the Canada Presbyterian Church," and was invited to address the court. The "fathers and brethren" were kind to me that night; some of them thought me an "enthusiast," and pitied me. Dr. John Hall of New York was on the platform, as deputy from the Presbyterian Church of the United States; and when I had finished speaking he led the Assembly in prayer, commending "the young missionary" to the care of the eternal God, praying for "journeying mercies" and the sure guidance of the Jehovah of Israel.

In those days the church in Canada was divided and weak. The union of 1875, that consolidated Presbyterianism in British North America into one harmonious, strong, and aggressive church, and that has made the Presbyterian Church in Canada not the least in the great family of the churches of the Reformation, had not yet been consummated. The missionary effort of the church was directed almost entirely to work at home. Now that a new move had been made, it was necessary that funds be provided to meet the expense. To assist in awakening an interest in the cause of foreign missions I was appointed to visit various congregations in Quebec and throughout Ontario during the summer of 1871. I visited a good many churches between Quebec and Goderich, carrying out Paul's injunction to Timothy; but when I discussed the "Master's great commission," and undertook to "reprove, rebuke, exhort," some of the congregations did not take kindly to the exercise. Some very uncomplimentary things were said, and I was called "an excited young man." There was a great deal of apathy, and the church was very cold. It seems to me that was the "ice age." But there were some noble exceptions. Several good meetings were held in Montreal, and I was greatly cheered by the kind and encouraging words of Principal MacVicar and the great geologist, Sir William Dawson. A union meeting was held in Ottawa.

Rev. Dr. MacLaren was minister of Knox Church, and Dr. Moore of Bank Street. Their noble words of commendation and appeal stirred more hearts than mine. At Ayr I had the good fortune to meet the pastor of one of the churches, the late Rev. Walter Inglis. He was himself a veteran missionary who had spent a quarter of a century in the Dark Continent. He felt the coldness and apathy of the church, but his royal nature touched it all with warmth and sunshine: "Never worry, young man. People will lecture you and advise you and talk about the cost. Put it in your pocket and go your way. Things will change, and you'll see a brighter day."

I look back on the experiences of that first tour of the churches, and I contrast them with things to-day. Surely the predicted change has come. Rip Van Winkle saw no greater in his day. Ministers now are all as "excited" as I was twenty-three years ago, and they are much better informed. Congregations are all organized for mission purposes. Missions is the most popular of all topics. People crowd to hear the story of missionary work abroad. There are "mission" evenings at every General Assembly. Missionaries are designated and sent out every year. The "brighter day" has come. Thank God, I have lived to see it. The past is forgotten in the joy of the present, and the future is pregnant with still greater things. To-morrow will be as to-day, and much more abundant.

CHAPTER III

TORONTO TO TAMSUI

Ordination—Departure—On the way—Credentials—Alone—Japan—With
English Presbyterian Missionaries—In South Formosa—At Tamsui
—" This is the land ! "

THE Presbytery of Toronto, in accordance with the instruc-
tions of the General Assembly, made arrangements for
my ordination and designation on Tuesday, September 19th.
I appeared before the Presbytery in the afternoon and delivered my " trials." In the evening the ordination service was
held in Gould Street Church. The pastor, the Rev. John M.
King, D.D., now principal of Manitoba College, Winnipeg,
preached on the text, " His name shall endure forever." At
my side that evening was another candidate for the holy office,
George Bryce, who was under appointment to missionary and
educational work in Manitoba. Dr. Bryce has served the
church with honor and success, and has risen to distinction
among Canadian educationists and authors. That evening
we stood together before the Rev. J. Pringle, the moderator,
knelt together, and by "laying on of the hands of the Presbytery"
were together set apart to the work of the gospel ministry and
designated to our respective fields, he to go to the newer West
and I to go to the older East. The convener of the Foreign
Mission Committee came up from Ottawa and delivered the
" charge " to the foreign missionary. My companion was
similarly addressed in the name of the Home Mission Com-

26

mittee by the Rev. Dr. Laing, now minister in Dundas. The speakers recognized the importance of the occasion as marking a forward movement in both the home and foreign work, and as suggesting a union of aims and interests that must never be sundered. The church's work is one, and conflict will be fatal.

One month after ordination, October 19, 1871, I bade farewell to my old home in Zorra, to meet again an unbroken family circle only when life's sea is no more. What was said or what was felt need not now be told. God only knows what some hearts feel. They break, perchance, but they give no sign.

It was nearly noon when the west-bound train pulled out of the station at Woodstock. Our first run was to Detroit. Chicago was next reached—a dreadful sight—dust and ashes and smoke. The " great fire " had just swept over the city, and was still smoking and smoldering. The third run was to Omaha, where I spent the first Sabbath day, and had the privilege of preaching the blessed gospel to a crowd assembled in the open air on the outskirts of the city.

Traveling was not the simple affair it is to-day. There were no through tickets from Toronto to Hong Kong. The missionary traveled over several roads and had to deal with various companies. There was no recognized " missionary rate." But the railway authorities were generous, and granted me a reduction over their roads. At Omaha the agent looked doubtful when I told him I was a missionary bound for a heathen land and asked for the favor granted by the three roads over which I had already traveled. " I do not know you," he replied. " Where are your credentials? " I had no credentials, nor any formal document by which I might be certified. I was at a loss what to do. No one knew me. Then like a flash the thought of my Bible came to me. It was the parting gift of the Foreign Mission Committee. I produced it from my satchel and asked the agent to read the inscription on the fly-leaf:

PRESENTED TO

REV. G. L. MACKAY,

First Missionary of the Canada Presbyterian Church to China, by the Foreign Mission Committee, as a parting token of their esteem, when about to leave his native land for the sphere of his future labors among the heathen.

WILLIAM MACLAREN, *Convener.*

OTTAWA, 9th Oct., 1871.

Matt. xxviii. 18–20.   Psalm cxxi.

These were my credentials. None could be better. No other was required. I was soon on my way again, and on October 27th arrived at San Francisco. Here I was the guest of a kind-hearted Canadian, Mr. William Gunn. On Wednesday, November 1st, I boarded the steamship " America," bound for Hong Kong. My host and two city missionaries, Messrs. Condit and Loomis, accompanied me on board to say farewell. The signal was given, the guns were fired, the stately ship weighed anchor, slowly steamed out through the " Golden Gate," and I was at last alone. Such experiences are common enough now, but then they were new and strange. I did not feel afraid, nor sorry, nor glad. Thoughts of home came, thoughts of the loved ones more than three thousand miles behind, and thoughts of what might be before. The sea was wide. The regions beyond were dark with the night of heathenism and cruel with the hate of sin. Would I ever return to my native land? And my life—what would it matter against such fearful odds? Could it be that I had made a mistake?

Such hours come to us all. They came to our Lord. They are hours of testing and trial. Sooner or later the soul enters Gethsemane. I found mine that day, and in the little state-room the soul was staggered awhile. But it was not for long. The Word brought light. The psalm marked by the committee on the fly-leaf of the Book began, "I will lift up mine eyes unto the hills;" and the promise was, "Lo, I am with you alway." And then the Forty-sixth Psalm! Oh, how often it has brought comfort and peace! When the waves dashed in fury I read it. Aye, and when storms arose wilder, more relentless, and deathful than any that ever vexed the broad Pacific; when heathen hate and savage cruelty rose like the hungry sea, the blessed words, "God is our refuge and strength," opened wide the door into the secret of His presence. On that day in my state-room I read it again and again —precious truth; glorious refuge; God, the eternal God. Hark, my soul! he speaks: "Certainly I will be with thee." Begone, unbelief! God in heaven is the keeper of my soul. The glorified Jesus says, "Lo, I am with you alway."

Voyaging on the Pacific is a pleasure now. A quarter of a century ago it was otherwise. There were no palatial Canadian Pacific steamers then. After twenty-six days the snow-clad peaks of Fuji-yama, the Holy Mountain of Japan, was a welcome sight. There were several other missionaries on board, whose fellowship was refreshing and helpful. From the ship's library I derived benefit and pleasure through such works as "The Social Life of the Chinese," by Justus Doolittle; "The Middle Kingdom," by S. Wells Williams; "China and the Chinese," by John L. Nevius; and "China and the United States," by Spears.

While our ship was lying at anchor in the harbor of Yokohama I had my first introduction to life in the Orient. Everything was new and interesting. The boatmen in the harbor, with their rice-straw waterproof coats, reminded me of pictures of Robinson Crusoe. Large, heavy wooden carts were rolled slowly along with much pulling, pushing, and interminable grunting. The smart rickshaw, a sort of overgrown perambulator, whisked by, the runners shouting, in their Japanese gibberish, " Clear the way, clear the way ! "

Leaving Yokohama, we sailed along the coast of China until we entered a narrow strait, and, following its serpentine course, were soon in the spacious harbor of Hong Kong. Magnificent view!—houses ranged tier after tier far up the steep sides of granite hills; and high over all waved the flag of " a thousand years." I had scarcely got rid of the coolies, who in their eagerness for the job of carrying my baggage had been pounding one another with bamboo poles, when a Saxon accent greeted my ears: " Are you MacKay from Canada? " That night I was the guest of Dr. Eitel. Next day I took the steamer for Canton. There on the pier I was hailed by McChesney, a Princeton fellow-student. The night was spent with the Rev. Dr. Happer, a veteran American missionary.

Having returned from Hong Kong, I took passage on the steamship " Rona," and on the following Sabbath we dropped anchor in Swatow harbor. No sooner had the ship's ladder been lowered than two Englishmen, whom we had been watching as they rowed out in a sampan, climbed on deck and called out, " Is MacKay from Canada on board? " It did not take long to make myself known, and the strangers proved to be Mr. Hobson of the Chinese Imperial Customs and Dr. Thompson of the English Presbyterian Mission at Swatow.

Before my designation the Foreign Mission Committee in Canada had correspondence with the committee of the Presbyterian Church in England. Mr. James E. Matheson of that church had written inviting the Canadian church to share with his the privilege of work in China; and in appointing me to China the General Assembly made special mention of coöperation with the English Presbyterian missionaries. The brethren at Swatow were, therefore, made aware of my coming, and right cordial was their welcome.

There were strong inducements presented in favor of settling in the Swatow district, but I resolved first to see Formosa. An up-the-coast steamer carried me to Amoy, and there I got a British schooner, " Kin-lin," and crossed the channel to Formosa. I had no plans, but invisible cords were drawing me to the "Beautiful Isle." The channel passage was the last and worst of the entire voyage from Canada. It was a night of thick darkness, howling blasts, and a plunging sea. We landed at Ta-kow, on the south of the island. Here I was met by a noble young physician, Dr. Manson, who took me ashore in a sampan. On the following Sabbath morning, in a British hong (warehouse) at Ta-kow, to a congregation of captains, officers, engineers, and merchants, I preached the gospel of a crucified Saviour. It was the last day of the year 1871, and that was my first sermon in Formosa.

On New-Year's day, 1872, I set out from Ta-kow to find the Rev. Hugh Ritchie, of the English Presbyterian Mission. He was at A-li-kang, twenty-six miles away. It was an interesting walk, even though my Chinese guide was a man of "strange speech." In the evening, as I drew near the village, I saw a man dressed in blue serge and wearing a large white sun-hat. I took him to be Mr. Ritchie, and so accosted him. "Is this MacKay from Canada?" he said, and with both hands he made me welcome to Formosa. For twenty-six days I enjoyed the hospitality of his home, and found him a friend with a large heart, a Christian with a high ideal, a missionary full of self-denying zeal, and his estimable wife a laborer of like mind. I learned much about the island and the methods of work in the south, and traveled many times over the district occupied by the nine stations under Mr. Ritchie's charge. I made good use of his Chinese teacher, and mastered the eight "tones" of the Formosan dialect.

Where shall I settle? was a question still to be answered. The missionaries on the mainland pointed to the "white fields " in the Swatow district. Here in the south they told me of North Formosa, with its teeming population in city and plain and mountain fastnesses, for whose souls no man cared. No missionary was there. The foundations of a mission were not laid. To that work I felt called. " I have decided to settle in North Formosa," I said to Mr. Ritchie one day. " God bless you, MacKay," was his glad response.

On March 7, 1872, Mr. Ritchie and I set out to explore the field chosen for my future work. We took passage to Tamsui, a seaport on the north of the island. At Tai-wan-fu, in the southwest, the capital of Formosa, where the English Presbyterian Mission was established by the noble Dr. Maxwell in 1865, we were joined by Dr. Dickson, leaving the Rev. W. Campbell in charge of the southern chapels. The " Hailoong " rolled and pitched for two days, and then we steamed into the mouth of the Tamsui River and anchored there. One look toward the north, another toward the south, another far inland to the dark green hills, and I was content. There came to me a calm, clear, prophetic assurance that here would be my home, and Something said to me, " This is the land."

CHAPTER IV

A beautiful parish—First glimpses—Prospecting—First night at an inn
—Malaria—A Pe-po-hoan village—With the aborigines among the
mountains—Parting company—Alone in Tamsui

BEAUTIFUL indeed was that first view of North Formosa,
as seen from the deck of the steamer in the harbor at
Tamsui. We all stood and gazed, deeply impressed. In the
evening we wandered out over the broad table-land and the
downs toward the sea. The fine large fir-trees, not found
near Ta-kow, attracted Ritchie's eye and reminded him of his
Scottish home. But when he saw the situation of Tamsui,
standing over against a solitary mountain peak that rose seventeen hundred feet, and backed on the east and south by
range after range climbing two thousand, three thousand, and
four thousand feet high, his soul was stirred to its depth, and
sweeping the horizon with his hand he exclaimed:

" MacKay, this is your parish."

" And far more beautiful it is than Ta-kow," added Dr.
Dickson, with equal emphasis.

The next day was the Sabbath. There was no preaching
done that day. I could not speak the language, and Ritchie
and Dickson deemed it prudent not to arouse the opposition
of the people by untimely service. No preaching had ever
been done in Tamsui, or anywhere else in North Formosa, and
we left the people to surmise about us what they chose. We

spent the day quietly in a room in the hong of John Dodd,
Esq., the pioneer British merchant at Tamsui.

As the purpose of Messrs. Ritchie and Dickson was to visit
the most northerly stations of their field by overland route
from Tamsui, I resolved to accompany them and "spy out
the land" in which I was to labor.   It was one hundred and
ten miles southwest to their nearest point.   Early Monday
morning we arose and made ready for the journey.   It was to
be taken on foot.   Ritchie and Dickson brought with them
one man each to serve as carriers.   Our outfit was simple
and soon prepared.   Some salted buffalo-meat, a few cans
of American condensed milk, pressed meat, biscuits, and
coffee formed our food-supply.   Ritchie wore a blue serge
suit, Dickson a Scotch tweed, and I my Canadian gray.   We
started out three abreast, with the carriers behind in single
file.   Walking toward the harbor along the north bank of the
Tamsui River, we soon reached the ferry and crossed to the
opposite shore.   Our shoes were off, and stowed away in the
carriers' baskets.   With feet bare and trousers rolled up to
the knees, we sprung from the ferry-boat to the shining sand.
It was a glorious morning.   The tide was out, and our path
lay along the sandy flats, left clean and cool by the receding
waters.   All were in high glee.   Soon we struck the trail,
that wound inland among little rice-fields, and in an hour or
two were on the high plateau.   The scenery was charming.
Here and there were groves of fir, and around an occasional
farm-house waved the tall bamboo.   It was early spring, and
the grassy sward was decked with innumerable dandelions,
violets, and other wild flowers.   The air was vocal with the
sweet song of the sky-lark singing clear up against the blue.
We descended into a large rice-plain and soon reached the
public road.   Toward evening we arrived at Tiong-lek, a
town of about four thousand population, and got quarters for
the night at the best inn.   It was on the main street, a low,

one-story building of sun-dried bricks. This was my first experience in a Formosan inn. Our room was small, allowing
no space for anything but the three beds it contained. There
was no stand, table, or chair. The beds were of planks with
legs of bricks, and, instead of springs and bedclothes, had
each a dirty grass mat, upon which coolies had smoked opium
for years. There was no window or other opening to the
fresh air. The glimmer that came from a pith-wick in a
saucer of peanut-oil revealed the black, damp earth floor, the
walls besmeared and mouldy; and crawling everywhere were
three generations of creatures whose presence did not add
to the "barbarians'" comfort. A stupefying smell of opium-
smoking, the odor of pigs wallowing in filth at the door, and
the noisome fetor of the whole establishment were almost too
much for my unaccustomed senses, and I thought surely my
companions were giving me a "strong dose." I soon learned,
however, that the inn at Tiong-lek was regarded as first-class,
and in some respects excelled any I afterward saw anywhere
in Formosa. We came to regard it as the "Queen's Hotel."
Other inns make no arrangement for meals or feeding travelers, but this one had in the open court an "earthen range"
for the use of travelers, and an open room with a table, two
chairs, and a bench. Many a time have I been grateful for
that "range" upon which to cook our food, and that room
in which to eat it. To be sure, the floor was earth, and the
hens and ducks had easy access, and the pigs grunted indoors
and out; but it was the most homelike place we ever found in
any public house in all our travels on the island.

Leaving Tiong-lek, the road ascended to an upland, the
edge of which, called Table Hill, three hundred feet high,
overlooked a rich plain with many little farms. The houses
were encircled by bamboo, which gave the whole place the
appearance of a waving forest. Descending by stone steps,
we passed through the fields and bamboo-plantations, and in

the evening entered the walled city of Tek-chham, with its forty thousand inhabitants. That night we spent in an inn compared with which the one at Tiong-lek was palatial. Next day we passed small fields of barley and wheat, and trudged over the weary sand-dunes, and at night were grateful for the grass hut at the halting-place for coolies, where the inevitable pig, with her swarm of little ones, took up her headquarters under our bed.

Next day Mr. Ritchie succumbed to malaria. He had been in Formosa only four years, but his system was honeycombed by the poison, and that day he had to take the sedan-chair. The dirty walled town of Tai-kah was next reached, and our path lay over a low piece of country toward Toa-sia, an inland Pe-po-hoan village. We were now within the territory of the English Presbyterian Mission, and at Toa-sia there was a small chapel and a number of converts. They had been advised of our approach, and about fifty of them came out to meet us. They received us with great joy, for only once before had a Christian missionary ever visited them. We stayed there nearly a week. On the Lord's day the chapel was crowded with eager Pe-po-hoan worshipers, and many Chinese from a neighboring town were attracted by the strange "barbarians." Our next move was to Lai-sia, a Pe-po-hoan village not far away, where we remained until the next Sabbath, when we returned to Toa-sia. On Monday we started out for Po-sia, a Pe-po-hoan settlement within savage territory, far in among the mountains. No white man had ever been in that plain. Many of its inhabitants had moved in from Toa-sia, and now fifty-five of their relatives accompanied us on our journey. They provided themselves with food for the way. The men carried knives at their belts, and a few matchlocks, fearing the mountain tribes, who regarded them as traitors. The first night we spent in the woods. The fires were kindled and burned all night.

The entrance to Po-sia was through a narrow pass made by some volcanic eruption among the rocks. At places the pass was not more than six feet wide, with the perpendicular walls of rock on either hand two hundred feet high.

On Tuesday we emerged into a plain six miles long and five miles wide, completely inclosed by densely wooded mountains. This was the Po-sia plain, and here lived six thousand Pe-po-hoan. At the edge of the rocks we were met by an outlook party that had been sent to welcome us, and on the way had been hunting the wild boar. There was great jubilation when friends met friends. They gave us an ovation, and as we did not wear the cue they called us their kinsmen. That night a great ox was killed, and a powwow of huge dimensions was held to celebrate our coming. They sang their wild chanting songs and awakened the echoes among the mountains. We remained there for over a week. Mr. Ritchie held service every evening, and on Sunday a great crowd assembled. There was no church there, nor had the gospel been preached there before, but here was illustrated the self-propagating power of Christianity. Some of these Pe-po-hoan had heard the truth at the English Presbyterian chapels in the south, and, according to Christ's commandment, had returned to their homes to show how great things the Lord had done for them.

We returned to Toa-sia, and there we parted, Ritchie and Dickson continuing their journey to Tai-wan-fu, and I with one Chinese started back for Tamsui. I returned by another route and reached Tamsui on April 6th, after an absence of twenty-three days. Here began my work, alone, without an interpreter, and among those who hated and despised the "barbarian." What I had already picked up of the Chinese language I must now utilize or submit to being imposed upon. After four days I succeeded in renting a Chinese house that was intended to be used for a horse-stable by military mandarins.

For this building I agreed to pay fifteen dollars per month. It was a filthy place. A steep hill being dug out furnished the site, and the road around separated it from the river. Situated as it was, it could not be healthy at any time. In the dry season the atmosphere was hot and oppressive, and when the rains came the water streamed down the sloping hill and ran through the building across the floor into the river in front. One room was floored with unplaned boards, another with tiles, and the others with nature's black soil. I moved into my new home with all my furniture—two pine boxes. The British consul, Alexander Frater, Esq., lent me a chair and bed; a Chinese, Tan Ah Soon, gave me an old pewter lamp; and I employed a mason to whitewash the whole establishment. It was thoroughly cleaned, portions of the walls hidden with newspapers, and openings curtained with red cotton. In full possession of this retreat, here is the record entered in my diary under the date of April 10, 1872: "Here I am in this house, having been led all the way from the old homestead in Zorra by Jesus, as direct as though my boxes were labeled, 'Tamsui, Formosa, China.' Oh, the glorious privilege to lay the foundation of Christ's church in unbroken heathenism! God help me to do this with the open Bible! Again I swear allegiance to thee, O King Jesus, my Captain. So help me, God!"

THE ISLAND

CHAPTER V

GEOGRAPHY AND HISTORY

Position—Climate—Rainfall—Depression—Malaria—First attack of fever
—Struck by a typhoon—A cloud-burst—Historical sketch—" Ilha
formosa ! "

THE island of Formosa lies off the east coast of China,
opposite the Fu-kien province. It is separated from the
mainland by the Formosa Channel, which varies in breadth
from eighty to two hundred miles. On the northeast and
southeast the island is washed by the waters of the Pacific
Ocean. It is about two hundred and fifty miles from north to
south. The average breadth is about fifty miles. It contains
an area of about fifteen thousand square miles, being about
one half the size of Ireland. Forest-clad mountain-ranges at-
taining the height of from seven thousand to fifteen thousand
feet run through the center from north to south, and from their
bases extends a broad stretch of lowlands, plateau and ravines.
This plain is drained by three large streams which run into the
Tamsui River. Precipitous cliffs from three thousand to six
thousand feet, clothed with vegetation except on the sea-face,
with two large and many small plains, which are silted inlets,
compose the eastern side of North Formosa.

Formosa is under tropical conditions. It lies between
20° 58' and 25° 15' north latitude and 120° and 122° east
longitude. The Tropic of Cancer runs through it not far from
the center, so that only the south is really within the tropics.

On account of its position and the altitude of its mountains there is a considerable variety of climate, not only in that part that lies within the tropics, but also in the north.

The climate of North Formosa is excessively trying to foreigners. Those who have traveled in the Orient will understand that statement, but to the average Westerner it will be meaningless. In fact, it cannot be fully comprehended save by those who have spent a number of years in such a climate. From January to December flowers are in bloom and the whole country is green. Foliage is renewed as fast as it decays. We have no frost or snow, and those accustomed to invigorating atmosphere cannot understand how at times in Formosa we long for just one breath of the clear, crisp air of a frosty winter morning. About once a year we do get a glimpse of the snow's refreshing whiteness, but it is only a glimpse, for it lies on the top of the highest mountains, and around Tamsui remains only a few days.

March, April, and May may be called our spring season. June, July, August, and part of September are very hot, and the months most dreaded, because, although the temperature varies from forty-two to one hundred degrees at Tamsui and Kelung, yet on account of the weight of moisture carried by the atmosphere the heat is much more oppressive and enervating than in other and drier regions of South China. In August and September the tropical storms and typhoons come, which help to clear the air. October and November generally bring delightful weather in the north. About the end of December our rainy season sets in, and continues through January and February. It is rain, rain, rain, to-day, to-morrow, and the next day; this week, next week, and the week after; wet and wind without, damp and mould within. Often for weeks together we rarely get a glimpse of the sun. All the year around we have to fight against depression of spirits, and say over to ourselves as cheerfully as possible:

" Be still, sad heart, and cease repining;
  Behind the clouds is the sun still shining."

Not only during the rainy season, but almost any time throughout the year, we may expect heavy floating clouds to be arrested by the mountains and to empty themselves into the plains. Especially is this the case during the northeast monsoon. As the warm waters of the Japanese "Black Stream" sweep northerly along the eastern coast of Formosa, vapors ascend and are driven toward the island, there to become heavy clouds, which condense, touch the mountain-tops, and torrents of rain result. This accounts for the heavier rain on the eastern than on the western side. During the southwest monsoon, however, the wind drives these vapors away from the northern part of the island, and then we have our finest weather.

Keeping in view the dampness of Formosa and the powerful influence of the broiling tropical sun, it will be easily understood that growth is very rapid. Scarcely a barren spot is to be seen. The rocks are clad in moss and festooned with vines; the very trees in their wild state are covered with creepers. But if growth is rapid, so is decay, and hence man's deadliest foe—malarial fever. This is the blackest cloud that hangs longest over our beautiful island. Because of it disease and death work terrible havoc among the inhabitants. Almost every form of disease is directly traced to this one source. Seldom do three months elapse without one or more members of every household being laid low. In the hot season the natives are suddenly attacked, and in many cases succumb in a few hours. The bacteria of Asiatic cholera and malarial fever, carried on the wind, sweep over the country like a deathful pestilence. Sometimes the fatal effects of the climate do not appear for many months; but they manifest themselves so suddenly and unexpectedly that the physician has little chance to save life. Therefore we have often been called to follow the beloved members of our little community to the grassy resting-place out on the hill.

My first attack of fever was exactly one year after my arrival on the island. I had been on an extended tour with Captain Bax of her Majesty's man-of-war. We penetrated far into the mountains, and were for a considerable time in savage territory. Bax, although strong and healthy when we set out, had to be carried back in a sedan-chair. On returning to Tamsui I found my rooms chilly, damp, and mouldy. While I was absent the place was not occupied, and when I returned and lay down to sleep I became cold as ice, shook and trembled like an aspen-leaf, my teeth chattering so loudly that A Hoa heard it in an outer apartment. He came to my relief and remained at my bedside the whole night. As there was no fireplace in the building, it was impossible to get warmed. Heavy doses of quinine broke the fever, but my system was not free from it for years. Many times, on trips among churches and in the mountains, have the mats under me been wet with perspiration during the hot stage of the disease.

Personal experience has convinced me that but few foreigners can resist the enervating influence of the climate in Formosa, and hence I have pleaded for a native ministry to carry on the work of the mission. If European merchants in their well-built houses in Tamsui or Kelung find it impossible to maintain their health, what would become of them had they to live in Chinese houses on the east coast, or be exposed to the wind and weather in inland traveling?

The position and topography of Formosa expose it to the dreadful typhoon which sweeps across the Malay Archipelago, over the Philippine Islands, and then northward to Japan, taking Formosa in its course. The name is from the Chinese *ta-fung* or " great wind." The intense heat in southern latitudes conspires with other causes to produce this fearful outbreak of the elements, that results every year in untold loss of life and property. As the main path of the typhoon is along the Chinese sea-coast, the greatest destruction is on the ships and islands. Trees are torn up by the roots, buildings are swept away like chaff, great ships are broken to pieces or lifted from their anchorage and deposited elsewhere, and thousands of lives are lost. My first experience was in 1874, when the great typhoon swept over the land. I was hurrying alone from Kelung to Bang-kah. I came to a deep stream, and was feeling my way across a narrow plank bridge, when a great roar was heard, and before I reached the opposite bank the typhoon broke. I was hurled headlong through the darkness into the mud and water below. How I regained the slippery bank and made my way through the storm-swept bamboo and along the narrow winding path I cannot tell. It was nearly midnight when I reached Bang-kah, and right glad I was to find some shelter with the students there. That night a British merchant steamer bound for Tamsui was struck outside the Kelung harbor, and in the morning only the fragments of a wreck could be seen. Nearly all on board were lost, and now on a rock a white marble cross commemorates their loss.

Some years afterward, with Sun-a, one of my students, I was traveling to Kelung. When on the last mountain we looked seaward across the harbor, and behold! a black wall stood between the troubled sea and the lowering heavens. Thousands of sea-gulls were pressing forward with long, loud cries. We understood the signs and made all haste. Just as we were entering the town, with one indescribable roar the storm burst. First a few drops of rain, then the wind loosened and the torrents fell. Every living creature sought refuge. We rushed into a half-finished hut, and were companions in distress with a number of black pigs. There we stayed the whole night, listening to the fury of the terrific gales and surging waves.

Early in the morning we looked out to see the streets two feet deep in the water, gardens and rice-fields flooded, and everywhere marks of destruction and loss.

Turning now to the history of Formosa, we find many of the annals untrustworthy, being both inaccurate and fanciful. The Chinese claim to have sent an envoy to the island during the Suy dynasty, which was overthrown in 620 A.D. This claim is entirely probable. With junks, such as the Chinese possessed hundreds of years ago, it is not credible that they could sail through the Formosa Channel year after year without seeing the island and touching it somewhere. The first Europeans to visit Formosa were Portuguese, who settled there in 1590. The Dutch landed in 1624, and two years later were followed by the Spaniards. The Dutch expelled the Spaniards in 1642, and they themselves were driven out by Koxinga, the famous Chinese pirate. Koxinga was loyal to the Ming dynasty, and when the Tartars came down from Manchuria, and Sun-ti was proclaimed emperor, Koxinga refused to submit to the usurper. He continued to molest the coast to such a degree that in 1665 the emperor ordered all the people to retire nine miles in and to escape Koxinga's grasp. One might suppose that an emperor strong enough to secure such obedience from his subjects might easily have defended his maritime provinces against attack; but such is Chinese strength and weakness. Having thus failed to reach the subjects of the empire, Koxinga crossed the channel, drove the Dutch out of Formosa, and proclaimed himself first king of the island. His reign was brief and stormy, and in 1683 his successors were dethroned by the Chinese emperor and Formosa made a dependency of the Fu-kien province. In 1874 the Japanese invaded the eastern part of the island, but left immediately after the Chinese government made reparation for the loss sustained by the Japanese junks that had been attacked by the savages. In 1887 Formosa first became a separate province of the Chinese empire.   In 1894 war broke out between China and Japan, and at its close the island of Formosa was ceded to Japan and is now under the flag of the " Rising Sun."

The aboriginal or Malayan name of the island was Pekan or Pekando.   In 1430 the Chinese named it Ki-lung-shan (" Mountain of Kelung "), and the best port in the north still retains that name.   Subsequently they called it Tai-wan (" Terraced Harbor "), and by that name it is known to all Chinese to this day ; and the capital of the island was therefore called Tai-wan-fu (" capital city of Tai-wan ").   " Formosa " is a Portuguese word.   It is a descriptive name meaning " beautiful," and was first applied to the settlement at Kelung in 1590.   Sailing along the east coast, their brave voyagers, sighting the green-clad mountains with peaks piercing the scattered clouds, cascades glimmering like silver in the tropical sunlight, and terraced plains waving with feathery bamboo, exclaimed with glad surprise, " Ilha formosa, ilha formosa! " (" Beautiful isle, beautiful isle! ").

CHAPTER VI

GEOLOGY

Formosan natural history unwritten—A great subsidence—The island
given back—Geological formation—Minerals found—Physical changes
—Earthquakes—Loss and compensation—The eternal Refuge.

THE natural history of Formosa is as yet an unwritten
book. Even in the best authorities information is
meager and unreliable. Anything pretending to be Chinese
science is empirical and must be carefully sifted; and foreign
scientists have done little personal investigation on the island.
But the subject was too important and too interesting to be
neglected, and so in all our travels, establishing churches and
exploring in the savage territory, I carried with me my geological hammer, chisel, and lens, and brought back on nearly every
occasion some valuable contribution to my museum at Tamsui. I ever sought to train my students to have eyes to see
and minds to understand nature's great message in sea and
grove and mountain gorge. In the hope that readers may be
interested without being burdened I shall set down here only
sufficient to convey a general idea of the formations, deposits,
and contents of the mountains and plains, and refer briefly to
the influences and agencies at work in modifying the topography of the island.

Formosa is a continental island which became separated
from the mainland of China by the subsidence of the intervening land some time during the Tertiary period, and similar sub-

sidences have taken place all along the Chinese seaboard.
Beginning at the south point of Kamtchatka Peninsula, and
embracing the Kurile, Japan, Loo-choo, Philippine, Borneo,
Java, and Sumatra islands, we have Formosa about the middle
of this line, which once formed the eastern boundary of the
Asiatic continent. The Okhotsk, Japan, Yellow, and China
seas, with the Formosa Channel, cover the submerged lands.
Formosa is still connected with the mainland by a bank submerged to the maximum depth of one hundred fathoms. This
is, indeed, the deepest sounding anywhere near the island, but
thirty miles off the eastern coast the soundings suddenly fall to
the depth of one thousand fathoms, and going farther seaward
to two thousand, three thousand, and four thousand fathoms,
until the dark unsounded depths of the Pacific are reached.

There have been, too, partial and total subsidences and elevations in the geological history of the island, and there are
evidences of a total submergence to the depth of at least one
hundred fathoms, during which period the coral insect built a
layer to a considerable extent over its surface. Then came a
sudden upheaval. The fierce energies within broke out with
mighty volcanic action amid the terrific thundering of nature's
heavy artillery. The igneous rocks were lifted to the height of
fifteen hundred feet above the surface of the ocean, and Formosa was given back to the light of day. The coral was carried up to these mountain-peaks and then sent in huge masses
tumbling down the sides. Heavy rains and sweeping storms
carried it as debris out to sea. Remains are still found at the
height of two thousand feet, and this, together with the coral
reef whose arms are stretched out beneath the waters around
the shore, attests the convulsions and changes of prehistoric
times.

The *rocks* of the island consist principally of sandstone,
slate, graystone, gneiss, limestone, shale, granite and trappean
compounds, basalt, clinkstone, coal, and coralline. In the

northern, northeastern, and western sides there are ferruginous, argillaceous, gritty, and silicious sandstones, intermingled with carboniferous quartzite and solid schistose rock. The eastern precipitous cliffs exhibit beautiful contorted gneiss and graystone masses. The curves and flexures in the lines of stratification are marked with wonderful distinctness. Around So Bay, on the eastern coast, and extending south and north, pyritiferous slate is dominant. The iron pyrites are very abundant in the entire formation. Gray, brown, and reddish shales are common in the northern parts. Mica-schist and micaceous sandstone alternate with gneiss, and appear contorted, displaced, and filled with lodes of quartz, varying from one eighth of an inch to several inches, which ran through the fissures when the mass was in a molten state. Massive limestone of bluish-gray color is found with shales and gritty sandstones. On the right bank of the Kelung River, near Pat-chien-na, there is an interesting formation of quartzose sandstone, composed of quartz-grains colored with iron oxide. It was evidently carried by the waters through the valley and deposited along the flanks of volcanic rocks which were vomited as molten material long before the now valuable quarry became cemented into hard rock. Tai-tun range is itself a mass of dark-blue igneous rock, with an extinct crater twenty-five hundred and seventy-five feet high on the southwest side. Quan-yin Mountain is of the same material, and is extensively quarried and dressed for door-steps, lintels, pillars, and the foundations of buildings. Already such rocks are called quanyin stone by natives.

Coal is known to abound in two thirds of the island, and it is more than probable that seams of different depths extend the whole distance from north to south. The best-known mines are at Poeh-tau, near Kelung. It is all bituminous, and is so dislocated by upheavals and convulsions that the strata are full of faults and fissures, which render the work less remunerative than it might otherwise be. Europeans employed by a governor sank a shaft, but there was so much blasting and cutting of sandstone that it has never been a profitable enterprise. Natives start at the outcrop at the side of a hill, following the seam on its incline; they dig with picks, and with a small hand-sleigh drag the pieces out. Opposite the Sin-tiam church there is a seam two feet thick, tilted almost perpendicular, and there it stands between the equally dislocated sandstone rocks. Lignite occurs in a few sandstone ranges on the western slopes.

Petroleum is found at several points between West Peak and Au-lang. At the seaside I took up a bottleful and kept it for ten years. It appeared like olive-oil and burned with ease, giving a bright light. Two Americans from Pennsylvania were employed by the Chinese to sink a shaft, but at three hundred feet the drills broke and the enterprise was abandoned.

Natural gas is obtained in several localities, and one has only to remove the black soil to the depth of a foot or two, strike a match, and in an instant the whole will be ablaze.

Salt.—Rock-salt has not been found in the island, but the aborigines in the Kap-tsu-lan plain have a process by which they extract the salt from the sea-water. Large quantities of the water are poured over the hot sand on the beach until for an inch or two in depth it becomes thoroughly impregnated. This sand is then collected into a large iron leach-tub, to which heat is applied, and into which more sea-water is poured. The water, percolating, carries the salt with it, and when evaporated a beautiful white salt remains.

Sulphur is found in great abundance, especially in the north. The best springs are at Kang-tau, near the Kelung River. I visited them in October, 1872. That was the first time I had seen so strange a sight. Descending from the height overlooking the Bang-kah plain, we found a winding path, along which we hurried up the valley till we reached the springs. The ground, as we approached, resounded to our feet like the rumbling of distant thunder. The narrow valley was a place of interest and beauty. A score of springs boiling and roaring, hissing like a great Mogul engine, sent up clouds of steam and poured out volumes of hot sulphur-water. The sides of the boulders and the lips of the crevices were all flaked with beautiful golden-colored sulphur. A bath at any temperature could easily be obtained, but the Formosans know nothing about the medicinal properties of their sulphur-springs. A valuable sulphur industry is carried on by the government. Coolies are employed in the neighborhood of the springs, digging up raw material, a lava-like substance, grayish in color. When this is melted in huge pans the sulphur comes to the surface, the sediment, when hard, being a beautiful specimen of igneous rock. There is another region, northeast by north, with solfatara springs; but by far the largest spring is seaward from Vulcan's Peak, fifty-six hundred and fifty feet high, on the way to Kim-pau-li. There it is hissing, roaring, and bellowing, like tons of blazing oil in a seething caldron. Sea-captains often mistake Vulcan's Peak for an active volcano. In from Sin-tiam, within the mountains, there is a region where the fires became extinct less than one hundred years ago.

Iron in some form must exist in the interior of the island, for at the sea-shore one can easily fill a cup with hematite of iron by dipping a magnet and collect ng the particles adhering to it. There are also chalybeate springs along the bases of many hills and mountains.

Gold was discovered in 1890 by a Chinese workman who had been in California and Australia, and who was engaged in excavating for the erection of a railway-bridge over the Kelung River. Reports of this fact having been circulated, multitudes were soon attracted to the place, and were from daylight to dark digging for the precious metal. Gold-bearing rocks in the interior are carboniferous quartzites, slaty and schistose, with lodes of quartz. It is difficult to estimate the quantity procured annually, although it must be considerable.

Great physical changes are continually taking place on the island. What was once a large and beautiful lake is now the fertile Bang-kah plain. Storms and freshets brought down vegetable matter from the mountains, and the bottom of the lake was gradually elevated. Meanwhile the waters were grinding and pressing against the spur that joined the Tai-tun and Quan-yin mountains, forming the lower bank of the lake. At some time a violent earthquake-shock rent this spur, and the waters rushed madly down to the sea, leaving behind a rich alluvial plain, and cutting what is now the channel of the Tamsui River.

Earthquakes are very common and do enormous damage. In 1891 on one day four shocks were felt, and a month later two more. Years ago at Kelung rumbling sounds were heard, and the waters of the harbor receded until fish of all sizes were left wriggling and floundering in the mud and pools. Women and children rushed out to secure such rare and enticing prizes, but shrieks from the shore warned them of the return of the water. Back it came, furious as a charge of battle, overleaping its appointed bounds, and sweeping away all the houses in the low-lying land along the shore. The story of that tidal wave is handed down as one of the great catastrophes in history. At Kim-pau-li, not many years ago, a shock was felt. Rice-fields suddenly sank three feet, and the sulphurous water rose and still covers the place. Sugar-cane is now cultivated in large tracts where boatmen plied their oars in 1872, and the waters of the Tamsui River glide over places where stood villages in which I preached the gospel twenty-three years ago. Changes are taking place, too, all along the shore. One might suppose that the hard rocks on the east coast would be able to resist all forces and influences. But no ; tides and waves of the great Pacific tunnel, undermine, and wear away the bases of the rocks, till needles, stacks, and arches stand up to attest the inward march of the water. On the west coast, however, there is compensation, for there the land is encroaching fast upon the sea. During heavy rains the rivers transport large quantities of mud, sand, and gravel from the mountains into the Formosa Channel, building sand-bars, mud-banks, and extensive shoals, as though the island sought to bridge again a pathway back to the parent land.

What mighty changes! What resistless power! Atmospheric, organic, aqueous, chemical, and volcanic agencies are ever at work lowering the mountains, elevating the seas, changing the face of nature. But note it well: they are blind and mighty forces, but they are all under control of Him who layeth the beams of his chambers in the waters, who maketh the clouds his chariots, the flaming fire his ministers, who walketh upon the wings of the wind, and by whom the foundations of the earth were laid that it should not be removed forever. We will not fear though the earth do change, though the mountains be carried into the midst of the sea. The eternal God is our refuge, and underneath are the everlasting arms. I will sing unto the Lord as long as I live; I will sing praises unto my God while I have my being.

CHAPTER VII

TREES, PLANTS, AND FLOWERS

THE richness of the soil and the humidity of the climate conspire to produce a luxuriant vegetation in Formosa. Trees, plants, and flowers literally cover the ground. Apart from a few exposed rocks, the crevices, ravines, and boulders are overgrown with ferns, plants, grasses, and creepers of all kinds and sizes. The trees are not tall, but large, having enormous branches. The mountain-sides are clothed from top to bottom with tangled undergrowth and trees of every possible shade of yellow and green. Reference will be made in this chapter to the many varieties found in this botanical garden of nature. For the sake of brevity the names only of many common or unimportant plants and flowers are mentioned.

I. *Forest-trees*

1. Shaulam (*Thuya Formosana*) is found in the mountains, in rocky places, and upon the bare rock. It is an excellent lumber-tree, has a beautiful grain, and when varnished with certain Chinese preparations it takes on a fine finish that reflects objects like a mirror, and is the best in Formosa for cabinet-work. It is nothing unusual to see boards and planks of it from two to eight feet in breadth.

2. Oak (*Quercus ilex*), a pretty evergreen, of which there are several varieties. It is hard red wood, which is used in the manufacture of hoe, ax, and adz handles.

3. Tallow-tree (*Stillingia azebifera*). The berry of this tree, after the covering falls off, is about the size of a pea, whitish in color, and hangs in clusters from the branches. The tallow is extracted from the berry by pressure, and is made into candles, which, when painted red, are used for idol-worship, especially in Buddhistic temples. The leaves of the tree resemble those of the Canadian poplar, but in autumn they assume the red and yellow tints of the soft maple.

4. Mulberry (*Morus nigra*). This tree is indigenous and grows everywhere. An attempt was made to establish a silk industry on the island, and the silkworm was introduced. But the leaves of the mulberry proved coarser than those on the mainland, and the raw silk being of inferior quality, the enterprise was abandoned.

5. Fir. This is planted to protect the tea-plantations from winds and storms.

6. Pine. Only a few small pines are found, and they are seen on the sides of the mountains.

7. Camphor (*Laurus camphora*). Camphor-trees are the largest in the forests. On measuring one I found it twenty-five feet in circumference. There is in my possession a plank which a hundred years ago was the end of a native chief's house. It is a single piece of more than eight feet square, and on it are many aboriginal carvings. Camphor-gum does not run like sap from the sugar-maple, nor does it exude like pitch from the pine. It is procured in the following way: An adz half an inch broad, and with a handle two feet long, is used as a gouge. With this the roots, stumps, and branches of the tree are chipped. These chips are collected and placed in a sort of covered steamer over boiling water. In due course the gum is distilled, and sublimates on the inside of the vessel like hoar-frost. The process of distilling is continued until a sufficient quantity is collected, when it is put up in tubs for export. As the demand is great in European countries,

the camphor industry is one of the most important on the island.

8. Paper-plant (*Aralia papyrifera*). The so-called rice-paper is made from the pith of this plant. The roll of pith, varying from half an inch to three inches in diameter, is cut into pieces according to the width of paper desired. It is then placed upon a very smooth tile, shaped somewhat after the fashion of a slate, with a brass frame the thickness of the paper raised above the edges. The operator, having made the pith perfectly smooth and cylindrical, rolls it backward over the tile with his left hand, and with his right pares it concentrically with a long, sharp, thick-backed knife. The knife rests on the brass frame, which serves as a gauge, and is drawn steadily back and forth. A beautiful paper is thus cut, which is used in making artificial flowers, or is exported to Hong Kong, where it is used in the manufacture of sun-hats. Chinese artists find large employment in painting cards of this paper, which are readily disposed of to European and American tourists.

9. Pung-tree (*Liquidambar Formosana*). This beautiful tree resembles soft maple. The leaves, especially when pressed between the fingers, are quite fragrant.

10. Bead-tree (*Melia Azedarach*). This tree grows very rapidly. When about a foot in diameter its wide-spreading branches and lovely lilac flowers present a picture very attractive to a lover of nature.

11. Banian (*Ficus Indica*). There can be no doubt that the banian is a long-lived tree. Of all the several hundred trees now in the college grounds at Tamsui, I planted every one from small branches, two inches through and five or six feet long. These were cut from large trees which survived several centuries of tropical storm. The banian is an evergreen, with rootlets running from the branches, which, if not interfered with, eventually reach the ground, take root, and grow as a support to the tree. The process of extension and

reduplication may go on until the branches, supported by their self-produced pillars, cover a vast area, and the original tree becomes an evergreen canopy under which thousands may find shelter.

12. Willow (*Salix*). As is to be expected, willows of different varieties are found growing on the lowlands and on the banks of streams.

13. Screw-pine (*Pandanus*). The leaves of this tree are arranged spirally in three rows, and bear some resemblance to those of the pineapple; thence the name screw-pine. The fruit, when ripe, is also similar in appearance to the pineapple, but is not edible. These trees are planted in the sandy districts for hedges. The leaves, when withered, are used for fuel, and the rootlets, cut a foot in length and hammered out, are used for brushes.

14. Varnish-tree (*Rhus vernicifera*). The exudations from this tree become an excellent varnish; but it must be used in a dark room, and the varnished article must be left there until it is thoroughly dry. It is very poisonous, and the effect on different persons is very singular. I was once in a cabinet-maker's establishment, remaining only a few minutes; but such was the effect of the varnish-poison that for three days afterward my fingers were swollen to three times their normal size, my face had a dropsical appearance, and my eyelids could scarcely be opened. It was not so painful, but it was very irritating and intensely disagreeable. The natives now eat the fruit, though doubtless in days gone by they dipped their arrows in the excretion to make them deadly weapons.

15. Thorn. This, as a tree, or as a creeper along the ground, with spines of different lengths, is often met with on the hillsides.

16. Tree-fern. This lovely plant is unsurpassed in beauty by even the stately palm. In well-sheltered valleys it stands fifty or sixty feet high, with fronds varying from ten to fifteen

feet in length. It is used for posts, and its wood is manufactured into cigar-boxes.

17. Rattan (*Calamus rotang*) is a species of palm. It grows from twelve to twenty feet high; then it begins to creep along in a vine-like fashion over other plants and above the branches of trees, until it reaches fully five hundred feet. In pulling it out the woodman often falls a prey to the savage head-hunter. The exportation of rattan is an important industry.

18. Red bamboo. This is an ornamental tree, with reddish stems and leaves, but it does not belong to the bamboo family. It is a *Dracæna ferrea*.

19. Betel-nut (*Areca Catechu*). This is an elegant tree, straight as a rod, rising sometimes to the height of fifty feet. Leaves are found at the top only. Its fruit is the well-known betel-nut, which is extensively used for chewing by the Malayans in Formosa and other islands, as a kind of intoxicant. This nut is the pledge of reconciliation. When offered by one and accepted by another, it is understood that the hatchet is buried.

20. Betel-pepper (*Chavica Bet'e*). This is a creeper that is often planted by the aborigines beside the betel-tree, up which it is trained to grow. The leaf of this creeper has a pleasant taste and is much relished by the native tribes, who chew it all day long with the betel-nut dipped in lime. This is a filthy and injurious habit.

21. Castor-oil plant (*Ricinus*). There are two species in the north—the one with green stems and leaves, the other, more lovely, with purple branches, leaves, and stems. Although indigenous and of rapid growth, the seeds from which the oil is produced are not utilized by the people.

22. Soap-tree (*Sapindus Saponaria*). The fruit is about the size of marbles, grayish in color, with a kernel inside. Savages and others on the border-land use it when washing clothes. But the style of washing is unique. Whether it be done at

ponds, creeks, or rivers, the garments are laid upon a plank or a flat stone at the edge of the water. With a stick two inches thick and two feet long, the garments are first pounded, then rubbed with soap-tree seeds, turned over, and pounded and rubbed again and again. When the clothes are considered sufficiently clean they are given a final rinse and taken home.

23. Chestnut-tree (*Castanea vulgaris*). This tree grows to a height of fifty or sixty feet in the mountains, and produces fruit similar to that of the same family in America.

24. Cedar (*Thuya orientalis*). These are not large, and are grown more for the purpose of ornamentation than utility.

25. Cayenne pepper (*Capsicum Sinense*). "Chilli" is the Mexican name for all the varieties. That in Formosa is a shrub two or three feet high, is very common, and the pods are much used for domestic purposes.

26. Kiu-kiong (*Lagerstrœmia Indica*). This is a very hard, firm, close-grained wood, and is used for seals, knobs, and other articles of that nature.

27. Wild mango (*Cerbera Odollam*), which grows to the height of twenty feet, has evergreen, waxy leaves. Its fruit is very peculiar and is about the size of a hen's egg. At first it is green, but afterward it becomes a beautiful reddish pink. But how deceptive! Inside it is nothing more nor less than dry fiber, neither useful nor ornamental.

28. Pho-chhiu (*Celtis Sinensis*). This tree resembles the peach, but its wood, which is soft and white, is not valuable as timber.

II. *Fruits and Fruit-trees*

1. Longan (*Nephelium Longanum*). This is about the size of a cherry, with a thin, bark-like rind. Within that rind there is a pulp which is edible, and in the center a kernel, black outside and white within.

2. Loquat (*Eryobotrya Japonica*). This is a yellow, juicy fruit, with a kernel edible both in the natural state and when preserved.

3. Persimmon (*Diospyros*). Of this there are several varieties, but one is peculiar to Formosa. The most common is red and about the size and shape of a tomato, for which, indeed, it might easily be mistaken. The other is hard and green, and is eaten after being cut and dipped in water.

4. Arbutus or strawberry-tree (*Arbutus Unedo*). It resembles a strawberry, but one has to acquire a taste for it before relishing it. It is often pickled and used as a condiment.

5. Angular fruit (*Averrhoa Carambola*). This is a peculiar fruit of angular shape, two inches long, and of yellow-green color. When ripe it is very juicy, of a green-gooseberry flavor, and is much relished.

6. Pomelo or shaddock (*Citrus decumana*). The formation of this fruit is sectional, similar to that of the orange; but it is considerably larger, being about the size of a citron. There are several species of it. The fruit of one is reddish, and of another whitish. The latter is preferred by foreigners.

7. Banana (*Musa textilis*). The stem of the banana is soft and does not resemble that of hard trees. The young shoot springs near the old plant, which falls after the fruit is ripened. In one year there may be three successive bunches, each weighing about forty pounds. The ground around a banana-tree is always wet, and where cultivated the neighborhood is more or less malarious.

8. Orange (*Citrus Aurantium*). The sweet and bitter grow here. There is a wild orange found in the forest, but it is much smaller than the cultivated one. There is one species which bears white flowers and golden fruit at the same time. The natives call it the "four-season" orange.

9. Plum (*Prunus domestica*). Considering the little attention paid to its cultivation, the Formosa plum must be described as

excellent. One kind is reddish to the pit and makes a delicious preserve.

10. Pear (*Pyrus communis*). This is hard and woody, like its wild uncultivated cousin in the West.

11. Crab-apple (*Pyrus Malus*). The apple is indigenous. How interesting and suggestive the fact that we have in Formosa the original of the northern spy, maiden's-blush, pippin, baldwin—indeed, of all the varieties of apple known in the world; and that the difference between these fine fruits and this scrawny crab is the result of horticultural care and cultivation!

12. Guava (*Psidium*). The tree which bears this fruit is to be found growing eight or ten feet high all over the hills; but it is also cultivated in gardens or orchards, and its fruit is improved thereby. The natives salt it when green and eat it when ripe.

13. Pomegranate (*Punica granatum*). The dark scarlet flowers of the pomegranate are of surpassing beauty, but as compared with that of Palestine the fruit is not to be desired.

14. Lime (*Citrus Limetta*). The rind of this fruit is dense, of a greenish-yellow color, and really excellent when ripe. It has a bitter taste. There are also "four-season" limes, producing fruit and flowers at the same time.

15. Citron (*Citrus medica*). It is much larger than the lime, and has a thick, tuberous rind. Its pulp is not so acid as that of the lime.

16. Peach (*Persica vulgaris*). The wild peach is small, round, and hairy, but the grafted variety is delicious when fully ripe.

17. Pineapple (*Ananassa sativa*). The best pineapples grow in light loam in the vicinity of the sulphur-springs. The plants are two feet high. One looking at them growing in the distance might mistake them for a garden of cabbages. Exportation is more disastrous to this fruit than to any other. One who has eaten the rich and luscious pineapple in its native For-

mosa cannot endure the very best offered for sale in foreign markets.

18. Mango (*Mangifera Indica*). Nothing can be said in praise of this fruit as it is found in North Formosa. It has the taste of turpentine.

19. Papaw (*Carica Papaya*). The tree which produces this fruit grows to the height of about twenty feet. The fruit itself is very edible, is yellow when ripe, and has a milky juice. Formosan mothers boil this fruit in the raw state, and eat it with pork, for they believe that on such a diet they can more liberally nourish their babes.

20. Jujube (*Zizyphus Jujuba*). The jujube-tree grows to the height of thirty feet. Its fruit is eaten by the natives, but is somewhat insipid.

21. Breadfruit (*Artocarpus incisa*). This fruit is used by the aborigines exclusively. The plant has a viscid, milky juice.

22. Lichi (*Nephelium Litchi*). It has a soft pulp, which is very delicious. It is often dried with sugar and used as a preserve.

23. Hong-kaw (*Nauclea cordifolia*). This is a yellow fruit, and is slightly larger than the egg of a common gray-bird.

24. Raspberry. Both red and black varieties grow in abundance everywhere on the cleared hills; but though the fruit looks full and enticing when ripe, it has not the flavor of the Western berry, and is never eaten, unless, indeed, occasionally by the herd-boys.

25. Fig (*Ficus*). The only indigenous fig is a creeping one, which is a parasite. Starting out self-dependent near a tree, it will fasten itself to the trunk and climb up till it reaches and overshadows the topmost branches. The Chinese regard the fruit, when boiled to a jelly, as valuable for medicinal purposes.

26. There is a creeping plant which produces a berry somewhat similar to the strawberry.

III. *Fibrous Plants*

At the outset it is well to state that there is no hemp, flax, or cotton in North Formosa.

1. Jute (*Corchorus capsularis*). This grows ten or twelve feet high, and is manufactured into cords, bags, and cables.

2. Grass-cloth or rhea (*Bœhmeria nivea*). It is cultivated with great care, fertilized with liquid manure, and made into grass-cloth and cords. It is found in Assam, Nepaul, and Sikkim.

3. Triangular rush (*Cyprus tegetiformis*). This grows in brackish water, and is cultivated in the Tai-kah region, at the boundary of our mission. That place, indeed, has become famous for its bed-mats made from this material. The mats vary in price from two to five dollars each.

4. Banana. Out of the fibers of the stem a thin summer cloth is manufactured.

5. Pineapple. Very luscious. Out of its leaves a cloth is made, similar to that made from the banana fibers.

6. Dwarf palm. Cords are made from the fibers of the bark.

7. Rain-coat (*Chamœrops excelsa*). The brown fibers near the leaf-sheets are sewn together with threads of the same material. The product is converted into coats which are worn during the heavy rains by peasants and boatmen. The coat is certainly a durable one, for even though exposed to sun and rain for fifteen years it will not rot.

8. Paper-mulberry (*Broussonetia papyrifera*). The bark is stripped from the trunk and lower branches, and afterward immersed in tubs containing water; but the liquid is not ready for use for several days. When it is prepared, a framework four feet square is made, and on it is fastened a coarse material like bag stuff. The frame is held on an incline and the liquid is poured gently over the canvas. The lower end of the framework is then raised until the liquid spreads evenly over

the surface and begins to thicken. It is then returned to the inclined position and exposed to the drying rays of the sun. The result is a sheet of gray paper resembling the material in a wasp's nest. This paper is oiled and used in umbrella manufacture instead of cloth.

9. Géthô (*Alpinia Chinensis*). It grows wild on the hills, among shrubs, everywhere. The leaves are long, and the flowers are white and waxy, and yellow within. The fibers are used in the manufacture of soles for one kind of grass sandals.

IV. *Leguminous Plants*

1. Indigo (*Indigofera tinctoria*). There are two species. One, with a small leaf, is cultivated in a sandy loam; the other, with large leaves not unlike the Irish potato, is cultivated in new land, sometimes around stumps.

2. Ground-nut or peanut (*Arachis hypogæa*). The appearance of this plant in the field is like clover. It has pretty yellow blossoms. The legumes are produced underground; hence the Chinese name, lok-hoa-seng. To dig the nuts is very laborious work. The Chinese, therefore, make what pioneers used to call a "bee," and from fifty to one hundred men, women, and children can be seen together digging with little scoops in the right hand, and picking up the nuts with the left. They are usually boiled and have salt thrown over them, or else roasted. Every rice-stall throughout the country has these useful peanuts on the table. From them an oil is expressed which is used for both food and light.

3. Beans, of which there are many varieties, are cultivated extensively.

4. Peas are less common and have fewer varieties.

5. Siusi (*Arbus precatorius*). This has long, narrow leaves and very lovely round yellow flowers. There are rows of it in the college grounds, and when all the branches are a

mass of yellow the sight is charming. Nearly all the tea-plantations have these trees planted around to protect them from the wind.

6. Sensitive-plant (*Mimosa sensitiva*) grows wild in cultivated localities.

7. Vetch (*Vicia Cracca*). This is not unlike the bean, and is found both wild and under cultivation.

8. Cessimum, sometimes called til. It is a *Cessimum orientale*, and has black seeds, from which a bland oil, dark in color, is made. This is very highly prized by the Chinese; in fact, it is considered almost a household necessity.

V. *Grasses*

1. Rice (*Oryza sativa*). This is the great staple of the land. Its culture is explained at length in another chapter.

2. Wheat (*Triticum vulgare*). This cereal is sown in November and harvested in May. At best the crop is poor, and now that American flour is imported its cultivation is rapidly diminishing.

3. Barley (*Hordeum vulgare*). There is but little barley grown anywhere on the island.

4. Maize (*Zea Mays*). This is cultivated by both Chinese and savages. When the grains are quite hard it is boiled and eaten off the cob.

5. Millet (*Panicum miliaceum*). Of this there are different varieties. One kind is only three feet high, while another, the *Sorghum vulgare*, grows to the height of ten feet in good soil.

6. Oats are not cultivated. I experimented with Canadian seeds. They produced straw four feet high, which was like stalks of reed, but the kernels were worthless.

7. Sugar-cane (*Saccharum Sinense velolaceum*). There are two kinds of sugar-cane cultivated, the one for chewing, and the other for the manufacture of brown sugar for export.

8. Bamboo (*Bambusa arundinacea*). There is one large species which is split and made into baskets, hoops, etc. Another kind grows to about the size of a large fishing-rod. There is still another with small and feathery leaves which is planted for hedges. The young shoots are cut off and used for pickles. Boats, houses, bridges, baskets, chairs, hen-coops, bird-cages, jars, water-vessels, pipes, lamps, beds, masts, doors, hoops, mats, paper, are all made from this indispensable grass. The savages also make earrings out of it, and the only musical instruments they possess. It is to the Chinese what the cocoa-nut is to the South Sea Islander and the date-palm to the African. It rarely flowers or produces seed, so that when flowers are seen those who are very superstitious declare that some great change will certainly soon take place.

9. Couch-grass (*Triticum repens*) grows wild.

10. Sand-grass (*Psamma arenana*).

11. A most useful reed (*Saccharum procerum*).

There are numerous grasses, many of which bear red, white, or black seeds. These seeds are used as beads by the wild mountaineers. A most useful reed, lo-tek or arunde, is used by builders; and the cellular tissues of lampwick (*Lepironia*) we used in the early days in our little bamboo lamps.

VI. *Bulbous Plants*

1. Sweet potato (*Batatas edulis*). This is really a convolvulus, with pretty flowers, creeping tendrils, and large bulbs underground. It must be distinguished from the ordinary potato which produces such nutritious tubers, and which belongs to a different order, the *Solanum tuberosum*. The bulb of the sweet potato is planted in March. In about six weeks the vines are cut into pieces eight inches long, which are planted in drills, and from these vine-cuttings the bulbs grow, and are ripe about the end of June. A second crop is planted

in a similar way in July and is ripe in November. Bulbs are never grown from bulbs, but invariably from vine-cuttings. There are three varieties, which differ in size, shape, and color.

2. Yam (*Dioscorea sativa*). There are several kinds—one white, another reddish, a third grows in water, while several others are produced on dry land on the hillsides. The dye-yam, which is procured from the mountains, is used mainly by the fishermen for dyeing their nets, clothes, and ropes.

3. Hoan-koah. This has a leaf in seven divisions, palmate in form. Above-ground it is a creeping vine. The tubers, one foot long, are beneath the surface. They are dried, grated to powder, and used for food.

4. Taro (*Aracaceæ*). Also edible, similar to the yam.

5. Turmeric (*Curcuma longa*). The branches of the root-stalk are used as a coloring-matter, medicine, and condiment. The powder which is made from the root-stalk is of a lemon-yellow color. This enters largely into the composition of curry-powder.

VII. *Vegetables*

1. Pumpkin (*Cucurbita maxima*). It grows to a large size. One can occasionally be found weighing as much as sixty pounds. The savages have a small, sweet variety.

2. Squash (*Cucurbita Melo-pepo*). Of considerable size.

3. Cucumber (*Cucumis sativus*). The common variety grows larger than in America, and besides there is a large, soft, and good species which is pickled and used extensively with rice.

4. Melon (*Cucumis Melo*). This compares favorably with that found in the West.

5. Watermelon (*Cucumis Citrullus*). This is extensively grown on sandy soil, and is very refreshing.

6. Bottle-gourd (*Cucurbita Lagenaria*). When young and tender this vegetable is sometimes eaten, but it is generally

cultivated for its value as a water-bottle, water-dipper, water-jar, or a jar for holding coral-lime.

7. Water-cress (*Lepidium sativum*). An excellent water-cress is found in running streams, but it is rather strange that people who eat and enjoy so many herbs and vegetables of all descriptions should never partake of the wholesome cress. The European sailors, however, especially the blue-jackets from her Britannic Majesty's ships, soon found it out, and now they can often be seen with their bonnets full, returning to the ship to enjoy a fresh delicacy at mess.

8. Tomato (*Solanum* or *Lycopersicum esculentum*). The tomato is truly indigenous, for it grows wild on cleared spots within the mountains, among shrubs, and beside pathways. For years I tried to induce the Pe-po-hoan to grow and use the tomato, but so far my efforts have been in vain. The Chinese themselves have an intense dislike to the taste. This is to be regretted, for the large cultivated variety could be grown with little trouble.

9. Brinjal (*Solanum Melongena*). The fruit is of a purple color, five or six inches in length and an inch in thickness. It grows on a plant somewhat like a standing tomato when about eighteen inches high. It is sliced lengthwise, boiled, dipped in sauce, and eaten.

10. White cabbage (*Brassica*). There are several varieties, which have been derived from *Brassica oleracea*, the original species. The foreign drumhead cabbage has been introduced and cultivated successfully. Occasionally one is found weighing twenty pounds.

11. Onion (*Allium Cepa*). The bulb is very small. The whole plant, having been boiled to dissipate the phosphoric acid, is eaten as a relish with rice.

12. Leek (*Allium Porrum*). This is used as the onion, but it is preferred when it is in blossom.

13. Garlic (*Allium sativum*). This is extensively cultivated

and used for its well-known irritant, stimulating, and diuretic properties.

14. Celery (*Apium graveolens*). This is used green, never blanched. It is boiled, cut into pieces an inch long, and eaten with rice.

15. Spinach (*Spinacia oleracea*). It is used as an esculent pot-herb.

16. Turnip (*Brassica rapa*). The different varieties are all white. One large kind resembles that in Western lands. It is sliced, salted, and thus prepared for future use. The small round variety is very sweet and succulent.

17. Bean (*Papilionaceæ*). Many types of bean are found, some white, others black ; some flat, others round ; some large, others small. They are all edible. The pods of a creeper in the forest are sometimes two feet in length, while the cultivated bean, which grows over water on trellis-work, is eighteen inches long. The *Dolichos soga* might be designated the oil-bean.

18. Pea (*Papilionaceæ*). It is planted, not sown broadcast, and its pods, when small, are picked, boiled, and used as a vegetable.

19. Lettuce (*Lactuca sativa*). This is never used in the raw state, but is always boiled before being eaten. Its property of alleviating pain and inducing sleep is well understood.

20. Parsley (*Petroselinum sativum*) is cooked in lard before it is put on the table.

21. Mustard (*Brassica Sinapis*). This, when salted, is the staple vegetable among the peasants.

22. Coriander (*Coriandum sativum*) is used as a salad, dipped in soy.

23. Fennel (*Fœniculum vulgare*) is sometimes used as a food, but more frequently as a medicine.

24. Ginger (*Zingiber officinale*). This very useful plant attains the height of about a foot, and has long, pointed leaves. The rhizomes or roots are taken when green, sliced, and pre-

pared as a relish. Around the city of Tek-chham there has sprung up quite an industry in preparing it for market. It is preserved dry, in sugar, in small earthen pots. It is not in any way like the preparation in Canton which is brought into Western lands. Plums, peaches, and pears are preserved in small earthen pots like the Tek-chham ginger.

25. Ka-pek-sun (*Cyperus*). This is a sedge found in drains, watercourses, and rivulets. The shoots, in the autumn, are used daily at meals. The root, when sliced, is of a whitish color, with black spots. It is truly a well-flavored, palatable vegetable.

VIII. *Other Kinds of Plants*

1. Tobacco (*Nicotiana Tabacum*). On the eastern coast tobacco grows sometimes ten feet high. I never saw a living creature put to death more expeditiously than was a venomous serpent one day when we were erecting Oxford College. He was found under a heap of tiles. One laborer pinned him to the ground with a pole. Another took from his tobacco-pipe a small quantity of nicotine and put it to the mouth of the reptile. Instantly his snakeship drew himself up, stretched himself out, shuddered, and, being released, turned his whitish belly upward and expired. I would have thought this incredible had I not witnessed it. It should be stated, however, that the said pipe was an heirloom for four generations. No wonder the nicotine was somewhat rank.

2. Tea (*Camellia theifera*). The tea-plant is grown on the uplands and hillsides. It is generally planted in rows, and attains a height of several feet. The pickers, stooping down, go between the rows and pluck the tender leaves with both hands, depositing them in baskets strapped on their backs. Tea-leaves are first of all dried in the sun. At times they are trampled with the bare feet, then partially dried in heated

pans, after which they are taken in sacks to the tea-houses in the city. There they are refired with great care, picked, and graded according to quality. Hundreds of women and children can be seen on low stools engaged in sorting during the tea season. Flowers are used to flavor the tea, especially the gardenia, which is cultivated in fields for this express purpose. Tea is the universal beverage, and it is the badge of hospitality. The moment one enters a cot, however humble, the order is issued, "Tsoa te" ("Infuse tea"). A few leaves are put into a tea-cup and boiling water poured over them, and that cup is the one from which the tea is sipped. Neither milk nor sugar is ever used by the natives in their tea.

3. Dandelion (*Leontodon Taraxacum*). This is similar to its New World relative.

4. Common thistle (*Carduus*). Similar to the common bull-thistle, but smaller. This is the only variety found on the island.

5. Mint (*Mentha*). The three varieties are found—peppermint, spearmint, and pennyroyal.

6. Plantain (*Plantago major*). This is said to follow in the wake of man, and I suppose it does, for he would be a clever botanist who could distinguish between the Canadian or Scotch and Formosan plantains.

7. Rush (*Juncaceæ*). This is used for cleaning tables, buckets, and benches, as in North Britain and America.

8. Water-caltrop (*Trapa bicornis*). It is found in shallow water, and is called by the Chinese "dragon's horns." Blackish outside, it certainly resembles the horns of the water-buffalo. It is boiled before being eaten.

9. Fern. There is an almost endless variety, but the brake is the most common. There is a beautiful creeper of such variegated form that separate sections of the same plant would be pronounced by any but skilled botanists to be parts of different species.

10. Duckweed. This is the weed which causes the farmer so much arduous toil in the rice-fields.

11. Thorn-apple (*Datura Stramonium*). It has a prickly capsule, and grows in great abundance in some localities.

12. Artemisia is put up over the doors with green branches of the banian, and is supposed to confer health and prosperity upon the family.

13. Wood-sorrel (*Oxalis Acetosella*) has beautiful flowers, and trifoliate leaves which resemble the shamrock.

14. As might be expected in that climate, fungi, mushrooms, puffballs, mildew, rust, dry-rot, and moulds are very common. The *Penicillium glaucum* is very destructive of books in hot, damp weather, utterly ruining the best bindings in a few days.

15. Cactus with anomalous ferns is common.

16. Seaweed (*Algæ*) is found in green, red, and black varieties in shallow water, and cast up in large quantities on the beach by the waves.

IX. *Flowers*

1. Convolvulus (*Convolvulus Byroniæ folius*). It grows so as to entirely cover large shade-trees. After the sun rises this morning-glory is truly gorgeous.

2. Rose. There are the creeping rose, which trails along the ground, the white single rose, and *Zephyranthes rosea*, with its purple flowers. They grow wild on the hillsides and in open spaces.

3. Magnolia (*Fuscata*). Owing to its choice fragrance this is the favorite flower in all Formosa, the women especially prizing its sweet-scented odor above all others. The *Magnolia pumila* is also found.

4. Chloranthus (*Inconspicuæus*).

5. Gardenia. Cultivated for flavoring tea.

6. Hibiscus.

7. Crested cockscomb (*Celosia cristata*).

8. Honeysuckle.

9. Marigold.

10. White lily. During the months of March, April, and May this beautiful flower, so much prized in Western greenhouses, and called the Easter lily, bedecks a thousand hillsides. I had several planted on good, rich, and prepared soil at Tamsui, and they grew to the height of four or five feet.

11. Azalea.

12. Hollyhock.

13. *Vinca rosea.* This bears purple-and-white flowers for fully one half the year. So tenacious is it of life that it is found at the seaside and in all kinds of soil, and the smallest fragment of root left in the ground will spring up and grow.

14. Wild violets. Violets, intermingled with lovely little yellow blossoms, beautify all the uplands.

15. Bluebells (*Campanula rotundifolia*).

16. *Pardanthus Chinensis.*

17. *Asclepias curassavica.* This has a small yellow cup-like flower, delicate and charming; grows wild on little knolls.

18. Be-te (*Tabernæmontana recurva*). This has attractive white flowers.

19. Kui-hoe (*Olea fragrans*). This flower is highly appreciated by the Chinese women as an adornment in their headgear.

20. Balsam. Cultivated in gardens.

21. Lotus (*Nymphæa Lotus*). Found in ponds.

22. Chrysanthemum. Many varieties, carefully cultivated, and brought to a high state of perfection.

23. To-tiau-lien (*Bryophyllum calycinum*). The white flowers of this plant are often seen hanging over walls and rocks.

24. Un-tsu-chio (*Costus speciosa*).

25. Kim-chiam (*Hemerocallis disticha*). This is also used as a vegetable.

26. Peony (*Pæonia Moutan*) is cultivated.

27. Sien-tan (*Ixora apperis*). It has bright scarlet flowers. Several varieties were doubtless introduced from China.

28. Orchids. A common and interesting variety is the lady's tresses (*Neottia spiralis*), called by the Chinese "corkscrew." It seems to me that this orchid family surpasses all others in the island for beauty and fragrance. Orchids are pretty when seen in conservatories, but to be viewed to advantage they must be met in their home in the dense forests, on the ground or on the branches of trees. The exquisite fragrance of some, and the varied forms and colors of others, resembling, as they do, spiders, birds, and butterflies, render them all objects of indescribable beauty and interest. At times one stands as if on enchanted ground. In those primeval forests the traveler becomes suddenly conscious of an influence that soothes and charms, making him for a while oblivious to all things else. It is the matchless fragrance of the orchid that there year after year "wastes its sweetness on the desert air."

The botany of Formosa presents a subject of intensest interest to the thoughtful student. For the missionary there is a tongue in every leaf, a voice in every flower. Do we not, as the great naturalist, Alfred Russel Wallace, said, "obtain a fuller and clearer insight into the course of nature, and increased confidence that the mighty maze of being we see everywhere around us is not without a plan"? Who can tread the ever green carpet of grass; who can see the many-colored flowers and blossoms on plant and vine and shrub; who can look up at the tangled growths of the bamboo, the palm, the elegant tree-fern, or the stately pride of the silent forests, and not be struck by the harmony between God's work and Word? Understanding something of the flora of Formosa, what missionary would not be a better man, the bearer of a richer evangel? What convert would not be a more enduring Christian? With reverent delight and adoration we exclaim, "O Lord, how manifold are thy works! In wisdom hast thou made them all. The earth is full of thy goodness."

CHAPTER VIII

ANIMAL LIFE

Mammalia—Birds—Reptiles—Fishes—Insects—Mollusca

IT would require a volume rather than a brief chapter to discuss in detail the zoölogy of Formosa. The subject has not yet received the attention of naturalists, and no lists or classification has been made. There is being manifested both in the East and in America a desire for information about the animal life of the island, and to meet in part the acknowledged want I have prepared lists under the various subdivisions of mammalia, birds, reptiles, fishes, insects, and mollusca. Those interested in the subject will be able to fill up the outline, and the general reader may not find this chapter uninstructive reading.

I. *Mammalia*

Mammalia Peculiar to Formosa

1. Monkey, pouched (*Macacus cyclopis*). Many of this class are found. We fed and cared for half a dozen from babyhood upward, and observed how similar they were to the earliest fossil monkeys.
2. Tree-civet (*Helictis subaurantiaca*).
3. Wild boar (*Sus taivanus*).
4. Flying-squirrel (*Sciuropterus kaleensis*).
5. White-breasted flying-squirrel (*Pteromys pectoralis*).
6. Red flying-squirrel (*Pteromys grandis*).

7. Field-rat (*Mus losea*).
8. Country rat (*Mus canna*).
9. A smaller rat (*Mus Koxinga*).
10. Fruit-bat (*Pteropus Formosus*).
11. Blind mole (*Talpa insularis*).
12. Mountain-goat (*Nemorhædus Swinhoii*).
13. Deer (*Cervus Swinhoii*).
14. Spotted deer (*Pseudaxis*).

Mammalia not Peculiar to Formosa, but Found There

1. Squirrel (*Sciurus*).
2. Squirrel (*Sciurus castaneorentris*).
3. Indian rat (*Mus Indicus*).
4. Rat (*Mus bandicota*).
5. Gem-faced civet (*Peguma larvata*).
6. Spotted civet (*Viverricula Malaccensis*). All these civets are wild, ferocious, and untamable.
7. Chinese tiger-cat (*Felis Chinensis*).
8. Marten (*Martes flavigula*).
9. Musk-rat (*Sorex murinus*).
10. Large-eared bat (*Nyctinornus cestonii*).
11. Black-and-orange bat (*Vespertilio Formosus*).
12. Leopard (*Felis pardus*).
13. Bear (*Ursus Malayanus*). We had one to keep company with the monkeys. It was amusing to see them tease and torment poor Bruin until he was enraged. Then he would stamp with his feet. But when he was pleased he would put his head between his fore legs and turn a series of somersaults, like a ball rolling round and round.
14. Hare (*Lupus Sinensis*).
15. Scaly ant-eater (*Manis longicauda*). It abounds in the mountains, is covered with scales, and is toothless. It burrows in the ground, and, as its name suggests, feeds mainly on ants, with

which the island is infested. It has power to raise its scales, which are hard and horny, and after disturbing the ants' nest it allows the inmates to cover its entire body. Then it either crushes them between its close-pressed scales, or, plunging into a pool, releases them on the water. In either case it secures its prey. The Chinese, referring to a man who would feign weakness in order to accomplish mischief, have this saying: " The manis feigns death to entrap ants." They have also a superstition which leads them to pluck the seventh scale from the end of the tail of this animal, and to hang it as a sort of charm around the necks of children.

16. Wildcat (*Felis viverrina*).

17. Otter (*Lutra vulgaris*).

Domestic Animals

1. Black goat. Smaller than the brown goat of Western lands.

2. Dog. This animal is wolfish in appearance and habit.

3. Cat. Similar in appearance and nature to the Western house-cat.

4. Horse. There are only a few horses in the island, and the few that are there have been brought from the mainland of China. They are small and used only for riding.

5. Water-buffalo and ox. There seems to be a misconception regarding these two animals. Wallace writes of *Bos Chinensis*, the South China wild cow, as being the same in form; Wright refers to the wild Formosan cow; and Blyth says it is a cross between the zebu and the European bos. I never saw and never heard of such an animal in the island. Under the family *Bovidæ* there is first the ox (*Bos taurus*), descended from the *Bos primigenius*, the origin of all domestic cattle. The Formosan cattle are smaller, of Jersey breed, and are not milked, so that there is no butter, milk, or cheese made in North

Formosa. Then there is the now almost extinct bison, the *Bos Americanus*. The so-called buffalo-robe is really a bison-robe. The bison family is not found in Formosa. The third branch of this family is the buffalo (*Bubulus buffalus*), which is distinctly Oriental, takes the place of the horse in Formosa, and is by far the most valuable animal reared there. It is called water-buffalo because pools of water where it may wallow are necessary to its existence. (See chapter on Rice-farming.)

II. *Birds*

Land Birds

Formosa may not have as many or as beautiful birds as some other tropical countries, but the island is not without its songsters, and has several species that are not found elsewhere.

Birds Peculiar to Formosa

1. Thrushes (*Turdidæ*).
2. Warblers (*Sylviidæ*). Three species.
3. Orioles (*Oriolidæ*). One species.
4. Crows (*Corvidæ*). One species.
5. Babblers (*Timaliidæ*). Eight species.
6. Pheasants (*Phasianidæ*). Two species.
7. Partridges (*Tetraonidæ*). Three species.
8. Pigeons. Three species. Early in the morning the bamboo-groves resound with the cooing of these beautiful birds.
9. Woodpeckers (*Picidæ*). One species.
10. Flycatchers (*Muscicapidæ*). One species.
11. Shrikes (*Campephagidæ*). One species.
12. Tits (*Paridæ*). Two species.
13. Weaver-finches (*Ploceidæ*). One species.
14. Goat-suckers (*Caprimulgidæ*). One species.
15. Owls (*Strigidæ*). Two species.

16. Jays (*Corvidæ*). Two species.

17. Skylarks (*Alaudidæ*). Two species. This is the sweetest singer in Formosa. Many a time, traveling over the plateau, where the dew-gemmed tea-plantations and tall fir-trees sparkle in the morning sun, have I been charmed by the cheery notes of the skylark poured out now almost within reach, and now falling faintly from the deep empyrean.

Birds not Peculiar to Formosa

1. Kingfisher (*Halcyon coromanda*).
2. Hawk-eagle (*Spizaëtus Nipalensis*).
3. Kite (*Milvus ictinus*).
4. Swallow (*Hirundo rustica*).
5. Magpie (*Pica caudata*).
6. Quail (*Coturnix Dussumieri*).
7. Owl (*Bulaca Newarensis*).
8. Cormorant (*Glaculus carbo*).
9. Sandpiper (*Totanus hypoleucus*).
10. Snipe (*Scolopax gallinago*).

Sea Birds

1. Common gull (*Larus canus*).
2. Black gull (*Larus marinus*).
3. Tern (*Sterna hirundo*).
4. Wild duck (*Anas boscas*).
5. Teal (*Querquedula crecca*).

Domestic Birds

There are no turkeys on the island, but the universal custom is to castrate male chickens of the hen family, and so there is reared a capon which in flavor and size is not much inferior to the gobbler. This fowl walks about the door quiet and tame, and sometimes attains a weight of fifteen pounds. The goose, common duck, and large Muscovite duck are common domestic fowl.

III. *Reptiles*

Serpents

1. One day, on returning from the country, and going up the steps to the door of our house in Tamsui, I found a large serpent, eight feet in length, lying across the threshold. With help I succeeded in despatching him. The following day, when about to leave my study-room, I was confronted by its mate, of equal size and very fierce-looking. A loud call brought two or three students, and we ended that one's life. They belonged to the species *Ptyas mucosus*.

2. Once, as I entered a small shed like a hen-coop, a snake which resembled the hoop-snake sprang from the roof and fell coiled up in front of me. Its head was up in a moment, and ready to spring. I jumped backward, and with the assistance of others I succeeded in securing this rare specimen for my museum.

3. A few years ago we had a pigeon-cage, made of bamboo wrought into the requisite shape. One night the poor birds were flying about, greatly frightened. Upon investigation we found a large snake of the python family bent over with its head moving at the pigeon-hole. One vigorous blow brought it down. When fully stretched out it was more than eight feet in length.

4. At Tamsui, near the mission bungalow, I erected a second story above an old kitchen for a small study-room. One night, about eleven o'clock, I heard a noise among papers which were lying over a hole in the floor. Supposing that the noise was produced by rats, I called to those below. Presently Koa Kau ran up, looked into the room, then darted downstairs again, and in a twinkling pinned the exposed part of a monstrous serpent to the wall below. By this time fully three feet of the body was through the hole into the room above. It was

exceedingly violent, but I soon thrust its head through with a long Chinese spear. It measured nine English feet. Its triangular head was protected by nine plates, the body highly marked, the fangs not very pointed, and the teeth small and inclined backward. The thought of that midnight companion was by no means pleasant. It was similar to the hamadryad type. The Chinese were greatly alarmed and would not rest until it was buried out of sight.

5. Walking across the harbor, making the ascent to the plateau, one day, my eye suddenly caught sight of something green in the midst of the bushes at a turn in the path. At the same instant it sprang to strike my hand; missing its aim, it grabbed the end of my sleeve in its teeth. It proved to be a green snake of the *Dryophis fulgida* species, eighteen inches in length, with flat, triangular head. It is now preserved in alcohol in my museum at Tamsui. The Chinese have a great horror of this species.

6. When among tall grasses and rocks, ascending the high mountain-ranges, I was more than once struck at by the deadly cobra-de-capello. Owing to the tall grass on each side I did not observe him, but fortunately he missed his aim. One successful charge would never need to be repeated.

7. I procured one of the species *Naja tripudians*, and found that keeping his head and neck in spirits of ammonia only made him writhe in agony and lash his tail with fury. He was four feet six inches in length.

Turtles

1. Green turtle (*Chelonia viridis*). They are found in large numbers along the shore of eastern Formosa, and are from three to five feet in length. They vary in weight from two hundred to four hundred pounds. Going up from the water at night, they dig holes in the sand on the beach with their flappers, lay their eggs, cover them over, then with head erect

start back for their home in the sea. Hundreds never reach their destination. The savages are on the beach, with fires kindled, awaiting their game. The turtles fight bravely, but being clumsy they are soon turned on their backs, in which position they are helpless.

2. Hawk's-bill turtle (*Chelonia imbricata*). The mouth is similar to that of the hawk; hence the name. It is the one from which so many useful and ornamental articles are made.

3. Mud-turtle. These may be found in many of the fresh-water streams.

IV. *Fishes*

Fish abound both in the waters around the shore and in the rivers and streams, and every conceivable method is used in fishing. Among the varieties may be mentioned:

1. Flounder (*Platessa flesus*).
2. Mullet (*Mullus barbatus*).
3. Mackerel (*Scomber*).
4. Shad (*Clupea alosa*).
5. Blackfish.
6. Shark (*Carchariidæ*). The peculiar hammerhead (*Zygæna malleus*) is eaten by the poorer classes. The blue shark (*Carcharias glaucus*), from five to twelve feet in length, is caught on the west coast, a day's journey south from Tamsui. The flesh is eaten, though not relished. Oil is made out of the liver. The fins, however, are counted a choice delicacy in all parts of China.
7. Flying-fish (*Exocœtus volitans*).
8. Trout (*Salmo fario*).
9. Sunfish.
10. Remora. An extraordinary creature with a suctorial disk with which it attaches itself to other animals and sucks their blood. A shark was once discovered in the mouth of the Tamsui River, floundering about helplessly. We surrounded

and secured him, and found a remora about six inches long in his ear. This little creature had power to make the monster of the sea utterly stupid.

    11. Globe-fish (*Diodon hystrix*).

    12. Diodon (*Ostracion cornutus*).

    13. Porpoise (*Phocæna communis*).

    14. Eel.

    15. Thornback (*Rija clavata*).

    16. Sole (*Solea vulgaris*). This is the most palatable of all the finny tribes in Formosan waters, and is most prized by Chinese as well as Europeans.

    17. Periophthalmus. It is found in mud or muddy water, as if depending on two leg-like fins for locomotion. With these it jumps and bounds with great agility. They are the keenest-eyed creatures I have ever seen. They are never caught napping. The slightest movement is observed, and like a flash they disappear into the mud. It was years before I succeeded in securing a specimen.

V. *Insects*

    1. Cicada. If the sacred beetle engaged the attention of the ancient Egyptians, the cicada won the affections of the Grecians. Homer and Hesiod sang of the light, bloodless, and harmless cicada. In modern times, Byron, making use of the Italian name, spoke of the "shrill cicalas." The males have an apparatus for the production of musical sounds, while the females are dumb and silent. There are three important species in Formosa; one reddish, another green, and a third large and black. The last, the *Fidicina altrata*, is most frequently seen. The female deposits her eggs on the branch of a tree. In due time little grubs are hatched and creep down the bark and into the earth, where they feed on the juices of roots and bulbs. In a couple of months, as large, living

beetles, they come up again, earth-stained, out of the ground, and climb up the stem of a tree, very often a banian. Having selected the sunny side, the beetle crawls on a fresh green leaf, forces its claws through it, and there remains with its back to the sun. The heat of the sun cracks its shell between the shoulders; a whitish-looking, soft-winged creature comes out, leaves its coffin, and flies away, singing "Katy did" and "Katy didn't." Its after-life continues for a couple of weeks, and then, dizzy-like, it drops, turns over, and life is extinct. Its little course is soon run.

2. The praying mantis. What a misnomer! The "praying" is really waiting in that attitude in which he can seize the prey which seldom escapes his vigilant glance. This insect is savage and cannibalistic in habits. A large female came near my study-room one day. She was captured and put into a paper box with a perforated top. I watched her movements closely and soon had the rare privilege of seeing her deposit one hundred eggs in a thick, spongy bag which she produced and affixed to the side of the box. This spongy bag hardened, and in a fortnight eight dozen small cannibals came forth, and were soon devouring one another without mercy. These emptied bags are seen on thousands of branches, but I never met a native who knew what they were.

3. Cockroach (*Blatta orientalis*). In summer this cockroach is almost as common as the house-fly. It is found among dishes, in bureaus, and on sideboards. One night at eleven o'clock, in my small upper room, I observed a cockroach moving slowly up the wall. Suddenly a gecko (chickchack) appeared within three feet right above. With little jumps and sudden movements he was soon close to the cockroach—so close, indeed, that he grasped the left wing in his mouth. Then he began to pull, shake his head, and show other signs of pleasure. Slowly the pair were moving upward, when a small lizard appeared, but was warned by very significant tail

movements to stand off. Soon the cockroach fell from his enemy's grasp and tumbled to the floor. He was too unwieldy for that active little chickchack.

4. Beetle. There are several species. Chinese boys make a very ingenious and extraordinary-looking toy out of a variety golden in color. The materials used in its construction are a string about three feet in length, a tube four inches long, and a stick slightly larger than an ordinary lead-pencil. One end of the cord is put through the tube, and secured there by a little key or fastener, so as to rotate without twisting. The other end is attached to the center of the stick, to each end of which there is tied a golden beetle. The boy, now holding the tube in his hand at arm's-length, gives the beetles an opportunity of exercising their wings. Faster and faster they go on their miniature merry-go-round, until they appear like a yellow circle. Sometimes the effect is enhanced by fastening little bits of bright-colored delf at intervals on the stick. I have seen a foreigner give a Chinese boy a dollar for an exhibition of this plaything.

5. Grasshopper (*Acrida viridissima*). There are numerous varieties. One large green kind, which might indeed be called a locust, lays its eggs on paths. The female makes a hole the size of a lead-pencil, and putting her body down into it deposits a heap of eggs, which are hatched by the heat of the sun.

6. Water-bug (*Nepidæ*).

7. Water-boatmen (*Notonectidæ*).

8. Bedbug (*Acanthia lectularia*).

9. Mole-cricket (*Gryllotalpa vulgaris*).

10. Field-cricket (*Gryllus campestris*).

11. Dragon-flies (*Libellulidæ*). This is a large family. One member has a red body and is of surpassing beauty.

12. White ants (*Termes*). They are not ants, but *Termis bellicosi*, and belong to the order *Neuroptera*, while the true ants belong to *Hymenoptera*. They work in the dark, and if

moving from place to place on the surface of an object they invariably construct a tunnel or incasement of earth and dust, with a passage somewhat larger than a large quill, and through this they pass and repass, carrying on their work of destruction. They are extremely destructive of all kinds of woodwork. They penetrate and riddle the large beams of a house from end to end in a few months, leaving nothing but a thin shell on the outside and the hard heart within. When they have done their work in the sill of a house there remains only a crust, sometimes no thicker than paper. They work up through board floors, pierce the bottoms of trunks, puncture furniture of every description, leaving the outside whole and complete, but so honeycombed within as to be easily crushed in the hand. Once we left a chest filled with clothes in our house at Tamsui while we were absent for two months. When we returned we found pecks of white ants in it, the clothes in shreds, and the boards of the chest so eaten away that it could not resist the slightest pressure.

13. Glow-worm (*Lampyris noctiluca*).

14. Death-watch (*Anobium striatum*). This insect bores into furniture and makes a ticking noise.

15. Stag-beetle (*Lucanus*).

16. Sacred beetle of Egypt (*Scarabæus sacer*). This interesting creature may be seen almost any day along the pathways in the college grounds. It is small, but of remarkable strength. The female deposits her larvæ in the interior of a ball about the size of a plum, made out of the excreta of some herbivorous animal such as the ox. When this ball is prepared it is transported to a hole already excavated, into which it is rolled, and where the eggs are hatched by the sun's heat. The living creature eats its way out of the ball and comes out the sacred flying-beetle, so famous in Egyptian mythology. The transportation of this ball, sometimes over considerable distances, is a very interesting sight. All principles of propul-

sion are employed, but the commonest is for the male to push the ball from the rear with his hind legs, while the female goes in front to steer its course and assist by pulling.

17. Golden beetle.

18. Tiger-beetle (*Cicindela campestris*).

19. Water-beetle (*Hydradephaga*).

20. Whirligigs (*Gyrini*).

21. *Elater* or skipjacks (*Elateridæ*).

22. True ants. Of these there are several species. One kind makes large nests, like those of wasps, in a tree; another raises hillocks on the ground; but the most provoking of all is a tiny brown species. Unless the legs of a dining-table are standing in bowls of water it is impossible to keep the food from being literally covered by the ants. Everywhere, at every corner and every turn, they can be seen during the summer months, moving in long lines.

23. Wasps (*Vespa*).

24. Bees (*Apis*). Hives are kept, but bees are often found in nests in the woods.

25. House-fly (*Musca domestica*).

26. Mosquito (*Culex pipiens*). The female alone stings, but so efficiently does she perform this service that there is not a bed in the emperor's palace or the beggar's hut that is not furnished with a mosquito-curtain to protect the sleepers.

27. Hawk-moth (*Acherontia atropos*).

28. Clothes-moth (*Tinea rusticella*). So destructive is this insect that a second suit of clothes is an unprofitable care.

29. Atlas-moth (*Atlacus atlas*). I procured one which measured from tip to tip of its wings nine and three quarter inches, and of exquisite beauty.

30. Moon-moth (*Atlacus luna*).

31. Sphinx.

32. Walking-sticks (*Bacillus natalis*).

33. Incased insects (*Psychidæ*).

34. Fleas. As great a pest as anywhere else on earth.

35. Lice.

36. Butterflies.

(1) Swallowtailed (*Papilio machaon*). Numerous and beautiful.

(2) Peacock butterfly (*Papilio io*).

(3) Leaf-butterfly (*Kallima paralekta*). When this beautiful specimen is on the limb of a tree one would require the eye of a naturalist to distinguish it from a dead leaf. The resemblance is almost perfect, alike to form, color, and position.

37. Myriapod (*Julus terrestris*).

38. Centiped (*Scolopendra*). Next to venomous serpents most dreaded by the natives.

39. Spider (*Araneina*).

40. Earthworms.

VI. *Mollusca*

To secure the glassy, shiny appearance of shells we place them when alive in the ground. In a few days they are removed and thoroughly washed. Those found at the sea-shore dead are never perfect, for the water and sand grind and wear off the external coat. These animals are found in sand and mud, on timber, and resting on seaweed as they sail the sea.

1. Fountain-shell (*Strombus*).

2. The buckie of Scotland (*Fusus* or *Cehrysodomus antiquus*). This is a shell in which the sound of the sea is always heard.

3. Whelk (*Buccinum undatum*). This has a rasp-pointed tongue, with which it bores the shells of other mollusks when in search of a delicious breakfast.

4. Cone (*Conus imperialis*).

5. Cone (*Conus aulicus*).

6. Money-cowry (*Cyprœa moneta*).

7. Tiger-cowry (*Cyprœa tigris*).

8. Snail (*Helix aspersa*).

9. Chiton (*Magnificus*).

10. Oysters (*Ostreidæ*).

11. Pecten.

12. Mussel (*Mytilus edulis*).

13. *Unio littoralis.*

14. Razor-fish (*Solen vagina*).

15. Limpet (*Patella vulgata*).

16. Boring-shell (*Pholas dactylus*).

17. Sea-urchin (*Echinus esculentus*). On the sea-coast of Formosa pickled sea-urchins are used as a condiment with rice.

18. Starfish (*Asterias rubens*).

19. Sea-anemone.

20. Hermit-crab (*Pagurus bernhardus*). This is one of the most interesting of all the living mollusks on the sea-shore. The fore parts are furnished with claws and feelers and are partially protected, but the hinder parts are soft, sensitive, easily injured, and entirely defenseless. The hermit-crab has no home, but is a semi-parasite, a kind of sea "tramp." It depends on finding a home in the shell of some dead whelk or other mollusk. I have often watched it on its search for a suitable shell. One would be too large, another too small, a third might be already inhabited, in which case a fight for possession sometimes ensued. When a satisfactory one was found and proved to be untenanted, the crab would whisk its unprotected parts into it and march off, its house on its back, as lordly as if it had a legal right to undisturbed possession.

21. King-crab (*Limulus gigas*). This resembles the ancient trilobite. It is found in the shallow water on the land side of Kelung harbor.

22. "Holy-water pot" (*Tridacna squamosa*). This receives its name because it is often used to hold the consecrated water in Roman Catholic cathedrals in France and Italy. There is an enormous one in a cathedral in Paris. In the Malacca Straits it grows to a large size, and has been found to weigh several hundred pounds. Large ones are brought in junks as

ballast from the China coast to Formosa, but smaller ones are found around the island. The preparing of them has become quite an industry, especially in the city of Tek-chham. The Chinese use a toothless hand-saw, sand, and water, as granite-cutters do in sawing granite. The pieces of this shell which are sawn off resemble marble. They are cut as desired, three or four inches thick, ground on sandstone, and then converted into bracelets, armlets, and other ornaments which are worn by the savages, who value them very highly, and give in exchange rattan, camphor, dye-root, and pith.

23. Periwinkle.

24. Triton (*Triton variegatum*).

25. Trumpet-shell.

26. Conch-shell.

27. Cockle (*Cardiidæ edule*).

28. Harp (*Harpa ventricosa*).

29. Thorny woodcock (*Murex tenuispinus*).

30. Trochus (*Trochus Niloticus*).

31. Scallop (*Pecten maximus*).

32. *Haliotis tuberculata*.

33. Sea-acorn shells (*Balanus sulcatus*).

34. Lobster (*Homarus vulgaris*). Large; bluish green when alive; a reddish-brown color when boiled.

35. Shrimp (*Palæmon vulgaris*).

36. Pea-crab (*Pinnotheres pisum*).

37. Paper-nautilus (*Argonauta argo*). It is difficult to conceive of anything more lovely than this thin, translucent, boat-shaped shell, which is propelled by water ejected from its funnel.

38. Octopus (*Octopus vulgaris*).

39. *Sepiidæ* (*Sepia officinalis*). "Cuttlebone," which is placed in the cages for canary-birds, is the calcareous internal shell of this animal.

40. Pearly nautilus (*Nautilus pampilius*). Its mouth is like a parrot's beak, the outside white, with brown stripes.

CHAPTER IX

ETHNOLOGY IN OUTLINE

Two classes—The dominant race—Ethnological table—The aborigines
Malayan—Traditions—Foreign opinion—Migration—Habits and
customs—Features—Linguistic differences

THE inhabitants of North Formosa may be classified as belonging to either one of two great races; the aborigines,
both civilized and savage, are Malayan, the Chinese are Mongolian. To be sure, there are "foreigners" from Europe and
America; but their number is so small, and the part they play
in the life of the island so inconsiderable, that they may be
excluded from our present reckoning. The two great classes
have not to any extent mingled, and so there is no mixed race
on the island. The purpose of this chapter is not an exhaustive
study, but rather to set forth in outline the ethnology of North
Formosa, and to indicate the argument in support of the
opening statement classifying the people as either Malayan or
Mongolian.

The dominant race, first in numbers, intelligence, and influence, is the Chinese. They do not present any problem of
difficulty to the ethnologist, as their origin and racial relations
are easily traced. They are immigrants, or the children of those
who in earlier years crossed the Formosa Channel from the
thickly populated provinces of the mainland. They brought
with them their habits of life and their household gods. They
found the island wooded down to the water's edge, and the

home of tribes of wild, roaming savages, whose appearance was strange to them, and whose speech was rude and barbarous. Their entrance was disputed at every point, but their greater numbers and superior skill prevailed. The savages were driven back out of some of the richest plains; rice-farms and tea-plantations took the place of forest tangle and wild plateau; the rude hamlets of another race vanished; towns and cities with their unmistakable marks of the " Middle Kingdom " took their place; and the Chinese became a superior power in Formosa. They are in the main industrious and aggressive, showing all the characteristics of their race, and retaining their ancestral modes of life and worship. The large majority have emigrated from the Fu-kien province, and speak what is called the Amoy dialect. These are called Hok-los. A few are the descendants of a tribe who moved from the north of China and settled in parts of the Canton province, whence they afterward crossed to Formosa. These are called Hak-kas ("strangers"), with distinct forms of life and language.

The Chinese call all the aborigines of the island barbarians, and classify them according as they live in the plains or on the mountains, and according as they have resisted or submitted to Chinese rule. In a large plain on the east coast are those who have acknowledged Chinese authority and adopted their mode of worship; these are called " Pe-po-hoan " ("barbarians of the plain "). In a second plain farther down the coast is another settlement of aborigines; these are called " Lam-si-hoan " ("barbarians of the south "). Unsubdued mountaineers they call " Chhi-hoan " ("raw barbarians "). A few who have settled among the Chinese in the west are called "Sek-hoan " ("ripe barbarians "). These names are all Chinese, and indicate the relations of the dominant race to the aborigines. Now that Japan has possession of the island a new element will be introduced. The relations of the Japanese to the present inhabitants cannot as yet be set forth, but the indications are that they will treat the aborigines with fairness. The following table will show the ethnology of the people:

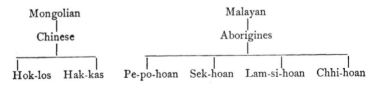

Mongolian		Malayan			
Chinese		Aborigines			
Hok-los	Hak-kas	Pe-po-hoan	Sek-hoan	Lam-si-hoan	Chhi-hoan

The classification of all the aboriginal tribes as Malayan may, however, be regarded as an open question, and proof of the statement may be demanded. There are several reasons which have forced me to the conclusion that they are all descendants of settlers from the islands around the Malay Archipelago, and these I now submit.

1. *Aboriginal Tradition.*—I have picked up at first-hand from various tribes traditions which support the contention that they are of Malayan origin. One is that their forefathers came from a southerly direction; that, being in boats, they were wrecked; that they lived near the sea on level ground, and afterward, when others came, moved inward even over the mountain-ranges; that they caught fish and turtle, entrapped the wild boar, shot the deer with bow and arrow, were clothed in deerskins, reckoned the time by tying knots on the stem of a tall grass, and when their numbers in any one place increased to upward of one hundred or two hundred they moved a little distance away, cleared the ground, and called themselves the "other village," "south village," "new village," or "large village." Their houses were made of reeds, rattan, and bamboo. New-comers, bringing knives and similar utensils, presented them to the head men, and afterward, when the Chinese put in an appearance, they exchanged skins and horns of deer for guns, powder, and knives. They remembered the coming of the "red-headed kinsmen," who treated them kindly, and with whom they had free mercantile intercourse. These the

Chinese drove out and began to make settlements themselves. Hatred sprang up, and head-hunting, which was prosecuted by their fathers in their ancestral home, was resorted to.

There is a second tradition and a memorial custom which point to the same conclusion. On the Ki-lai plain, on the east coast, where the Lam-si-hoan are settled, two canoes are kept to commemorate the coming of their fathers to the island. As one shows marks of decay it is renewed or replaced. They are kept under a thatched cover in the open plain not far from the sea. Once a year the Lam-si-hoan assemble and carry these canoes to the water's edge, when a number of their men enter them, paddle out a short distance, and return. Then with rejoicings the canoes are restored to shelter. The Lam-si-hoan declare that their forefathers came in similar canoes from places south and east of Formosa, and this custom is intended to preserve that tradition.

At Lam-hong-o, a Pe-po-hoan village near So Bay, men of eighty years of age told me how in the days of their grandfathers forty or fifty strong fishermen took a dislike to the rainy weather in the Kap-tsu-lan plain and longed for their old home. They lashed planks together and formed rude boats, in which they set out in a southerly direction, bound for their fatherland. My informants were of the opinion that their ancestral home was one of the Philippine Islands.

At Sin-sia the villagers assert that their forefathers came, not from the islands, but from the mainland of China, and were non-Mongolian. It is certain that only one other village in the Kap-tsu-lan plain speaks the same dialect as Sin-sia, and these two villages recognize each other as kin, and are so looked upon by all the rest. It is entirely probable that they are descended, as they claim to be, from the aboriginal tribes still found on the mainland of China.

2. *Consensus of Foreign Opinion.*—Travelers see in the various tribes of Formosa the features and manners of the inhabitants

of Luzon, Polynesia, the Malay Peninsula, the islands of Loo-
choo, Sunda, and Borneo, and of Siam and Yunnan; and there
is great unanimity of opinion that the aborigines of Formosa are
descendants of emigrants from the Malay Peninsula and the
islands of the China Sea. It is contended by some, however,
that the aboriginal inhabitants of Formosa were of the negro
race, and that they were driven back into the mountains by the
Malayans. I cannot admit the contention, as I have failed to
find the slightest trace of the negrito element, nor is the presence within the mountains of such a people suspected by any
known tribe. I have made careful inquiries among the mountain tribes near Ta-kow in the far south, among the tribes at
Po-sia Lake in the center, and among more than a dozen tribes
in the north, as well as among the Pe-po-hoan and Sek-hoan, and
everywhere I received the same reply. They were all positive
that there were no woolly-headed races within the mountains
or anywhere else in the island. Superficial observers frequently
make strong assertions. Indeed, I was told a few years ago
that a white tribe, finely developed and with grayish eyes, was
to be found among the mountains. So persistent was the contention that I resolved to put it to the proof. Making my way
into the place where they were said to dwell, instead of the
descendants of the Dutch, I found short-set, brown-featured,
black, lank-haired Malayans.

3. *Natural Migration.*—The ocean current that sweeps between Sunda, Java, and Sumatra on the one side and Borneo
on the other runs north through the China Sea and between
Formosa and the mainland. Another current sweeps between
Borneo and Celebes, through the Celebes Sea, and touches
the north Pacific current, which runs as a black stream (Kuro
Siwa) across to the eastern side of Formosa. This ocean current would very easily and naturally carry mercantile boats
and fishermen in their smacks from the islands in the Malay
Archipelago to the shores of Formosa. Indeed, examples of

such migration have taken place within my own time. Some years after my arrival in Formosa strange-looking outriggers sailed into the harbor of Kelung. In them were a number of famished boatmen with tattoo marks from head to foot. They were kindly treated, and in the course of time were taken to Hong Kong, and thence conveyed to their home on the Pelew Islands. Not infrequently boat-loads from the Loo-choo Islands are wrecked on the shore of Formosa.

4. *Habits and Customs.*—The habits and customs of the aborigines of Formosa will be referred to at length in subsequent chapters. Suffice it to say here that in nearly every point they bear a marked resemblance to the habits and customs of the aborigines of Borneo. The tattoo marks follow the same well-established pattern. Their dress and ornaments are similar, and their houses suggest a common architecture. Like Malay Islanders, they worship their ancestors, and within the mountains they have the unmistakable head-hunting proclivities of the Dyaks of Borneo.

5. *Physical Features.*—The Chinese in Formosa are round-headed, the aborigines medium between long and broad. The sutures or lines where the bones of the skull are united, I find in the skulls of the young to be only slightly traced; the skull has the appearance of a round ball or bone. This is characteristic of the islanders belonging to the lower races. So, too, prognathism or projection of the jaws—"maxillary angle," "facial angle"—points to kinship with the islanders of the Malay type. The hair is round, thus showing that in its possessor there is no trace of the woolly-headed race. Its color is black, identical with the Malayan. The eyes are Malayan in color, and the nose conforms to the same type.

It may be objected that the various aboriginal tribes cannot have had a common origin inasmuch as they now speak different dialects. Linguistic differences, however, are not conclusive. Scandinavians in Caithness, Finland, Orkney, and

Iceland speak dialects or languages quite different from their kinsmen in Norway and Sweden. Different circumstances explain the difference. Similar changes have taken place among the Chinese in Formosa. A mainland man can be told at once from his Formosan cousin, and the " Kap-tsu-lan twang " marks the Chinese in that plain. In like manner crews and passengers from the Malay Islands, shipwrecked at intervals on the coast of Formosa, would be absorbed by the larger community already settled there, and would acquire the dominant dialect; and where tribes have been isolated, with no means of intercommunication, and with tribal enmities keeping them separate, modifications and changes in their language are to be expected. Such changes have taken place in the Highland settlements in Canada, where the grandchildren of the pioneers are entirely ignorant of the much-loved Gaelic of their forefathers. An interesting instance came under my notice in one of the Kap-tsu-lan villages where we have a church. There is there a man who was shipwrecked on that coast. Years before, he, with others, started in a boat from the Philippine Islands. They passed Bashee and were driven out of their course and upon the shore of Formosa, and he alone survived to tell the tale. He was able, however, to understand a few words of the dialect of the aborigines among whom he landed. He soon learned the Pe-po-hoan dialect, and was subsequently married to a Pe-po-hoan wife, and became, to all intents and purposes, Pe-po-hoan.

The foregoing seems to me a cumulative argument, irresistible and conclusive, that numerous adventurers, fishermen, and traders from the islands south and east of the China Sea, and others from the north and east of Formosa, with perhaps a few from the mainland, entered the island at intervals, and formed what is now called the aboriginal race, and that that race is Malayan.

AMONG THE CHINESE

CHAPTER X

Chinese in Formosa—The Hok-los—The Hak-kas—The language—The
" barbarians "

THERE are nearly three million Chinese on the island. Of
these about one million are in the four districts served by
the Mission of the Presbyterian Church in Canada. They are
divided into two classes, the Hok-los and the Hak-kas. The
Hok-los comprise seven eighths of the Chinese population in
North Formosa. They are emigrants, or the children of emigrants, from the Fu-kien province, opposite the island. After
Koxinga, the Chinese pirate, drove the Dutch out of Formosa,
that rich and beautiful island was opened up for Chinese emigration, and became an outlet for the overcrowded province of
Fu-kien. They found it inhabited by aboriginal tribes who,
though they were friendly to the Dutch, resisted the aggressive-
ness of the Chinese. Gradually the Chinese crowded these
aborigines back into the mountains, and they themselves now
occupy the large and fertile plains on the north and west. Besides those who have made their home on the island, between ten
and twenty thousand come over every year from Amoy to engage in the tea industry. Of these a percentage remain. The
Chinese in Formosa have all the marks of their countrymen in
Fu-kien, except that emigration has done its work in changing
somewhat their customs and point of view. They speak the
Amoy dialect. The women bind their feet and wear the same
dress as those in Amoy.

The Hak-kas ("strangers") are supposed to be descendants of a tribe that emigrated from North China into the Fu-kien province and subsequently into Canton. There are about one hundred thousand of them in North Formosa. They are brave and vigorous, and have fought their way both on the mainland and in Formosa. The women do not bind their feet, and as a result are stronger and more robust than their Hok-lo sisters. They help their husbands on the farm and in all outside work, and are remarkably industrious. In consequence of this the Hak-kas will thrive and become wealthy where the Hok-los would fail and the aborigines would starve. They are found mainly in towns and hamlets in the Sin-tiak and Biau-lek districts, and are the pioneers in the border-land between the Chinese and the savages. They speak a dialect of the Cantonese. The younger generation learn the Hok-lo dialect, and in time the Hak-kas may become extinct.

It should be remembered that the written language in Formosa, as throughout the Chinese empire, is everywhere the same, although the spoken language is so varied. It is not easy for a Westerner to understand this. The written characters remain fixed and represent the same ideas to all the Chinese, but the names of these characters are different in the different provinces of China. Not only so, but in Formosa there are really two languages to be learned, the pronunciation of the characters by the literary class being entirely distinct from the colloquial. For instance, the character representing "man" is pronounced "jîn" by the literary class and "lâng" by the masses. There are no declensions or conjugations in Chinese, their place being taken by the "tones," of which there are eight in the Formosan vernacular. A word that to an English ear has but one sound may mean any one of eight things according as it is spoken in an abrupt, high, low, or any other of the eight "tones." Each one of these "tones" is represented by a written character; hence there are upward of sixty thousand written characters in the language. There are numerous other variations and complications which make the learning of the Chinese language no simple task. A sharp ear, a ready tongue, and a strong imitative faculty are requisite for proficiency in public speech. Many foreigners never become proficient in speaking the language, but may be none the less useful in other departments of service.

The Chinese in Formosa have great contempt for the aborigines, and treat them very much as the Americans have treated the Indian tribes, bartering with them, cheating them, and crowding them back into their mountain strongholds. The aborigines in the plains, whom they call " Pe-po-hoan," the Chinese regard with more favor than they do the savages, but they are gradually dispossessing them and forcing them back into territory to be reclaimed from the mountain tribes.

CHAPTER XI

GOVERNMENT AND JUSTICE

Form of government—The cue—Formosa a province—Official corruption
—Injustice in the yamen—" Mandarin eats cash "—Forms of punish-
ment—Money all-powerful—" Ridding up "—Punishment by proxy
—Oppression of Christians

THE government of China is patriarchal. The emperor
is in theory the father of two hundred and fifty million
Chinese. The present emperor, Kong-su, is ninth in the line
of the Tartar dynasty, which succeeded the Ming dynasty in
1644. The first emperor of the Tartar dynasty was Sun-ti, who
belonged to Manchuria. One of his " reforms " was the introduction of the cue. All Chinese men were compelled to shave
the forehead and dress the hair in a long braid, according to
the Manchurian custom. The cue was made the badge of
fealty to the emperor, and not to wear it is to endanger one's
head. Westerners are slow to learn that the cue has no religious or superstitious significance, but is purely political. It is
the " old flag " of the Chinese empire, the mark of loyalty to
the reigning dynasty. The people have become accustomed
to it, and what was once a disgrace is now regarded with pride.
A Chinese without a cue is a traitor and a rebel. When this
fact comes to be known by self-respecting people in the West
the emblem of Chinese loyalty will cease to be regarded with
ridicule, and the offensive " pigtail " will be blotted out of
English literature.

Theoretically the emperor rules China, but practically the affairs of the empire are managed by six boards, which appoint all the higher officials in the various provinces.

After Koxinga was dethroned, in 1683, Formosa became a dependency of the Fu-kien province. In 1887 it was raised to the rank of a province of the empire, and a governor was appointed by the imperial authorities at Peking, as in the other provinces. Under the governor were four officials, who had rule over the four districts into which North Formosa was divided. Under these magistrates others of lower grade, having jurisdiction over smaller sections, were appointed, and subordinate to these again were local officials and head men, whose authority was correspondingly reduced. All these superior officials were from the mainland, but the head men usually belonged to North Formosa. All these magistrates have judicial as well as governing powers. The administration of justice is in the hands of the governor and his underlings. Each subordinate official holds his office at the will of the next above him. The income attached to any of the offices is not sufficient to support the retinue which must be maintained. As a result there is universal official corruption. From the highest to the lowest, every Chinese official in Formosa has an "itching palm," and the exercise of official functions is always corrupted by money bribes. The mandarin supplements his income by "squeezing" his attendants and every man who comes within his grasp. His attendants have the privilege of recouping themselves by "squeezing" all who through them seek favors from the mandarin. In the matter of bribing and boodling the Chinese official in Formosa could give points to the most accomplished office-seekers and money-grabbers in Washington or Ottawa.

The chief opportunity for corruption is afforded in connection with the administration of justice. The yamen or court-house is the scene of unmitigated lying, scheming, and oppression. The mandarin comes in his sedan-chair, attended by his retinue. He takes his seat on the dais in the yamen. At his right stands his interpreter, an indispensable functionary, inasmuch as the mandarin, being a mainland man, is not supposed to know the local dialect. On either side, in two rows facing each other, stand the constables, and near at hand the lictors and executioners. The yamen is crowded by friends of the litigants and the rabble from the street. There are no lawyers or counsel, and no trial by jury. The mandarin has everything in his own hands. He sits in state, clothed with the awful authority of the "dragon" throne. The case in hand is presented, and the accused kneels before the judgment-seat, the picture of abject humility. The mandarin examines him through his interpreter:

MANDARIN. "Ask him if his name is Lim."

INTERPRETER. "The Great Man asks you if your name is Lim."

ACCUSED. "The little child's name is Lim."

INTERPRETER. "His name is Lim."

MANDARIN. "Ask him if he is guilty of the charge made against him."

INTERPRETER. "The Great Man asks if you are guilty of the charge made against you."

ACCUSED. "The little child would not dare to do such a thing."

And so the case goes on. Sometimes witnesses are called; this, however, is optional with the mandarin, who is subject to other influences than the weight of evidence. The "almighty dollar" turns the scale of justice. The financial strength of the litigants and of their friends has been inquired into, and the one who sends in the largest amount of sycee-silver is certain to get the verdict in his favor. To be sure, all this is *sub rosa*. There is the greatest parade of righteous judgment, and a hint at bribery would be shocking. But the people all know the facts. They have a saying commonly applied to their officials: " Koa chiah chi " ("The mandarin eats cash "). The magistrate has arbitrary power in the matter of punishment. The sentence depends not a little on the humor the mandarin may be in, but much more on the size of the bribe paid. The most common sentence is the fine, and this is graded according to the ability of the culprit to pay and according to the fee privately given the judge.

The next punishment is smiting on the cheeks. This is often administered to false witnesses; indeed, it often happens that a witness whose evidence is not pleasing to the mandarin is immediately beaten. The Great Man expresses his displeasure at the evidence, and the constables lay hold of the witness by the cue and turn up his face to the lictor, who gives him the appointed number of blows. If the witness continues obstinate in his evidence he may be beaten again and again.

Another punishment is the "bamboo." The culprit is stripped by the constables under the eye of the mandarin, and receives on the thighs from ten to one thousand blows with the bamboo cudgel. Sometimes the punishment is inflicted at intervals, as the "cat-o'-nine-tails" in the West. The "bamboo " is always painful, and at times the flesh is lacerated and mortification sets in, which ends the victim's life.

The cangue is an instrument of humiliation as well as pain. It is formed out of heavy oak planks, is nearly three feet square, with a hole in the center, and is worn on the neck in a public place for a month or two, in some instances both day and night.

Imprisonment for a limited time or for life is a common sentence. The prison is always a dark, dirty dungeon, where tortures, illegal according to Chinese law, but cruelly real in Chinese practice, are inflicted to extort money from the prisoners and their relatives.

Decapitation is inflicted for murder, theft, incendiarism, and other grave offenses. The burglar or firebug gets no mercy. Ordinarily it is a swift stroke from a sharp two-handed sword. In the case of parricide the culprit's body is literally hacked to pieces.

Pirates are punished by having their hands tied behind to a post facing the glaring sun, and their upper eyelids cut off. After several days of this torture they are beheaded in the most excruciatingly painful manner.

In all these cases money wields all-powerful influence. It corrupts the mandarin in his judgment, the lictors and executioners in carrying out the sentence, and the local officials in disposing of the bodies of the dead. The lictor has his opportunity to "squeeze" when the sentence is the "bamboo," the blows being heavy or light according to the bribe. The executioner carries out the death-sentence deftly in a short, swift stroke or with prolonged torture according to the money paid.

I witnessed the execution of four soldiers condemned for burglary. One was on his knees, and in an instant the work was done. Three blows were required for the second. The head of the third was slowly sawed off with a long knife. The fourth was taken a quarter of a mile farther, and amid shouts and screams and many protestations of innocence he was subjected to torture and finally beheaded. The difference in the bribe made the difference in the execution.

So manifestly corrupt is the whole system, and so difficult is it to bring influential criminals to justice, that a periodical "ridding up" is necessary. The imperial authorities at Peking every ten or twelve years appoint some high official, with power over all provincial magistrates, to go through the empire and examine into long-standing grievances. This storm of justice clears the air, and has done not a little to prolong the life of the Chinese empire. I happened to be in Tekchham once when this "avenger of blood" was making his rounds. There lived near the city a local magistrate who for many years had oppressed and imposed upon the farmers and fishermen in his locality. He was always able to bribe the superior magistrates, and was carrying on his extortions with impunity. When it was known that the imperial official would visit Tek-chham a petition was prepared complaining of the local magistrate's conduct. As these poor people would not presume to enter the Great Man's presence, they availed themselves of the privilege of constructing an effigy or " grass man " on the side of the road, in whose hands they placed their petition. When the judicial cortège passed that way, attendants, seeing the " dummy," brought the document, and the official read the appeal as he was carried along. On arriving at Tek-chham he made inquiries, and finding the complaints true he summoned the magistrate. Everything was prearranged. The magistrate prostrated himself before the high official, but while he protested that " the little child would not dare to do such a thing," a signal was given, and without warning the executioner severed his head from his body. This had fine effect on the community and on other magistrates.

Criminals are sometimes punished by proxy. If the guilty party cannot be found, or if he can bribe the magistrate, some careless fellow can easily be procured to suffer the punishment. A little " cash " will do it. Once when complaint had been made that a certain man had plundered one of our chapels, the mandarin at Bang-kah reported to the British consul that the man was under arrest. With several students I accompanied the consul to the yamen. No sooner had we entered than a man was brought in wearing a cangue. I at once saw that he was not the right man. When the consul told the mandarin that this was not the man charged with the offense he confessed that it was a case of proxy, but argued that by punishing this man the real culprit would be so afraid that the moral influence would be quite as salutary. Another instance happened at Sa-teng-po, on the way to Kelung, where the chapel was ransacked by runners of the mandarin. Complaint having been made, the mandarin investigated the case, and two men soon appeared before the chapel wearing the cangue. I was staying there at the time with my students. It was an open secret that these men had nothing to do with the case, but were bribed to wear the cangue for six weeks. We treated them kindly, and in wet weather allowed them to come inside the chapel, and in other ways relieved them. They did not forget this kindness, and years afterward, when the mob howled after me in the streets of Bang-kah, one of these men stood up in my defense.

My first experience of the duplicity and unrighteousness of the yamen was in the second year of my work. A merchant at Chiu-nih, a large village near Bang-kah, had heard me preach at other points, and invited me to his village and gave a room for a preaching-hall. The work grew wonderfully, and soon the country for many miles around became interested, and on the Sabbath packed the hall and the street. Among the converts was a teacher and his aged father. As the work grew the enemy became more enraged and insolent toward the converts. A prominent clansman forcibly seized the teacher's small rice-fields, and the head man refused to give redress. The teacher and his father prepared an appeal to the mandarin at Bang-kah. But meanwhile their enemies had forestalled them and prejudiced the minds of the yamen men, telling them that the whole country around was in rebellion, joining the "barbarian." A plot was laid. When the teacher and his father, accompanied by six other converts, one of whom was my friend the merchant, presented themselves before the mandarin in the yamen, and when the old man was on his knees before the judge, he was told by the Great Man that it was insolent and disloyal to forsake the religion of their fathers and to follow the "barbarian." Then the plot was revealed. All at once the constables shouted, rushed hither and thither, caught the Christians by the cues, jostled them, and holding up long knives in the air, they rushed to the mandarin, crying, "The converts brought these knives to assassinate you." The mandarin pretended to be furious, and gave orders to shut the doors and chain the prisoners. One of these was a boy, the son of the teacher, but, being under sixteen, was allowed to go; his little companion was chained along with the others. They were all dragged to the prison, and put in the stocks in the darkest dungeon. Mock trials were held, during which they were compelled to kneel on red-hot chains. Again and again they were bambooed and otherwise tortured. They were then taken down seven days' journey to Tai-wan-fu and imprisoned. The teacher and his father were dragged out one morning to the execution ground. The son's head was chopped off before his father's eyes. The old man was then executed, and the two heads were put into buckets and carried slowly back to Bang-kah. All along the way and at every stopping-place the crier called to the multitude to see the fate of those who followed the "barbarian." A poster with the inscription "Jip kon-e lang than" ("Heads of the Christians") was fastened over the buckets. In this way they succeeded in terrorizing the people. The heads were finally put on the gates of the city of Bang-kah. The others of the party were brought back to Bang-kah and imprisoned. Two of them died from torture and starvation. The merchant lived eight years longer, during which time he continued faithful to Christ and ceased not to exhort other prisoners to accept the Saviour. At first it was very difficult for me to receive letters from him. Several were sent inclosed in small bamboo quills. After some years the strictness was relaxed and I received letters from him regularly. The substance of all was this: "I, Tan Su-bi, believe all things—heaven and earth, angels and men—were created by the great God. I believe our Saviour Jesus became man and died for Su-bi. I believe God loves me in prison, and his Holy Spirit gives me comfort and keeps me cheerful. I thank God that the gospel came to Tamsui." The last letter closed with these words: " I believe Jesus my Saviour has power to save me and give me eternal life." He died shortly afterward. The instigators and participants were never brought to justice, but years after they all confessed the plot and that the Christians were entirely innocent.

This is only one instance of the corruption and inhumanity of officialdom, and of the violence and injustice inflicted upon Christians in North Formosa, witnessed during the past twenty-three years.

CHAPTER XII

INDUSTRIAL AND SOCIAL LIFE

Movement cityward—Chief centers—Industrial classes—Farming—The pig a pet—Home life in the country—Education—A Chinese school —A graduate—Theaters, plays, and actors—Amusements—Horsemanship—A novel device—Woman—Marriage—Betrothal—Breaking a betrothal—First Christian marriage—Change in public opinion

THE Chinese, like the Anglo-Saxons, are gregarious. There is a tendency to gather together and to live in towns and cities. In Formosa this movement gains headway by reason of the protection which it secures. With savages in the mountains not far away, and with desperate characters of all sorts watching their chance for plunder, the isolation of rural life is not very desirable. Life in town is thought to be safer, if not pleasanter, than in the country, and even country people themselves often live in close proximity, grouping their dwellings into little villages and hamlets. A dozen or a score of families may live together, the men carrying on their farming-operations in the neighborhood.

The three largest cities in North Formosa are Bang-kah, with a population of forty-five thousand; Tek-chham, with a population of thirty-five thousand; and Toa-tiŭ-tia, with a population of thirty thousand. Five other centers—Tiong-kang, Sek-khau, Sin-po, Sa-kiet-a-koe, and Ba-nih—have each a population exceeding ten thousand. There are a great many towns, a still greater number of large villages, and innumerable hamlets and peasants' homes.

In the cities and towns all classes of workmen and traders are to be found. All work is done by hand. The hum of machinery is never heard. A list of workmen would include blacksmiths, carpenters, cabinet-makers, undertakers, idol-carvers, silversmiths, jewelers, workers in pewter and brass, implement-makers, locksmiths, weavers, tailors, dyers, shoe-makers, masons, stone-cutters, brickmakers, lime and charcoal burners. Traders and merchants of all sorts have their shops and expose their wares. The silk merchants are important, and fruit and fish merchants do a thriving trade. Skilled workmen are paid from thirty to forty cents per day. Ordinary workmen earn not more than twenty-five cents. They are generally economical, and their expenses are light when compared with the expenses of workmen in Western lands. But their life is often empty and mean.

The farmer is not only more important than the mechanic or the merchant, he is also more highly esteemed. He is looked upon as being the real producer, and his work is more honorable than that of him who merely handles his goods and passes them on to the consumer. Farms are small and are all under cultivation. Rice has long been the chief among farm products. In a subsequent chapter on rice-farming the culture of this cereal is fully explained. Tea-culture is now becoming important, and Formosa tea is already a popular beverage in Britain and America. The large plateau to the southwest of Tamsui, that twenty years ago was a meadow broken in upon by little rice-farms, is now a magnificent tea-plantation. This industry gives employment every year to thousands of people, many of whom are brought from the mainland. Sugar-cane, sweet potatoes, and a little wheat are cultivated. Onions, leek, celery, spinach, cucumbers, water-melons, a Chinese white cabbage, and other garden stuffs are grown. The indigo and camphor industries are increasing in importance. The Chinese farmer, like the Pe-po-hoan in the

Kap-tsu-lan plain, uses the ox for dry plowing and the water-buffalo in the miry rice-fields. The plow, harrow, hoe, and sickle are his implements, and the ox, water-buffalo, and pig his stock. He brings all his produce in baskets to the town, and offers it for sale in an open space in the street. Failing to dispose of his supply in this way, he may hawk the remainder about the streets.

The pig is a great pet among the Chinese. It is always to be found about the door, and often has free access into the house. In our missionary journeys we frequently found ourselves room-mates of an old black pig with her litter of little ones. The affection of an Englishman for his dog is scarcely stronger than the affection of a Chinese for his pig. Foreigners in China should remember this, and not thoughtlessly excite enmity and antagonism. Not long after my arrival, when in my house at Tamsui, I heard loud voices and hurried tramping in the street in front. On opening the door I saw several European sailors, from a ship lying at anchor in the harbor, running in wild haste down the street toward me. As they came near, one of them, mad with rage, asked if I had a gun. They were followed by a mob that seemed to be furious and eager to overtake them. I directed the sailors down a narrow lane, by which they escaped to their ship. Turning to the crowd, I asked the cause of the disturbance. They replied that the sailors had been striking the pigs belonging to one of their families with their walking-sticks. The people were very indignant, and had they overtaken the sailors there would have been trouble. I appeased them by the assurance that should the offenders misbehave again complaint would be made to the authorities.

Farming in Formosa is very hard work, and only by strictest economy can it be made even fairly remunerative. Some farmers own the land they work, but the majority rent. Indeed, more than half of the cultivated land in North Formosa belongs to one man, who rents to others, the rent being paid generally in produce. These tenant-farmers frequently live all their days in the same place. The sons marry and still continue to live in the old home with their parents, two and sometimes three generations occupying the same house at the same time. They are, on the whole, hard-working, honest, reliable, and, as men go, moral. The peasants are indeed the best class in the community, instances of immorality being rare. Among themselves they are very friendly and sociable, the social chat of an evening, or what my Highland ancestors called a " ceilidh," being quite characteristic of rural society.

Education, as they understand it, is not by any means neglected among the Chinese. It is more than a thousand years since competitive literary examinations were established throughout the empire, and those who succeed in passing these examinations have always been the most honorable class in Chinese society. They are not only socially the superiors of all others, but from among them appointments are made to all the chief positions of influence and power. Parents are therefore very anxious to have their sons educated. There is in Formosa no system of public instruction such as now exists in the more advanced States of the American Union or the provinces of Canada. The competitive examinations, held by the government in the *fu* cities, provincial capitals, or in Peking, according to the degree, are conducted with tiresome attention to form and details. The Four Books are the textbooks, and some saying of Confucius or Mencius the theme of their essays. Without describing the system, which is very elaborate, it may be said that the higher degrees can scarcely be obtained by any who have not more than ordinary ability, and the physical strain of preparation and examination very frequently wrecks the health of the student. The percentage of the successful competitors is very small, but the reflex influence of this wide-spread interest in education is very powerful.

The unsuccessful candidates for the highest degree, and the graduates holding lower degrees, constitute the literary class. They are the teachers, and, being generally poor, their services may be obtained for very little financial remuneration. They find employment in the families of the rich or in teaching the village school. Rich men frequently pay the salary of a teacher for the children of their poorer neighbors. Ordinarily the teacher secures a room and arranges with the parents in the locality to have their children taught, the fees going to pay the teacher.

A Chinese school is the scene of great industry and of great noise. The students all study aloud, and their shrill drawling voices make a disagreeable babel. The text-books are the Chinese classics, and the parents have no cause of complaint on the score of frequent change. The books never change from century to century. The characters are first learned; but it is purely mechanical work, not the slightest attention being paid to the meaning of the words. The book-language is entirely different from the vernacular, and the boy has to commit to memory pages, and even whole books, without understanding anything of their significance. After years of such severe work the boys begin to prepare definitely for the competitive examinations. There is nothing really educative in the system. Unconsciously the style and sentiments of the books are absorbed, but originality, in either thought or expression, is not only undesirable, but utterly impossible.

When a young man succeeds in passing the examinations for even the lowest degree, preparations on a most elaborate scale are made at his home for honoring him on his return. No one but an eye-witness can imagine the scene. A feast is prepared, theatrical performers are often engaged, a procession goes out to meet the graduate, who affects all the airs imaginable, and his conceit is swollen beyond endurance. His swagger is supercilious to the point of silliness. To recognize his old companions is a condescension for which they feel extremely grateful. The whole performance tends to make these graduates the most obnoxious of all the people one meets.

Mention has just been made of theatrical performances, and it should be said that theatrical entertainments among the Chinese are very different from those with which foreigners are familiar. The actors as a class are numerous enough, but there are no opera-houses or halls erected for entertainment purposes. These shows in Formosa are almost invariably exhibited on a platform in the open air, and generally are associated with idolatry. In the open space in front of the temple plays are most frequently performed. No admission fee is charged, the expense of the show being borne by previous subscription, or defrayed by some wealthy citizen. There is not much art in a Chinese play; to a foreigner, indeed, it appears absurd and dreary. The *motif* is generally patriotic. Historical or fictitious scenes are presented, in which some rebel or traitor is the "villain," and after much intrigue, sedition, and other crimes against the government, he is arrested, condemned, and punished. This kind of play is patronized by the government as tending to inspire the common people with respect and awe for the emperor and his representatives. Love, marriage, and murder, to be sure, are the stock in trade of Chinese playwrights, and virtue is always rewarded, while vice is as surely punished. The costumes of the actors are exceedingly ridiculous, and the way in which they "speak the speech" would excite the disgust of less particular personages than Shakespeare, and make the "town crier" an artist in comparison. Everything is spoken in a shrill falsetto drawl, and accompanied with such endless, excessive, and excited action that Hamlet's judgment that "some of nature's journeymen had made men, and not made them well, they imitated humanity so abominably," would seem to have special reference to Chinese players. In truth, the text of the play, being in the book-language, is very imperfectly understood by the audience; and were it not for the colloquial "asides" and the explanations given by knowing ones to those about them, the performance would indeed be a "dumb show" to most of the auditors. I have frequently stood in the crowd and watched the players, and sometimes they would give spice to their parts by a reference to the "black-bearded stranger." There are no actresses in these companies, the parts of female characters being taken with remarkable skill by men. The social standing of actors is low, but probably as high as their merit or their morals deserve.

Puppet-shows are very popular among almost all classes of people, and are, in their way, decidedly clever. Kite-flying among the Chinese is a science compared with any like exhibition seen in Western lands. The children have their tops, which they handle with exceptional skill, and their jackstones, which never lose their popularity.

Boat-racing is a common sport, and at Bang-kah I once witnessed an exhibition of military horsemanship, that regularly draws immense crowds of spectators. The horses are run singly in a long trench several feet high, without bridle or saddle. They are trained, and are eager for the race. The rider carries a bow and arrow, and the object of the game is to shoot at a target set up on one side of the trench near the end of the course, after the principle of the game of tent-pegging. The horses require little urging once they enter the trench. A curious custom is slitting the horses' nostrils to increase their speed. Jockeys observed that after the race a horse seemed to have great difficulty in breathing, and this extra puffing they supposed was caused by an insufficient escape for the air from the lungs. To relieve this difficulty, and to add to the racer's speed, the nostrils are slit open.

Among the Chinese in Formosa the position of woman is higher than among pagan and savage races, but immeasurably lower than in Christian lands. The birth of a daughter is no occasion for rejoicing, if, indeed, it be not regarded as a calamity. The inferiority of woman to man is not an open question. She is regarded as useful, but her death, even when a wife and mother, is trivial compared with the loss of a brother or son. As she advances in years, however, she is treated with more respect, and in old age compensation is sometimes made for the neglect of earlier years.

Marriage is in every way encouraged, not so much as a satisfaction for cherished affections and a fulfilment of social instincts, but in order to obtain male posterity, who shall guard the graves of the dead and minister to the needs of the departed spirits of their ancestors. The bearing of this is shown in a subsequent chapter dealing with Chinese religious life. The social aspect of the question is one of the most perplexing problems facing the advocates of reform.

Marriage is arranged by the parents of the contracting parties, without regard to the feelings and preferences of the parties themselves. A third party—a match-maker or go-between—is a most important character. Through her the arrangements are made. Prenatal betrothal is rare, but not by any means unknown. The betrothal of children under ten years of age is more common, but the general age for a girl is between fifteen and twenty. The most common method is for the parents to purchase a young girl and bring her up in their own home to be a wife for their son. This is much cheaper, as she earns more than she costs, and no gifts or money need be paid her parents at the marriage. In such a case the girl is called Sim-pu, and is regarded as one of the family, but too often is treated with great harshness and cruelty.

Parents may choose out a suitable wife for their son, and it frequently happens that the son agrees in the selection and is delighted with his betrothed. But human nature is the same the world over, and sometimes the Chinese young man does not take kindly to his parents' choice. If the girl has been brought up with him in his home he may come to love her, and not to marry her would be a real grief. But should his wayward fancy fly far from home and picture maidens fairer than the drudge of his mother's kitchen, he may refuse to accept his betrothed wife, and if so he will find some way of evading the domestic arrangement and the custom of his country. It is looked upon as a calamity for the betrothal to be broken off, and it is believed dire calamities are sure to visit the family of one who violates so venerable a custom. Young men sometimes run the risks, however, and follow affection rather than custom.

An instance of the breaking up of an early betrothal came under my notice, illustrative of both the old and the new order of things. At Go-ko-khi, where our first chapel was built, there lived a man of great local influence, named Tan Phauh. He was a powerfully built man, who had been through several rebellions on the mainland, and was not used to having his plans thwarted by anybody. His services in connection with the establishing of our first church are told hereafter. He was a loyal Chinese, and, although he became one of our earliest converts, he never was unpatriotic or disloyal as a citizen. There lived with the family a girl who was betrothed to his second son. She was a good, hard-working girl, and was kindly treated, and really loved as a daughter. The whole family became Christian, and this son joined my class of students and traveled with us, preparing himself for the ministry. Association with other students, and college life at Tamsui, widened his horizon and greatly developed his intellectual powers. He began to think for himself, and self-consciousness developed independence. His ideals were enlarged and his standards of life changed. The thought of his betrothal began to be burdensome. He had nothing against the girl, but she was not his ideal, and he could not cherish for her the " supreme affection for one " that philosophers call love. She was uneducated, and took no interest in the larger subjects and ambitions that now fired his soul. Under such circumstances young men who, thinking themselves in love, voluntarily entered into an engagement without the advice or knowledge of their parents have been known to fret and become discontented. Poor Theng cannot, then, be blamed for fretting over a betrothal to which he was not a party, made years before he understood or cared. On the occasion of one of his visits home the question of his marriage to Sim-pu was raised, and he distinctly refused. He did not love the girl and could not marry her. The grief, disappointment, and anger of his parents were almost beyond control. They were Christians, but the custom was an old one, and, besides, they loved Sim-pu. The father went to bed and stayed there till his anger cooled. The mother felt even more strongly. I visited them and reasoned with them, explaining the nature and terms of Christian marriage, and the teachings of the Bible on the subject. The eldest son agreed with me, and thought his brother should be allowed to choose for himself. The younger son stood by the venerable social custom, and wanted to know what kind of a lady Theng would like for a wife, that he should refuse one whom they all loved so much. But Theng was unmoved. In the struggle between love and custom the tender passion prevailed. He would not give his hand, for he could not give his heart. The girl felt badly, for she had had her day-dreams. Theng married a girl he loved, and Sim-pu married a young farmer living a few miles away. The old man often told me that only Christianity and the grace of God could reconcile him to his son's action. The girl did not cherish any hard feelings, as she would have done were she not a Christian. When passing near where she lived, she insisted on my visiting her new home, and her welcome to myself and the students who were with me had no suggestion of animosity or secret regret.

Marriage, according to Chinese law, is consummated by the exchange of necessary documents between the parents of the prospective bride and groom. No license is required, and no one is authorized to perform the ceremony. There are endless social preliminaries, formalities, and ceremonies, and on the marriage day the bride is carried from her own home to the home of the groom, and there with him bows before the ancestral tablet of the family. Feasting and tablet-worship mark the occasion.

It was at Go-ko-khi, the first station established in the country, that the first Christian marriage was celebrated. The formal documents were exchanged, complying with the law of the land, and then the ordinance of marriage according to Christian form and teaching was performed. The young man belonged to the clan Tañ, and was twenty-five years of age; the bride was of the clan Ti, and was in her seventeenth year. He could not possibly marry one of his own clan. To do that would be to violate the most sacred and inflexible custom. Such a thing as the marriage of two persons having the same surname is not known among the Chinese.

The news that the missionary was about to perform a marriage ceremony spread rapidly through the region; and the whole neighborhood became excited, alarmed, and enraged. The wildest stories were told: "She is going to be the missionary's wife for a week;" "The missionary is to kiss her first;" "Her own eyes are to be taken out and others put in their places;" "The amount to be paid the missionary will ruin the family."

On the afternoon of the marriage day a great crowd gathered at the bridegroom's house. After a long wait music was heard in the distance, and the children began shouting, "They're coming, they're coming!" Presently a sedan-chair with an old woman, the go-between, appeared, and immediately behind a larger and more beautiful one, draped with red cloth. Then came twenty-five pairs of bearers carrying presents of all descriptions in tables turned upside down and suspended from poles borne on the bearers' shoulders. Firecrackers and squibs kept up an incessant noise, doing honor to the occasion. The bride's chair halted before the door, and the bridegroom, dressed as gorgeously as though he were a great official, stepped forward and removed the front part of the chair, and led his bride, whom he saw that hour for the first time, into the house. They were then called out into the courtyard, where hundreds of excited spectators—the majority of whom, of course, were women—crowded every available space, eager to witness the ceremony. A Christian woman acted as bridesmaid, and the groom was supported by a native preacher. I then addressed the people on the institution of marriage as ordained by God and sanctified by Christ, and emphasized the importance of monogamy and mutual respect and forbearance. The contracting parties were then exhorted, the " vows " put, and they were pronounced husband and wife.

As soon as the service was over the young couple were taken back into the house. In view of the suspicions of the people, I deemed it prudent to take leave at once, and set out with the students to the nearest chapel. In a few days the report of the Christian marriage spread far and wide, and now the missionary was praised as liberally as he had previously been blamed. The Christian ceremony was pronounced everything that was beautiful and good, and during all succeeding years, although I not only performed the ceremony hundreds of times, but also waited for the subsequent festivities, and even accepted invitations to heathen households, no unjust insinuations were ever again made, or anything said against the morality of Christian marriage.

CHAPTER XIII

CHINESE RELIGIOUS LIFE

Heathenism in Formosa—Gods and goddesses innumerable—A new candidate—Praying with divining-blocks—Idol-making industry—Wiping out devotional arrearages—An offering of two hundred hogs—"Seventh Moon Feast," a hideous spectacle—Ancestral worship—Annual family gathering—An "open sesame"—A burdensome curse—Lifted by the gospel

RELIGIOUSLY the Chinese in Formosa are related to the Chinese on the mainland, especially in the Fukien province. They are all idolaters. Transportation and separation from the huge mass may, indeed, have had the effect of loosening the bonds and making idolatry in Formosa less unyielding in its hold and less hopelessly blinded in its outlook than it is in China. The incessant struggle for life in a new country may also have done something. At all events, it would seem as though there were more laxity, more indifferentism, among the masses of the people than may be found on the mainland.

But the heathenism of Formosa is of the same kind and quality as the heathenism of China. It is the same poisonous mixture, the same dark, damning nightmare. The original element was Confucianism—a system of morality, with its worship of heaven, its deification of ancestors, and its ethical maxims. Centuries after, Tauism was added—a system of demonolatry, with its spirit-superstition and wretched incantations. Then from India Buddhism was brought—a system of idolatry, with its shrines and smoking incense. These three systems existed

125

side by side until the dividing-walls began to crumble; and now the three are run together, a commingling of conflicting creeds, degrading the intellect, defiling life, and destroying all religious sentiment.   In Western lands one hears much about Oriental religions, the beauties of Buddhism, and the like. One who knows is not deceived.   These indiscriminating laudations are false and vain, the outcome of ignorance or the enchantment of distance.   I know something of the delights of Buddhism, not as seen from the platform of a Parliament of Religions, but as Buddhism really is in its own country.   For twenty-three years I have been in the midst of heathenism, brushing against its priests and people; and I know the poison of its sweets, the fatal flash of its light, and the stagnant fetor of its life.

It is not needful that an exposition of the complex religious system of the Chinese be here presented.   Of late years the literature on that subject has greatly increased, and students will find in the works of such authors as Wells-Williams, Nevius, Du Bose, and others, intelligent and detailed discussion. What they have reported regarding the mainland is to a large degree true in regard to Formosa; and for the purposes of this book, beyond a general survey, all that is possible is some reference to points and customs not dealt with by the authors mentioned.

The Chinese in Formosa have innumerable gods and goddesses, many religious festivals, and countless superstitions that burden their life.   The names of their idols would fill pages, and the details of their beliefs and worship volumes.   There are gods having authority over each of the various powers of nature, departments of industry, relationships of life, states of feeling, physical conditions, and moral sentiments.   Some have been worshiped for centuries; others are of recent date.   Some are universal, receiving the adoration of all classes throughout the Chinese empire; others are local or special, and are reverenced only in particular localities or by certain orders. The origin of the worship of many of the idols is a mystery, but modern instances are suggestive. In 1878 a girl living not far from Tamsui wasted away and died, a victim of consumption. Some one in that neighborhood, more gifted than the rest, announced that a goddess was there, and the wasted skeleton of the girl became immediately famous. She was given the name Sien-lu-niu ("Virgin Goddess"), and a small temple was erected for her worship. The body was put into salt and water for some time, and then placed in a sitting position in an armchair, with a red cloth around the shoulders and a wedding-cap upon the head ; and seen through the glass, the black face, with the teeth exposed, looked very much like an Egyptian mummy. Mock money was burned and incense-sticks laid in front. Passers-by were told the story, and as they are willing to worship anything supposed to have power to help or harm, the worship of this new goddess began. Before many weeks hundreds of sedan-chairs could be seen passing and repassing, bringing worshipers, especially women, to this shrine. Rich men sent presents to adorn the temple, and all took up the cry of this new goddess. But the devotees were disappointed, for the divining-blocks gave no certain answers ; and while they might continue to reverence an unanswering goddess whom their ancestors had worshiped before them, they had not the same respect for a new candidate. One woman who had heard the gospel several years before, while we were preaching in the town of Kim-pau-li, was being carried to worship at this temple ; and when on a high narrow path, through some accident she was tumbled down the bank in her sedan-chair. She returned home very much displeased with herself, and angry at those who introduced this new object of worship. Her confidence in the idol was all the more easily shaken because of the secret working in her mind and heart of the gospel heard years before. Indeed, all attempts to make the worship of this new goddess popular and universal failed, and failed because "the light of life was in the field." A hundred years ago, however, she would soon have had millions before her presenting their offerings and beseeching her favor.

Idol-temples are common throughout the country, and idols may be seen under trees and near bridges for travelers and chance devotees to burn money and toss the divining-blocks. Their method of petition is saddening to behold. Divining-blocks are used. These are made of bamboo roots split into two pieces, each piece having one side convex, the other flat. With these two blocks, two or three inches in length, the petitioner stands before the idol and offers his prayer. The petition is presented in the form of a question; e.g., "O idol, will you give me wealth?" The blocks are then waved in the hands three times and tossed on the floor. If either the two convex or the two flat sides are turned upward the answer of the idol is in the negative; but if one convex and one flat side be upward the answer is in the affirmative. If the petition be granted the blocks are returned to their place, and vows may be made and mock money either burned or placed in front of the idol. The offerings presented are in accordance with the favors granted. Should the divining-blocks return a negative answer from the god, the petitioner, if very importunate, will try again and again, and this "heads or tails" form of prayer may be kept up until the desired answer is obtained.

Idolatry is the mother of a very extensive industry, as the manufacture of idols is a thriving business. There is little art about it, as the Chinese idols are inartistic in form, grotesque, hideous. They are made sometimes of stone or bronze, generally of wood or clay. The wood of the camphor-tree is often used in idol manufacture. After much use the idol is taken back for repairs—repainted, regilded, an arm or head to be replaced, an ear reset, or the eyes to be touched up or made new. The various parts are cut out or moulded into shape and put together by the idol-maker, and the devotee walks out of the place with the God of War or the Goddess of the Sea! The paper money used in worship is made out of tinfoil, beaten thin, and sold in packages. A great number of men are employed in the manufacture of candles for idolatrous purposes.

Many of the Chinese, especially the women, are devout worshipers; many others are skeptical, and the majority are careless. Idolatry has a powerful hold on their minds, but it is only when reverses and troubles come that the average man will resort to the temple. They believe the gods have power to help or to injure them, but so long as things go well they are careless about their devotions. There are great occasions when a feast is held or a general offering made, and then all devotional arrearages are wiped out. I once attended an immense gathering in honor of the God of Medicine, when an offering of two hundred hogs was made. It was on the birthday of the god, and in a grass hut on a small plateau five miles north of Tamsui the idol was seated. In front of the god, pork, fowl, rice, fish, eggs, tea, and spirituous liquors were set. A Tauist priest performed incantations, bowing, chanting, and beseeching the god to be favorable and to partake of the feast provided. Fragrant incense-sticks were burned, and at intervals mock money was offered. Outside the hut men were busy preparing the great feast for the god. Two hundred dressed hogs, on frames prepared for the purpose, were ranged all around in rows, an orange in the mouth of each, and a large knife stuck in the back of the neck. These hogs varied in weight from fifty to four hundred and eighty pounds. Fully four thousand men, women, and children were present, each family displaying its own articles to the best advantage. In the evening torches, music, and theatrical performances added to the honor done to the poor camphor-wood god in the grass hut.

The most elaborate and hideous scene I ever witnessed was

the "Seventh Moon Feast." The seventh month was the time for making offerings to all departed spirits. It was a time of great festivity and excitement. The custom prevailed in all the cities and towns in North Formosa of erecting, in an open space of several acres, great cone-like structures of bamboo poles, from five to ten feet in diameter at the base, and sometimes fifty or sixty feet high. Around these cones, from bottom to top, immense quantities of food, offered to the spirits, were tied in rows. There were ducks and smaller fowl, dead and alive, pork, fish, cakes, fruits, bananas, pineapples, and all manner of delicacies in season ; and fastened everywhere in the mass were hundreds of huge fire-crackers. On one occasion I saw fifty such cones at a feast at Bang-kah. It was a gruesome sight. When night came on and the time for summoning the spirits approached, the cones were illuminated by dozens of lighted candles. Then the priests took up their position on a raised platform, and by clapping their hands and sounding a large brass gong they called the spirits of all the departed to come and feast on the food provided. "Out of the night and the other world" the dead were given time to come and to gorge themselves on the "spiritual" part of the feast, the essence, that was suited to their ethereal requirements. Meanwhile a very unspiritual mob—thousands and thousands of hungry beggars, tramps, blacklegs, desperadoes of all sorts, from the country towns, the city slums, or venturing under cover of the night from their hiding-places among the hills— surged and swelled in every part of the open space, impatiently waiting their turn at the feast. When the spirits had consumed the "spiritual" part, the "carnal" was the property of the mob, and the mob quite approved of this division. But the time seemed long. At length the spirits were satisfied, and the gong was sounded once more. That was the signal for the mob ; and scarcely had the first stroke fallen when that whole scene was one mass of arms and legs and tongues. Screaming, cursing, howling, like demons of the pit, they all joined in the onset. A rush was made for the cones, and those nearest seized the supports and pulled now this way, now that. The huge, heavily laden structures began to sway from side to side until with a crash one after another fell into the crowd, crushing their way to the ground. Then it was every man for himself. In one wild scramble, groaning and yelling all the while, trampling on those who had lost their footing or were smothered by the falling cones, fighting and tearing one another like mad dogs, they all made for the coveted food. It was a very bedlam, and the wildness of the scene was enhanced by the irregular explosion of the fire-crackers and the death-groan of some one worsted in the fray. As each secured what he could carry, he tried to extricate himself from the mob, holding fast to the treasures for which he had fought, and of which the less successful in the outskirts of the crowd would fain plunder him. Escaping the mob, he hurried to his home, expecting every moment to be attacked by those who thought it easier to waylay and rob the solitary spoilsman than to join in the general scramble in the plain.

One cannot estimate the demoralizing effects of such feasts; and it is to the credit of that progressive governor, Liu Ming Chuan, that the barbarities of the " Seventh Moon Feast " have been entirely abolished in Formosa. Such a sight as has been described will never again be witnessed there.

In a general and broad sense all their worship is ancestral, as their gods are the deified spirits of some of the distinguished dead. But the worship of their gods is not the real religion of the Chinese, the idol-shrine is not their most holy place. Their real religion is the worship of their ancestors, their real idol the ancestral tablet. The worship of ancestors is certainly of very ancient date, and was sanctioned by the Chinese sage Confucius. Their doctrine is that each man has three souls. At death one soul goes into the unseen world of spirits, the second goes down into the grave, and the third hovers about the old homestead. For the first the priest is responsible. The second and third claim the services of living relatives, the grave being tended for the one, while the other is invited to take up its abode in a tablet of wood; and from that hour the ancestral tablet becomes the most sacred thing in the possession of the family. It is simply a narrow piece of wood, about a foot long, two or three inches wide, and half an inch thick, set in a low pedestal, and on one side are inscribed the ancestral names. The eldest son has charge of the tablet and its worship. It is placed in the main hall of the house, offerings are presented before it, and incense burned to it every day. The son regards that tablet as in very truth the abode of a personal being who is far more to him for weal or woe than all the gods of the empire. The gods are to be feared and their favor is to be propitiated; but ancestors are loved and their needs in the spirit-world generously supplied. The heathen Chinese have no knowledge of the "Father's house of many mansions," where "they hunger no more, neither thirst any more." To them the dead are dependent on their living relatives, and should they be neglected they would become beggar spirits, hungry, naked, penniless, with will and power to punish their undutiful offspring for their neglect. Food must therefore be offered before the tablet, to satisfy the hunger of the spirit; paper clothing must be burned to hide its nakedness, and paper money to give it independence in the world of shades.

There are some things that appeal to human nature in this ancestral idolatry. Its motive may be fear, but its basis is filial piety. And there is something very solemn about their annual family gatherings before the spirit-tablets of their dead. The most sacred time in all the Chinese calendar is the last night of the old year, when the chief family feast is held and sacrifices are offered to the ancestral guests. To be present on such an occasion, the son returns home, it may be, from beyond the

Pacific. The household assemble in their family oratory. No stranger is there. Before them are the sacred tablets, their household gods, and with reverence they present their offerings, burn their sacrifices, and bow themselves in worship. Pork, fish, fowl, vegetables, rice, and some spirituous liquor constitute the food, which is offered smoking hot, and the spirits feast upon its essence carried up in the ascending steam. Paper clothing and mock money are burned, and as the smoke curls up the spirits are clothed and enriched. Lest any vagabond spirit, neglected by its living offspring, should be hovering about seeking an entrance into this hallowed place, a supply of food is set outside the door, that the hungry soul may be satisfied and not intrude. This ancestral feast on the last night of the year is to the Chinese what Passover night is to the pious Jew.

It has been my custom never to denounce or revile what is so sacredly cherished, but rather to recognize whatever of truth or beauty there is in it, and to utilize it as an "open sesame" to the heart. Many, many times, standing on the steps of a temple, after singing a hymn, have I repeated the fifth commandment, and the words "Honor thy father and thy mother" never failed to secure respectful attention. Sometimes a frail old man, whose cue was white, and whose hands trembled on his staff, would nod approvingly and say, "That is heavenly doctrine." Having gained common ground, and having discoursed on the duties to earthly parents, the transition of thought to our Father in heaven is easily made. Prejudices have been overcome in this way, and minds disposed to the truth of the gospel. The worship of idols is first given up; but it may be months—perhaps a year—before the tablet can be forsaken. The truth about the soul, death, and the hereafter must be firmly grasped, or it will wring the heart to throw away the tablet.

Ancestral worship has its beauties, and in its exaltation of marriage it may indirectly have been a blessing; but it has its darker side, and in its train follow domestic infelicity, miscarriage of justice, and a social and moral bondage that subjects the millions of the living to the degrading service of the dead. A marriage that does not result in the birth of a son, who will guard his father's grave and worship at the ancestral shrine, is a source of perpetual misery, giving the husband just cause for ill-treating his wife, putting her away, or resorting to concubinage. Should an only son whose parents are dead be arraigned before a magistrate and found guilty of the most heinous crime, the fact that there is no one else to attend to the offices of ancestral worship would interfere with the execution of a just sentence, as the magistrate would shrink from the responsibility of depriving the spirits of the departed of the care and support they require. And this ancestral worship blocks the way of all change and progress, because to make any change in social customs or religious forms " would disturb the status between men and spirits, and thus prove fatal to the repose of the dead and the safety of the living."

This venerable cultus, the worship of ancestors, is indeed the most stubborn obstacle Christianity has to face. It is so engrained in the nature, and appeals so touchingly to the heart, that it requires the strongest conviction and the finest moral courage to break its thraldom and brave the scorn of friends and relatives, to whom neglect of one's ancestors in the spiritworld is the most inhuman and cruelest of crimes. The gospel of the risen Saviour, shedding light on the immortal life, and redeeming men from the heavy bondage of ignorance, superstition, and fear, is proving itself the only power that can save to the uttermost. It drives out the false by the expulsive power of truth, and under its vivifying influences the devotees of the tablet turn from the darkening past and look forward and upward to the hills of the Homeland, where the weary rest in the light of God.

CHAPTER XIV

BEGINNINGS OF MISSION WORK

Purpose—Learning the language—With the herdboys—First sermon—
The literati—Coming of A Hoa—Conversion of Go Ek Ju—A Christian family

IN April, 1872, I had secured a house in Tamsui, and faced
the question, Why am I here? Is it to study the geology,
botany, or zoölogy of Formosa? Is it to examine into questions about the racial relations of the inhabitants? Is it to
study the habits and customs of the people? No; not for
that did I leave my native home. Not for that did the church
in Canada ordain me and send me out. My commission is
clear; I hold it from the King and Head of the church: "Go
ye into all the world, and preach the gospel to every creature."
Whatever else may be done, that commission must be fulfilled.
More than that. Whatever else may be done must have a
real and positive bearing on the fulfilment of that commission.
Whatever of history, geology, ethnology, sociology, or of any
other subject may engage the missionary's attention must be
regarded in its relation to the gospel. To get the gospel of
the grace of God into the minds and hearts of the heathen,
and when converted to build them up in their faith—that was
my purpose in going to Formosa. I had it clearly before me
at the beginning, and nothing has been allowed to obscure it
or make it less than supreme.

But the question of ways and means had yet to be answered;

and taking things as they came, my first duty was to learn the language. Already I had mastered the eight tones of the Formosan dialect and had learned a few words. But what was that compared with the task scarcely begun ? I had no teacher, and there were then no books of much use to a beginner. My Chinese servant, who returned with me from the trip down the west coast with Messrs. Ritchie and Dickson, was my only helper. I spent hours with him pronouncing words and imitating sounds. He was not used to that kind of service, and at times would look at me doubtfully, as though he thought me a little daft. I kept away from the main street and wandered out into the country in the hope of meeting some peasant with whom I might converse, and from whom I might learn something of the language of the common people. Out on the downs I saw a dozen boys herding water-buffaloes. As soon as I went near they yelled, " Foreign devil, foreign devil !" jumped on the ground, waved their large sun-hats, and disappeared behind boulders. The next day I tried them again. They looked at me in silence, but on the alert, and ready to run at the first sign of danger. The third day I spoke to them, and as I had carefully practised my words they exclaimed, in utter astonishment, " He knows our language!" That the "barbarian" could speak even a few of their words interested them very much. I took out my watch and held it up for them to see. They were around me instantly, feeling my hands, fingers, buttons, and clothes. The herdboys and I became friends that day, and ever after they would wait my coming with eager interest. I was out there on the plateau with them every day for four or five hours, talking to them, hearing them talk, noting down new words and phrases, until my vocabulary began to grow with a rapidity that quite amazed my servant. I learned more of the spoken dialect from those herdboys than in any other way, and years after, when they grew to manhood, they continued friendly, and were always delighted to recall the first days on the buffalo-pasture. Several of them became converts to Christianity, one a student and preacher.

All this time I was working away at the written characters with my English-Chinese dictionary. It was slow and vexatious. Without a teacher or helper, and having none of the improved dictionaries, it sometimes took hours to find the meaning of one character.

In this way I learned the spoken dialect in the daytime from the herdboys, and studied the characters from the books at night, all the while practising aloud in order to train both tongue and ear. Something new was learned every day, and my old servant had to listen to new words and sentences and hear the old ones over again every night. It is entirely probable that he said some things I did not understand, and that were not very complimentary. I am quite sure he became sick and tired of my questions and cross-questions. After a few weeks in my service he collapsed, and left me to march up and down the room reciting and rehearsing by myself. I never saw him again. These exercises were not in vain, however, and as I shunned all Europeans and English-speaking Chinese, and spoke to every other man who would listen to me, within five months I had so far mastered the language that I was able to preach my first sermon; and while it was much shorter than the sermons I was accustomed to hear in Zorra, it was listened to by some of those heathen hearers with strict attention. The text was, "What must I do to be saved?" The room was full. Some sneered, others laughed outright, but some were respectful and attentive.

While studying the language I was also coming into touch with the people. The proud, conceited literati would enter my room, open my Bibles and other books, throw them on the floor, and then strut out with a grunt of contempt. I got a large sheet of Chinese paper, printed on it the ten commandments, and pasted it on the outside of my door. It was soon daubed with mud and then torn down. A second was similarly treated. The third was put up and remained untouched.

One forenoon a young man, prepossessing in appearance, and of more than ordinary intelligence, called upon me and questioned me on many subjects. When he was leaving I invited him to return in the evening and have another talk. He promised, and was there at the time mentioned, and remained during brief exercises and the singing of a hymn. I read one of our hymns, the subject of which is the brevity of human life, and presented him with a copy of the hymn-book. There was something about the young man that attracted my attention and made me think more about him after he had gone than about any of the others with whom I had met. He was intelligent and respectable, but there was a seriousness, a downrightness, that marked him as superior. I had been pleading with God to give me as the first convert an intelligent and active young man. Long before I had reached Formosa that had been the burden of my prayer. That night when I was alone in my room the thought flashed upon my mind that my prayer was heard, and that this young stranger was the man I had prayed for. So powerfully did the conviction come home to me that, although I had not a tittle of evidence of his conversion, I slept little that night for very gratitude.

In a day or two the young man returned, bringing with him a graduate of some note, who discussed questions of religion with me for some time. It was clear now that there was to be a conflict with the literati, and that day I began studying their language and religion with more earnestness than ever. The next time the young man came he brought with him six graduates, who remained for two hours discussing and questioning. A few days later he brought several others. Then he came with a literary man of a higher degree, a *ku-jin*, and twenty graduates and teachers. By this time I had become so interested that with the utmost eagerness I entered into the discussion and attacked them on their own ground. Question after question was put to them touching their three religions, Confucianism, Buddhism, and Tauism. They were surprised at the "barbarian's" knowledge of their sages and their teachings. Their spokesman was soon entangled, and in a little while they all left the room. Within half an hour the young man returned. He looked more serious than ever. I read the hymn "A day's march nearer home." His eyes brightened, and he said, "What you read now suits me. I love those words, and I am convinced that the doctrines you teach are true. I brought all those graduates and teachers to silence you or to be silenced. I have thought a great deal about these things of late, and I am determined to be a Christian, even though I suffer death for it. The Book you have has the true doctrine, and I should like to study it with you." I wrote down all the young man said in my journal, at his own request; and with the record now before me, my mind goes back to that day in the month of May, 1872. I recall something of the feelings of that hour—the strange thrill of joy, the hope, perhaps the fear, the gratitude, and the prayer. I look back through these twenty-three years, see the earnest face of that young man, and hear again his words of resolve and conviction. Were those true words? Who can say one syllable was untrue? That young man became a Christian, a student, a preacher, and to-day, after twenty-three long years of trial and testing, he is there still, the chief among the native preachers, the man to whom, more than to any other, the care of sixty churches in the mission in North Formosa falls. His name is Giam Chheng Hoa, better known as A Hoa. Will any one who knows anything about the history of mission work in Formosa say that A Hoa's brave resolution, made on that day so long ago, has failed?

Some time after A Hoa became a disciple, a painter in

Tamsui named Go Ek Ju persisted in disturbing our meetings and molesting us. When I was addressing the people at
night, with the door open, he would pass by and throw peb-
bles inside. When the door was closed he would look through
holes and listen to all that was said. His habitual custom was
to lie in wait for A Hoa when on his way home after worship.
First alone, then with others, he would jerk A Hoa's cue, slap
him in the face, stand right before him in the street, and insult
him in other ways. We just pleaded with God every day to
give the man light from above. One afternoon a medium-
sized, thin-faced, pock-marked, intelligent-looking fellow came
to me at our house and said, " I am sorry for my past conduct
toward A Hoa and you, and beg you to forgive me." It was
Go Ek Ju, the painter. He took his stand as a Christian that
night, and publicly declared his allegiance to Christ.

After his conversion he spent every hour of spare time in
study. But his aged mother—how she cried, raged, and
threatened when she heard what her only son had done!
How true it sometimes is that " a man's foes shall be they of
his own household "! His two sisters sent him word privately
to keep away from the house, lest something serious should
happen. The poor, warm-hearted son was to be pitied, and
A Hoa went with him to his former home. They were received with bitterness, for relatives, neighbors, and constables
goaded the mother on to desperation. At length I went to
the house with him and A Hoa. Go Ek Ju sat beside me.
The mother, who was engaged pounding rice, looked angry
and fierce. She gave a few replies to my explanations, then
flew into a rage and moved toward her son with a mallet in
her uplifted hand. I intercepted her, grasped the mallet, and
threw it outside. We walked out, subject to abuse from the
infuriated mother. We now prayed for that woman. In a
few days one of the daughters was prostrated with a severe
illness. Sorcerers, doctors, and idols were consulted in vain,

and the poor mother's heart was bleeding. Some one advised European medicines, and I was called in to prescribe. The malarial fever from which the girl was suffering soon yielded to the remedies. With the mother's heart now softened and gladdened, there was no difficulty in getting her consent to the son's continuance as a student. Before long, son, mother, and daughter all shared in the hope of the gospel. It became a Christian household, and all have remained steadfast until this day. The son has been a preacher for twenty-one years, and the mother a Bible-woman for a third of that time.

CHAPTER XV

A NATIVE ministry for the native church was an idea that
took shape in my mind before leaving Canada. My
prayer had been for a young man of such gifts as would mark
him out for the sacred office. The prayer had been answered,
and the coming of A Hoa seemed to indicate the mind of the
Head of the church. From the very beginning I began training the first convert for the work of the ministry. He became
at once both pupil and companion. On the morning after his
confession he came to my house, and as my old servant had
wearied of my everlasting Chinese chatter, he set to work and
made the room clean and neat. The result was that he joined
himself to me and took full charge of all housekeeping affairs.

The early life of this first convert and preacher is deserving
of notice. His family surname is Giam. When his father
was ten years of age the family came from the mainland
of China. Their old homestead was near Foo-chow. His
mother was born on Steep Island, northeast of Formosa, and
belonged to the clan Tan. When thirteen years of age she
moved to Tamsui, and five years later was married to Mr.
Giam. There in Tamsui, in the very house I afterward rented

in 1872, and in the very room I first occupied, their first-born son, who was to be so great an instrument in God's hand in overthrowing the heathen religion and bringing many of his countrymen to a knowledge of the world's Redeemer, was born.

A Hoa opened his eyes to poverty and a hard life, for his father died before he looked upon his face. His widowed mother was left poor, and could ill afford to provide nourishing food for herself and child. As a result he was weak and delicate, and his mother took him to an idol in the town, seeking advice. The answer was, " Let him be called my child, and name him Hut-a." In time this name, which means " Idol's Child," was changed to Hok-a, then to Hoa, and lastly to A Hoa. He grew up a filial son, and his care and respect for his mother, who is still alive, are very touching. During boyhood his days were spent with his mother and his evenings with his teacher, a relative, who belonged to the Squeers school of dominies. The years from ten to seventeen were spent almost entirely in study. He then entered the service of a mandarin, who gave him employment first as scullion and last as private secretary. He traveled considerably in China from Foo-chow to Tientsin, and spent six months in Peking. Shortly after this he returned to Tamsui, and not long after his return I landed in Formosa. How he was led to the gospel, and his decision to become a Christian, have already been told.

A Hoa proved a faithful servant and a most apt and diligent student. I began by teaching him to read and write the romanized colloquial, i.e., the Chinese spelled with English letters. His progress was simply astonishing. Nor was I losing time myself. With a helper like A Hoa, who was as eager as myself, I found my stock of Chinese words rapidly increase, and the difficulties of pronunciation more easily overcome. When in the house we read, sang, studied, drilled, the whole day long. A neighbor entered one day to see if we had both become altogether crazy. He meant well, but was a little afraid of us. He brought us two cups of tea as a specific, and suggested a visit to the nearest temple as a good thing for people affected as we were. There may have been some humor in the scene, but we started a hymn, and, fearing another outbreak, the man bolted out of the door, dropping the tea-cups on the floor in his frightened haste. He would not venture back, but in about an hour a little boy came in for the fragments of the dishes.

As A Hoa advanced in his studies I procured a map of the world, and it was amusing to watch him as his eye took in the vastness of other countries than China. His Chinese notions about geography were upset, and he soon began to have thoughts about the wide world outside the Chinese wall and beyond the broad Pacific. Astronomy, too, became a favorite and inspiring study. But the chief subject was the Bible and "that wonderful redemption, God's remedy for sin." He was with me every evening as I preached to the people, and their threats were as angry against him as against the "barbarian." He traveled with me, too, on short trips into the country. One morning we called on one of his old friends, a farmer, living not far from Tamsui. When they recognized us two fierce dogs were set on us, and the children yelled after us, pelting us with stones.

In all these services A Hoa was only a companion, and never did more than join in singing. The time had come when his own gifts must be exercised. One evening, when we were alone in our room, I asked him to engage in prayer. He had never attempted audible prayer in his life, and the request came upon him unexpectedly. Immediately he fell on his knees before a rickety old bamboo chair. He was terribly in earnest, and his halting words and broken petitions were charged with intense emotion. Grasping the arms of the chair firmly with both hands, he shoved it about the hard, uneven floor, making a hideous creaking accompaniment to his faltering sentences. By the time the prayer was finished he had moved half-way across the room. The scene had even to me a ludicrous aspect, and had others been present it would scarcely have been to their edification; but the prayer was sincere, and to God in heaven it was an incense of sweet smell. I noted the words: "Lord, thou art the true God. I did not know thee a few months ago. Help me to know more and more of thee. I know now that the idols our people worship cannot save their souls. I thank thee from the bottom of my heart that Pastor MacKay came to us. Lord, help me by the Holy Spirit to bring my mother, relatives, and neighbors to Jesus. We do not know much, but, O God, help me, help us. This is my heart's desire."

One morning early I started out with A Hoa, crossed the Tamsui River, visited a Buddhist priest in a temple, and then began the ascent of the Quan-yin Mountain, the side of which was covered with tall grass that would cut like a knife. When we reached the summit, seventeen hundred feet above the sea, our hands were sore and bleeding. The view from the mountain-top repaid us for the pain and toil. It was magnificent. But poor A Hoa was greatly perplexed, wondering what under the whole heavens could be my purpose. Like all other Chinese, he had no eye for the beautiful in nature, and to climb a mountain for the mere pleasure of gazing on the scenery was to him past comprehension. At first he was a little afraid as we looked down upon Tamsui lying at our feet, and far inland saw the broad stretches of the Bang-kah plain. His senses were dormant, however, not dead. Standing there together we sang the One Hundredth Psalm, and before the last verse was finished the great Spirit, who makes all things beautiful in earth and sky and sea, touched A Hoa's soul. His nature was stirred to its very depths. It was the birth-hour of the beautiful. His new-born soul had now an eye and ear for God's message in creation, and from that hour he became a devoted student and ardent lover of everything in nature.

In the autumn of the same year we visited Kelung for the first time. On the way we passed through Bang-kah, the largest city in the north, where the citizens showed signs of bitterest hostility, and many followed, reviling and pelting us with stones. A Hoa was now becoming familiar with the taunting cries that everywhere greeted us: " Foreign devil! Black-bearded barbarian!" At Sek-khau, on the banks of the Kelung River, broken bricks gave emphasis to the cries when our backs were turned. As dark came on we were making our way along a path through tall reeds and grasses, when, at a sudden turn, a band of robbers with their long spears flashed their lights in our faces. When I told them we had no money, and that I was a teacher, they repeated the word "teacher" and disappeared. We were carrying torches, but a storm was brewing, and soon a strong blast left us in utter darkness. We were then on a strange road in an unknown territory. Gusty winds came howling down from the mountains, driving sheets of blinding rain. What were we to do? We could not return. To stand still was alike out of the question. On we went, creeping along the wet and slippery path, a Canadian missionary, a Chinese convert, and a heathen basket-bearer. Here we stumbled over boulders, there one slipped into a crevice in the rock, and somewhere else we all three staggered into the mire of an unfenced rice-field. But underneath and round about us were "the everlasting arms." Kelung was reached before midnight, and the rest of the night was spent in a low damp hovel. A Hoa early learned that the path of duty in the service of Christ is sometimes rough and sore, as it was for Him who first went up to Calvary.

At Kelung we stood on the stone steps of a large heathen temple, sang a hymn or two, and immediately the crowd gathered, filling the open space and the street. It was a mob of angry idolaters. Some of them were A Hoa's old acquaintances and companions, and when they saw him stand beside the hated "foreign devil" their contempt for the Christian missionary was as nothing compared with their feelings toward the Christian convert. I turned to A Hoa and invited him to address the people. It was a moment of testing. He had never before spoken for Christ in the public street. It was only a few months since he himself had first heard the gospel. He heard the scornful and vile words of his old friends and comrades, and when I turned and asked him to speak he was silent and hung down his head. Immediately I read the first verse of a hymn, and we sang it together. The words were those of the old Scotch paraphrase that has so often put iron into the blood and courage into the hearts of trembling saints:

> " I'm not ashamed to own my Lord,
>   Or to defend his cause;
> Maintain the glory of his cross,
> And honor all his laws."

It was enough. A Hoa raised his head, and never again was he "ashamed." Looking out over that angry mob, he said, in the calm, clear tones of a man who believes and is unafraid, "I am a Christian. I worship the true God. I cannot worship idols that rats can destroy. I am not afraid. I love Jesus. He is my Saviour and Friend." His testimony was brief, but it was his first, and it was brave and true. It is easy for a young man now to take his stand for Christ; there are other converts to cheer and encourage him. But it was different then. That word uttered by A Hoa to that crowd of rough and bitter heathen before the idol temple in Kelung was the first ever spoken for Christ to that generation by a native Christian in North Formosa.

On the second Sabbath in February, 1873, exactly one year

after my arrival in Tamsui, at the close of service I announced that a number were to be admitted by baptism into the Christian church. The cry was raised outside, " We will stop him. Let us beat the converts." The house was filled, and the street in front was crowded. After the singing of a hymn five men came forward and made public confession of their faith in Christ. Each man spoke in clear, decisive tones. Their names were: Giam Chheng Hoa, aged twenty-two, scholar; Go Ek Ju, aged thirty-one, painter; Ong Tiong Sui, aged twenty-four, writer; Lim Giet, aged twenty-six, carpenter; Lim Poe, aged forty-two, farmer. They were then baptized into the name of the Father, and of the Son, and of the Holy Ghost, after which each addressed the people. There were many yells, jeers, and taunts, but A Hoa spoke with great boldness and effect.

The next Sabbath these five sat around the Lord's table. It was a memorable day for us all. Never before had they witnessed such a service. Never before had I presided at such a communion, and when I read the solemn warrant for the observance of this sacrament all were visibly affected. Poor Lim Giet broke down completely, sobbing out, " I am unworthy, I am unworthy;" and it was only after he had spent some time in prayer in the little room that he could be induced to partake of the sacred elements. That first communion marked an epoch in A Hoa's spiritual history, and from that day he regarded himself as no more his own, but fully committed to Jesus Christ and called to his service.

But God, who had so strangely led this young man, and who was so strangely fitting him for the work of the ministry, was at the same time preparing a place for the exercise of his gifts and making ready a people to hear his word. Ten miles up the river from Tamsui is a country village called Go-ko-khi. One day, while I was preaching in our rooms at Tamsui, a widow named Thah-so, from that village, attended the service, and at the close came up and said, "I am a poor widow living at Go-ko-khi. I have passed through many trials in this world, and the idols never gave me any comfort. I like the doctrines you proclaim very much, and I believe the God you tell about will give me peace. I will come again and bring others." Next Lord's day she was there with several other women. Week by week the number of her companions increased, until at last a boat-load would come down the river and enter the preaching-room. So interested were they, and so much in earnest, that they persuaded us to visit their village. At last A Hoa and I went up the river to Kan-tau, then to the right up a smaller stream that ran through fine rice-fields, until we reached Go-ko-khi. A number of the villagers met us and led the way to the house of Tan Phauh, the head man. He was a tall, strongly built, manly looking fellow, and when I gave him some commandment sheets he pasted them on the walls of his house in the presence of neighbors and others; then, turning to all, he said that he had lost all confidence in idols, and was determined to live by the ten commandments now put up.

I procured an empty rice-granary for a sleeping-room and preaching-place. There we began our work and made our headquarters for several months, during which time we preached the gospel in the beautiful valleys and villages in that vicinity. Tan Phauh, the head man at Go-ko-khi, gave a plot of ground opposite his own house for a chapel site. Stones were collected, sun-dried bricks prepared, and the work of building the first chapel in North Formosa begun. There was great interest manifested by the villagers, but when the walls were about three feet high a company of soldiers and constables sent from the prefect in Bang-kah arrived and ordered the work of chapel-building to cease. They were armed with guns, spears, and knives, and by beating gongs and drums, yelling, threatening, they thought to frighten the simple-minded villagers. When they entered the head man's house Tan Phauh drew himself up to his full six-feet-two and faced them. He was originally a mainland man, who had been in several rebellions, and the bluster of a few soldiers was nothing to him. Pointing to the commandment sheets on the wall, he said, "I am determined to abide by the ten commandments." The soldiers then made a rush for Widow Thah-so's house, but she held up her hymn-book and said she was resolved to worship only the true God. Very soon the soldiers left the village, saying that the "foreign devil" had bewitched the villagers, using some magic art; and their superior officer, the prefect in Bang-kah, reported the case to the British consul, and asked that the missionary be prevented from building a fort and taking guns up the river by night.

But despite all intrigues and plots the Lord's work prospered in Go-ko-khi, the building was finished, and on opening day the room was crowded, while many stood outside. That was our first chapel, and there more than one hundred and fifty declared their rejection of idols and their desire for Christian instruction. It was a great day for us, and that night our hearts were full of gratitude because of all that the Lord had done. We met in the chapel regularly for instruction and worship. Many of those who came were still heathen idolaters, and none of them were accustomed to anything like a Christian service or public addresses. Strange indeed are a missionary's first experiences. Sometimes when we had sung a hymn and I began to address them, one or two would take out their pieces of steel, strike a flint, light their long pipes, and when the smoke ascended I would pause and remind them that they wanted Christian instruction and should keep quiet. "Oh yes, yes, we must keep quiet," and with that they would nod their heads with great politeness. No sooner would I get fairly started again than some one would spring to his feet and shout, "Buffaloes in the rice-fields; buffaloes in the rice-fields!" Another reminder of their duty would bring another reply: "Oh yes, yes, we must keep quiet." And for a few minutes all do keep quiet and I go on with my address. Then an old woman with her little feet hobbles to the door and shouts out, " Pig has gone; pig has gone; pig has gone!" One interruption follows another; but we never blame those restless people, for such services are strange and new to them. Within two months, however, the congregation assembled in the chapel at Go-ko-khi was just as attentive as any I ever addressed anywhere in Christendom.

A Hoa, the first convert, was appointed preacher in the first chapel, and chief among his helpers was the first female con-vert, Widow Thah-so. She was baptized there three years afterward, when sixty-two years of age. A Hoa's natural abil-ity, kindness of heart, devotion, and sincerity of purpose gave him great influence in Go-ko-khi and the surrounding country. Thah-so grew into great beauty and strength of character. She continued to the close a firm believer and zealous worker. In 1892 she told me that she had one daughter in China, who had never heard the gospel. I could see that the old mother's heart had been greatly exercised, and that she was " again in travail until Christ be formed " in her daughter's soul. A passage across the channel was arranged, and Thah-so went in search of her child. Her visit was not in vain. After remaining with her daughter for several weeks she returned home, feeling that her work was done and the time of her de-parture at hand. The end came soon. I visited her a day or two before her death. For two days she was quiet and silent; then suddenly the familiar voice was heard again in clear, strong tones singing a verse of the psalm, " I to the hills will lift mine eyes," and one of the hymn, " Forever with the Lord." When she came to the line, " My Father's house on high," the voice ceased awhile. Then the eyes opened wide, the face shone as with a radiant light, and in accents sweeter than any sounds of earth the words came: "The golden gate is open. The large white sedan-chair is coming for me. Don't keep me. Don't call me back. I'm going home." Thus in the "white sedan-chair," too fair and beautiful for other eyes than hers to see, the strong heroic soul of our first "mother in Israel" passed away. Dear old Thah-so! For twenty years she served her Lord on earth, and at the last there was given her an abundant entrance into the eternal kingdom.

CHAPTER XVI

ESTABLISHING CHURCHES

CHRISTIANITY is not a system of philosophy that may be taught, but a life that must be lived. The religion of Jesus is distinguished from all other religions in its incarnation. Its power is the power of a divine Personality. It is propagated by personal contact. Christ gives life to men, and then says, "As the Father hath sent me, even so send I you." Every Christian is a missionary. He may have been nursed in the lap of Christendom and trained in a luxurious religious home, or he may have been born a pagan and "suckled on a creed outworn." It matters not. If he has been "born again," and feels the throb of the Christ-life, he is a missionary sent by the living Christ to touch dead souls to the newness of life. This primary truth needs heavy emphasis, for there is everywhere perpetual danger of its being neglected. The far-sweeping purpose of the election of grace is being ignored, and the churches are crowded with people whose largest thought of salvation is that their own souls shall be cared for. Not until Christianity is not only believed, but lived, will the churches either at home or in heathen lands become the power the Master meant them to be.

153

The success of missionary effort in North Formosa is in no small measure due to the inculcation of this primary truth of Christian discipleship. Converts are taught that the grace of God has been given to them, not for their sakes alone, but in order that they may be channels for the communication of that grace to others. One of the most delightful experiences in a missionary's life is to observe how eager converts are to be of service in helping others out of the darkness of heathenism from which they have so recently emerged. Looking back now and recalling the incidents connected with the establishing of churches, it is surprising to note in how many cases the way was opened, humanly speaking, not by the missionary's effort, but by the zeal and Christian enterprise of the converts. Some of the most conspicuous and useful workers in the mission were found as Andrew found Simon and brought him to Jesus.

One evening in 1873 a young man who had been attending our services, and whom I knew, entered my house at Tamsui, accompanied by a stranger who seemed reticent and bashful. The young man introduced his companion, saying, "This friend of mine has heard the gospel and is now a believer in Jesus Christ. We have talked it over a great deal, and he desires further instruction, that he may tell others of the Saviour." I had some conversation with the stranger, and was impressed by his earnestness and modesty. He was a farmer's son, known to several of the converts, and had been attending the services, in which he became deeply interested. As I came to know him better my confidence increased and he was enrolled as a student for the ministry, and one more faithful never studied in any college. He is now known as the Rev. Tan He, pastor of the church at Sin-tiam.

Sin-tiam is a compact and busy town nestling at the foot of the mountains some eighteen miles inland from Tamsui. A man living there had been at Tamsui and had heard the gospel. On his return home he reported to his friends, whereupon several others came out, followed us in our touring from place to place, and at last persuaded us to visit Sin-tiam. When we arrived there great crowds were in the town, it being a season of feasting the gods. Very few of the people had ever seen an Anglo-Saxon, and on all hands the familiar cries, "Barbarian! Foreign devil!" could be heard. Presently a rush was made toward a certain point, and angry voices were heard shouting, "The barbarian struck a boy." This was answered by wild cries from the outskirts of the crowd: "Kill him! Kill the barbarian; he is not very big!" As we were some distance from the center of attraction I pressed through the crowd until I came to the boy, who had indeed an ugly wound on the head, which was bleeding profusely. Having the necessary surgical instruments, I dressed the wound and bound it with my handkerchief. Now a new cry was raised by the crowd: "Ho sim, ho sim!" ("Good heart, good heart!"). A few days later an old man was injured by falling upon a heap of stones. One of the students carried him to a shelter under a tree, where his suffering was relieved, and again the cry, "Good heart, good heart!" was heard. As a result the people became friendly, and an old couple gave us the use of a room for our services. A congregation was soon gathered and a chapel became necessary. One rabid idolatress threatened to smash my head with a stone if we persisted in building a chapel; but the work went on, and the chapel of unplastered stones was finished and dedicated to the worship of God.

The present church at Sin-tiam is one of the finest buildings in North Formosa, and its situation one of the most picturesque. The church stands on the rising ground at one end of the town, its stone spire being the one conspicuous object visible for miles around. A stone wall incloses the church property. The Sin-tiam River sweeps round in a wide curve a few rods from the door, the space between being covered with "stone eggs," carried down by freshets and worn smooth by the water. At the back of the church stands a high bluff, the slopes of which are covered with verdure. In front, across the river, steep hills rise abruptly from the water's edge, ascending tier after tier, like a giant stairway, terminating in lofty mountain-peaks. Clinging to the slopes are groves of trees, feathery grasses, reeds and ferns of every description; the moss-covered rocks are festooned with great masses of purple morning-glory and trailing vines of pink and white roses; and everywhere blooming myrtle-trees, pure white Easter lilies, and the sweet-scented honeysuckle add to the luxuriant beauty of the scene.

What though idols of camphor-wood are enshrined in many houses in Sin-tiam! Here stands the church of Jesus Christ, and here are gathered, week after week, more than two hundred who bow in adoration before the God of all the earth. They have endured hardships for the name of Jesus. They have been robbed and persecuted, and in the dark waters of the swift-flowing river two of the converts faced the death and won the crown of martyrs for the faith.

The congregation worshiping in the beautiful Sin-tiam church is now self-sustaining, supporting their pastor, bearing all other expenses; and although by no means wealthy, they contribute to the general work of the church in Formosa, help the poor, and send voluntary offerings for the relief of famine-stricken districts. Tan He, their faithful and beloved pastor, wields a great influence, and is growing in intellectual and spiritual strength year by year.

Tek-chham, a walled city of forty thousand inhabitants, was one of the places visited on my first trip down the west coast the week after landing at Tamsui in 1872. I had a "prophet's chamber" there, and after frequent visits succeeded in renting a small house for chapel purposes. No sooner had we got the place cleaned out than indignant crowds filled the narrow street, jostling, reviling, spitting in our faces. After three days the turmoil ceased, largely through the influence of a literary man to whom I had given medicine on a previous occasion. Within a month thirty persons enrolled themselves as Christians, and larger premises had to be secured. The work grew until a still larger building was required. There is now a large preaching-hall, with real glass in the front windows; and there a once proud Confucianist graduate is preaching the gospel of Christ. In the country round about Tek-chham are many Christians, but as the city gates are closed at night they could not attend evening service. The Christians in the city contributed money, and in other ways assisted in securing a suitable building outside the wall, and there another literary man is preaching Jesus as the only Saviour.

Ten miles from Tek-chham, toward the mountains, is a Hakka village called Geh-bai. To this village we were led by several Hak-kas who attended services in the city church. The villagers assembled under a beautiful banian-tree, where fully a thousand people could find shelter from the broiling sun. They were greatly delighted, and one fine old gentleman welcomed us to his house for the night, one of the largest and cleanest in the island. The old man was genuinely interested, and walked many times to Tek-chham to the Sabbath services there. That evening a great crowd gathered in the open court to hear the new doctrine. One man, seventy years of age, exerted himself with such success that a house was rented, repaired, and fitted up for chapel services. The congregation became organized, and when a native preacher was sent among them four months of his salary was paid in advance. There in that Hak-ka village, high among the hills, is a flourishing, self-helping Christian congregation.

The church at Kelung was established largely through the instrumentality of Ko Chin, a convert who afterward became an elder and preacher. He had lived with his family among the beautiful green hills around the Kelung harbor. Becoming filled with the desire for more wealth, he moved to Sekkhau and became an extensive cattle-buyer, traveling through the whole of North Formosa. He was an intense idolater, and being something of a musician, became somewhat famous as a drummer and guitar-player in idolatrous processions. In 1872, a few months after I began to preach in Tamsui, he came to hear the "barbarian." The following Sabbath he was there again. When a chapel was opened nearer his home he attended there, walking generally ten miles to be present. In Kelung he rented a house and furnished it as a place of worship. On the appointed day I was escorted to the place to conduct the dedicatory services. More than four hundred were present. Ko Chin continued regular and faithful, and at the age of forty-five was baptized. Finding his business lucrative, but a hindrance to Sabbath observance, he gave it up, returned to the old homestead, and brought up his entire family to worship God. In due time he was ordained an elder in the Kelung church, and subsequently became a student and finally a preacher at the Margaret Machar Memorial Church on the east coast. During the French invasion in 1884 his dwellings at Kelung were destroyed by looters, his property was confiscated, and himself and family persecuted. In a very literal sense he "took joyfully the spoiling of his goods." His services as preacher were blessed of God, and when he fell a victim to the malarial fever the elders and deacons of his church gathered about his bed and sang the One Hundred and Twenty-first Psalm, the first he ever learned. His "going out" was kept by the God in whom he put his trust.

The missionary abroad, like the missionary at home, sometimes finds the bread cast upon the waters after many days. Back of the Quan-yin Mountain, near Tamsui, is a beautiful plateau in which stands a hamlet called I-khut ("Round

Pool "), where we have a chapel and congregation. The first man to show interest in our work there was a pugilist and gambler whom I had met shortly after landing in Formosa in 1872. Going through the valley, I passed a small rice-shop where were several gamblers squatted on mats on the floor. I entered into conversation with them and asked if their sage Confucius would not be displeased with them for their waste of time. The majority seemed indifferent, but one became very angry. He was a powerfully built man, and had distinguished himself as a pugilist. It was his custom, when he lost in gambling, to use physical force in compelling the winner to return the money. Everybody—even his own brother— dreaded him. He was very angry on the occasion of our first meeting, but something of the words spoken remained in his memory and touched his conscience. In after-years he frequently fell in with converts and native preachers, and began to take a lively interest in our work. In due time he joined our ranks, and with as much energy as he had put into the works öf sin he entered now on the service of Christ and his church. He visited the people in that locality, exhorting them to accept Christ, and the result of his enthusiastic efforts was a suitable building and a flourishing congregation.

Twenty years ago the most lawless region in North Formosa was round about Sa-kak-eng, a town of two thousand inhabitants, northeast from Toa-kho-ham. The people lived in terror of a large band of ruffians and highwaymen who had their headquarters in the mountains near by. The customary method of redress—punishing the kindred of such criminals— could not be adopted, as the relatives of these banditti lived either on the mainland of China or in out-of-the-way places in Formosa. They were all the more daring because the townspeople sometimes compromised with them, and when it suited their purpose joined with them in resisting official investigation and interference. The subprefect and retinue narrowly

escaped death on one occasion, his sedan-chair being pierced
by spears and lances. The banditti would form a company
and march into the town, singing boastfully, with a wild kind
of yell,   " Lin kho koa;
                       Goan kho soa; "

which means, " You trust the mandarins; we trust the mountains." I had very great difficulty in gaining an entrance into
Sa-kak-eng, and when the chief of a strong clan gave me a
room in the rear of his shop there were loud threats of drag-
ging us to the hills, gagging us, and gouging out our eyes. So
violent was the opposition that I had to change my quarters
to the outskirts of the town. The mob often surrounded the
building, and once when A Hoa and I came out of the door
a howl was raised, and a large flat stone flung by a man near
by grazed the top of my head, and, striking against the wall,
was broken into three pieces. Neither of us flinched, but,
turning round, I picked up the pieces of stone as mementos of
the day. One of the pieces weighed three pounds; another I
brought as a contribution to the museum in Knox College,
Toronto. Several months afterward, on entering the chapel, I
saw a man lying on a bench. He rose to his feet, and, bowing low, said, " Will you forgive me ? " He then confessed
that he was the man who threw the stone, and that his inten-
tion was to put an end to my life. For the next three months
he was with the native preacher every day, and before the
year closed he passed away rejoicing in the hope of salvation
through Christ. Sa-kak-eng is quite a changed place. The
desperadoes have been scattered, their forest retreats cleared
and cultivated, chapel buildings purchased, prejudices against
converts and preachers overcome, and every year marks progress. On our last visit we were escorted in high honor to the
next chapel, four miles away, a band of music leading the
procession.

At Pat-li-hun, across the harbor from Tamsui, at the foot of the Quan-yin Mountain, stands a solid and handsome chapel that was built within one month.   Our first place of worship there was a banian-tree, our next a fisherman's house, then a slender grass-covered structure, and then a building of dried mud.   This last being destroyed during the troubles with the French, we resolved on erecting a more substantial structure. On the first day of May the stones for the foundation were ungathered on the mountain-side, the lumber and bricks were up the Tamsui River at Toa-tiu-tia, the coral for lime was un-burned, and the clay undug.   The plans were drawn, masons and carpenters employed, and the work pushed forward.   The thermometer stood at times at one hundred and twenty, and the blowing sand inflamed our eyes; but on the last day of May the work was completed and the chapel ready for occu-pation.   The walls of sun-dried and burnt brick are two and a half feet thick, plastered white on the inner side, finished in stucco-work without, and strong as solid masonry, having with-stood rain-storms, hurricanes, and earthquakes.

The most beautiful church in all the mission is at Toa-tiu-tia.   This town stretches along the Tamsui River about a mile from Bang-kah, and almost connected with the new walled city of Tai-pak-fu, and is the most progressive place of business in North Formosa.   The railway-bridge across the river is fourteen hundred and sixty-four feet long.   All the British and other Western merchants have establishments there. Our church is a splendid structure of stone, with turrets and tower and a capacious auditorium.   I have seen that church crowded from platform to door with eager and attentive hear-ers; and on October 18, 1891, after preaching to over five hundred people from the text, " The Lord is a great God, and a great King above all gods," I dispensed the sacrament of the Lord's Supper to one hundred and thirty communicants. In the congregation there was a stranger, a Corean Christian, named Phok I Peng, who was traveling through Formosa in search of his brother. So impressed was he by the eagerness of the Chinese converts and the heartiness of their worship that he said at the close, "This is truly the kingdom of God come down to earth. I can never forget this scene. Peace to you all."

Ten miles east of the city of Bang-kah, on the south bank of the Kelung River, is a town of four thousand inhabitants, called Tsui-tng-kha. In 1890 a new building, costing seven hundred dollars (Mexican), was erected there by the native Christians. The entire cost of both site and building was paid by the churches in Formosa, and the deed of the property is stamped in the name of the native church. A Hoa planned the building and superintended its erection, and now a native preacher is stationed there.

The conduct of two members of the church at Tsui-tng-kha is an answer to the question often asked about the stability of Chinese converts. Several years ago a man of the Tan clan allowed his eldest son to attend the chapel services to see what kind of doctrine was taught. The young man became interested and brought two younger brothers. One of the members of the church taught them to read the romanized colloquial, and they studied the gospel with growing earnestness, until all three confessed their faith in Jesus Christ. Then they refused to worship idols and ancestral tablets in their home. This aroused the father's wrath, who, fearing there would be no one to worship at his grave, forbade his sons' going again to the chapel, and ordered them to attend idolatrous ceremonies every night. To pacify their enraged parent they resolved to "bow in the house of Rimmon," but while they held the lighted incense-sticks before the idol they turned their heads away. But they still attended the chapel services, which when their father found out, he visited the chapel secretly; and when he saw his sons singing praise to Jehovah-God he shrieked and ran about like one mad. After this they met together on the Sabbath in some quiet place in the mountains, and sang, prayed, and read the Word, praying most of all for their angry father. Then they would meet at night in a grass watch-house among the rice-fields. But nowhere were they long unmolested. Their father's anger became more cruel and watchful. At the close of the year preparations were being made for the customary idol festival. They refused to take part in the ceremonies. He became wild with rage, and, seizing a long knife, rushed at the eldest son. They all escaped and found refuge in a convert's house. The father would not be appeased, and drove his daughters-in-law, with their little children, out of the house. Neither the sons nor their wives dared come near the place. Then the mother's heart relented. She could not give up her children, and after much pleading the father gave her the knife and promised not to injure the sons should they return. They did return. The father forgave them, and they were permitted to worship God in the home ; and on every Lord's day, with their wives and children, they joined in the services in the chapel at Tsui-tng-kha.

CHAPTER XVII

HOW BANG-KAH WAS TAKEN

The stronghold—Waiting an opportunity—Forbidden—Expelled—Back
again—Mobbed—Victorious—Changes—Honored

BANG-KAH was the Gibraltar of heathenism in North Formosa. It is the largest and most important city, thoroughly
Chinese, and intensely anti-foreign in all its interests and sympathies. In 1872 I visited it with A Hoa and got a foretaste
of the reception awaiting me on every subsequent occasion.
In my journal of 1875 I find the following entry, made after
having experienced anew the malignant hate of the Bang-kah
people:

"The citizens of Bang-kah, old and young, are daily toiling
for money, money—*cash, cash.* They are materialistic, superstitious dollar-seekers. At every visit, when passing through
their streets, we are maligned, jeered at, and abused. Hundreds of children run ahead, yelling with derisive shouts;
others follow, pelting us with orange-peel, mud, and rotten
eggs. For hatred to foreigners, for pride, swaggering ignorance, and conceit, for superstitious, sensual, haughty, double-faced wickedness, Bang-kah takes the palm. But remember,
O haughty city, even these eyes will yet see thee humble in
the dust. Thou art mighty now, proud, and full of malice;
but thy power shall fall, and thou shalt be brought low. Thy
filthy streets are indicative of thy moral rottenness; thy low
houses show thy baseness in the face of heaven. Repent, O

Bang-kah, thou wicked city, or the trumpet shall blow and thy tears be in vain!"

We had previously established churches north, south, east, and west of Bang-kah. She sent hirelings to surrounding villages and towns to reprimand the magistrates, incite the people, and frustrate us in the execution of our work. Three large clans, through their head men, ruled the city. All the others had to acquiesce in every proposal. Foreign merchants never succeeded in establishing themselves there. Attempts were made, but their Chinese agents were dragged out of the city and narrowly escaped death. It might seem that mission work should have been begun in Bang-kah first. Indeed, I received a communication from a very devoted and excellent missionary in China—one who has now gone to his reward— in which he said, " I hear you have stations in several towns and villages. Why don't you begin at Jerusalem? " Now I did not begin at the " Jerusalem " of heathenism for the same reason that I did not go to Madagascar or to India. I sought to follow the lead of my Captain. He led me to Formosa, and to point after point where chapels were already opened. I knew the time would come when Bang-kah would be entered.

The authorities of Bang-kah issued proclamations calling on all citizens, on pain of imprisonment or death, not to rent, lease, or sell either houses or other property to the barbarian missionary. But in December, 1877, the time came for establishing a mission there, and in spite of all their attempts to prevent our entrance I succeeded in renting a low hovel on the eastern side. On getting possession I placed a tablet of paper on a wooden frame above the door, with the inscription, "Jesus' Holy Temple." Shortly afterward several soldiers who were returning to their encampment near by came, stood, looked up, read the inscription, and immediately threatened me with violence. Then they returned to their encampment and reported to the general, who despatched a number of

officers to order me out of the place, stating that the site belonged to the military authorities.   I demanded proof of their
statement.   It was produced, and it was at once evident that
I could not maintain my position there.   We must respect
Chinese law and act wisely if we would successfully carry on
the Lord's work, and so I at once admitted their claim, but
stated that, as I had rented from a citizen, I would not leave
that night.   Till long past midnight angry soldiers paraded
the streets, shouting threatening words.   At times they were
at the door, on the point of smashing it, rushing in, and disposing of me with their weapons.   Again and again they approached, and it seemed in that dark, damp place as if my end
were at hand.   On leaving the place in the morning great
crowds went in front; others followed after, jostling and sneering; and many viewed me from their low-roofed houses and
flung filth and missiles down at me.   It took me several hours
to make my way a short distance to the river's bank.   Entering a boat, I went down the river to the Toa-liong-pong
chapel, three miles away, to find my students.   We spent the
rest of the day there, and in the evening, after preaching in
the chapel, we entered the little room and prayed to the God
of heaven to give us an entrance into the city of Bang-kah.
Rising from prayer, we returned immediately to the city.   It
was dark, but some lights were visible.   Not knowing exactly
whither we were going, we met an old man, and inquired if
he knew any one who would rent even a small house for mission work.   "Yes," he replied, "I will rent you mine."   We
accompanied him, and, passing through dark streets and over
rubbish, came to a small back door opening into a dirty room
with mud-floor.   We entered and began to write a rental
paper.   The house had to be rented by a native, for foreigners
cannot hold property away from the treaty ports.   To be particular I said, "Do you own the site?"   "Oh no," said he,
"but I can secure the owner this very night."   In half an

hour the owner was with us, another paper prepared, and both contracts signed and stamped. I was in full possession, and that according to Chinese law, by midnight. He gave us possession at once, crept out a back way, and disappeared.

In the morning I put up a tablet over the door with the same inscription as before: "Jesus' Holy Temple." In less than an hour crowds filled the street, and the open space in front of a large temple was thronged with angry citizens. People came and went the whole day long. The second day the whole city was in an uproar, and the hubbub produced by their thousand voices fell very unpleasantly upon our ears. Still I walked the street among them, now and again extracting teeth, for we had friends even among so many enemies. On the third day lepers and beggars and other lewd fellows, hired to molest us, pressed around with their swollen ears and disgusting-looking features. They tried to rub against us, expecting us soon to quit the premises. About four or five o'clock the excitement grew to a white heat. Hundreds had their cues tied around their necks, and blue cloth about their loins, to signify that they were ready for the fray. One stooped down, picked up a stone, and hurled it against the building. In a moment their screams were deafening. They were on the roof, within and without, and the house was literally torn to pieces and carried away. No material was left. They actually dug up the stones of the foundation with their hands, and stood spitting on the site. We moved right across the street into an inn. No sooner had we done this than scores were on the roof and many more climbing the walls. The crash of tiles could be heard as they attempted to force an entrance. By this time the shouts and yells were inhuman. One who has never heard the fiendish yells of a murderous Chinese mob can have no conception of their hideousness. The innkeeper came to us with the key of the door in his hand and begged us to leave, lest his house be destroyed.

Then there was a lull. The Chinese mandarin, in his large sedan-chair, with his body-guard around him, and with soldiers following, was at the door. Just then, too, her Britannic Majesty's consul at Tamsui, Mr. Scott, put in an appearance. We sat down together. The Chinese official told the consul to order the missionary away from the city. The consul quickly retorted, " I have no authority to give such an order; on the other hand, you must protect him as a British subject." I love British officials of that caliber. When the consul left I accompanied him to the outskirts of the city. On my return the mandarin was literally on his knees beseeching me to leave the city. I showed him my forceps and my Bible, and told him I would not quit the city, but would extract teeth and preach the gospel. He went away very much chagrined, but left a squad of soldiers to guard the place. In two or three days the excitement subsided. In a week I was offered a site outside the city, and the promise of help from the Chinese authorities to erect a building there. I refused point-blank. As I was lawfully in possession of the site as well as of the building which had been destroyed, I was determined to have our mission building in Bang-kah, and on that spot. The officials then said that I would not be allowed to build in that place again because it was within only a few feet of the examination hall, although, in fact, the hall was a mile and a half away. Having exhausted their whole stock of excuses and subterfuges, they yielded. I erected a small building on the original site—not one inch one way or another—and opened it, with soldiers parading the street to preserve the peace. Still the three strong clans continued to be bitterly opposed to us and our work. Every citizen who dared to become even a hearer was boycotted. The former owner of the site had to flee for his life. In time a few became friendly. We purchased a larger site and erected a good, commodious place of worship, roofed with tiles. During the French invasion in

1884 that building was destroyed by the looters, the materials carried away, and indignities heaped upon the preacher and converts. Within three months after the cessation of French hostilities three stone churches were erected. One of these was in Bang-kah. It is a solid, handsome, substantial church, with stone spire seventy feet high, and lightning-rod three feet higher. It is of stone hewn at the quarry; has pillars and turrets of modern style; the inside is plastered beautifully white, the outside finished in stucco-plaster like colored stonework. There are rooms for the preacher, and an upper room —the only one in the mission—for the missionary.

In 1879 six students and I, on foot, and my wife in a sedan-chair, were going through one of the streets after dark on our way to the chapel. It was the tenth day of a heathen feast, and the idolatrous procession was about to disband, so that the devotees were wrought up to the highest pitch of fury and agitation. There were thousands of them in the procession, leaping and yelling as if under the afflatus of evil spirits. We were recognized. There was a pause, and a torch was thrust into the face of my wife in the chair, nearly destroying her eyes. A dozen dragged two students by their cues, while others were tumbling a third on the stone pavement. Wilder and wilder grew the infuriated mob. Louder and louder sounded their gongs and yells. Things looked dangerous, when an old man from a house right there rushed up and said, "This is Kai Bok-su, the barbarian teacher. Do not interfere with him or his company. Take my advice and go on in your procession." Fortunately there was a narrow lane at right angles to the street where we met the processionists. Into this he hurried us out of danger. We went directly to the chapel, where I preached on the words of the psalm, "As the mountain, are round about Jerusalem, so the Lord is round about his people from henceforth even forever."

Changes have taken place in that once proud city. In 1887

I was there during the time of idolatrous rites and processions. Perhaps there never was such a gathering of people in that city before. A Hoa and myself took our position purposely at various places near the temple, on the cross-streets, by the wayside, and on the wall of the new city. Once we were right above the gateway through which the processionists passed, but we were neither molested nor slandered. They went along with smiling faces. That very evening we sat in front of the large temple where years before the mob met to kill us. The same Bang-kah head men were in the procession, and as they came near us they halted and greeted us kindly. Before dark I extracted five hundred and thirteen teeth and addressed an immense throng. But what a change! Who ever dreamed of such a change! I never witnessed such a half-hearted, listless procession. By removing an idol or two the whole performance would have amounted to little more than a sight-seeing farce. But idolatry is far from being dead yet. There is indeed a great change, but hard battles must yet be fought before heathen hearts will yield to Jesus and follow him.

But it was on the eve of our departure to Canada in 1893 that Bang-kah gave evidence of the greatness of the change produced in that city. In the chapel, on the occasion of our last visit, two marriage ceremonies were performed in the presence of a large assembly. The head men of the city sent their visiting-cards, with a message to ask if I would be willing to sit in a sedan-chair and be carried in honor through the streets of their city. I begged some time to consider, and decided that, as in the past they had acted toward us as they chose, so now I would allow them to do the same. A procession was formed on the same level ground, near the same old temple. Eight bands of music, with cymbals, drums, gongs, pipes, guitars, mandolins, tambourines, and clarionets, took the lead. Men and boys with flags, streamers, and banners followed;

scores with squibs and fire-crackers set off after the manner of Chinese celebrations. Five head men, a magistrate, a military official, and two civil officials came next in order; and then three large red " umbrellas of honor," with three flounces each, presented by the people, with their names inscribed, were carried in front of me, as I sat in a handsome silk-lined sedan-chair. Following the chair were six men on horseback, twenty-six sedan-chairs, three hundred footmen in regular order, and various other parties behind. Thus we passed through the streets of Bang-kah, and on all hands received tokens of respect and honor.

On arriving at Bang-kah "jetty," where the steam-launch was waiting, our Christians stood and sang, " I'm not ashamed to own my Lord." Heathen and Christian alike cheered us as we boarded the launch. Two bands of music accompanied us all the way to Tamsui, and from the launch right up to our dwelling-house. In front of our door was the climax of the demonstration. And all this was from the head men and citizens of Bang-kah, the erstwhile Gibraltar of heathenism. And thus was Bang-kah taken. Not unto us, O Lord, not unto us, but unto thy holy name, be the glory!

CHAPTER XVIII

TOURING IN THE NORTH

Traveling on foot—" Perils of waters "—Sedan-chair—Rickshaw—Railway—Struggling with a donkey—Change and incident—With a hill-man—An old Confucianist—Doomed savages—Among pioneers—A man of faith—At Lam-kham—An opium-smoker—Pleasant memories

THE headquarters of the mission in North Formosa are at Tamsui, and from that point tours are frequently made, visiting the churches in order and exploring the regions beyond. This is a most important part of the missionary's work. Responsibility is put upon the native preachers settled at the various chapels, but oversight is required in matters of organization and administration. These periodical visits are encouraging to the preachers and stimulating to the members. In making tours of the churches I never travel alone, but always with a company of students, who are in this way introduced to the work and become acquainted with missionary methods.

There are many modes of traveling, the chief of which is traveling on foot. It is often dangerous and always wearisome. The paths are so rough—now over mountains, now across hot, blowing sands, now through jungle—and the mountain torrents, especially during the rainy season, are so numerous and difficult to cross, that there is little physical enjoyment. Sometimes the traveler is carried across the stream on the shoulders of a coolie. Generally we wade the streams, going in pairs, hand in hand, holding in the disengaged hand a long bamboo pole with which to feel the way. On one occasion Lien Ho, one of the preachers, was nearly drowned. His companion slipped and fell, and losing his hold, he was swept down by the current, tumbling over and over in the seething waters, until at a sharp curve in the stream he was rescued by two of the students who were on shore. At some points there are ferry-boats, and by holding on to a rattan stretched across the stream and spiked to trees at either end, the boatmen cross with ease and safety. Sometimes the boats are abandoned by their owners and left on the rocks. Once we came to a broad, rapid stream and saw a boat on the opposite shore. The boatman was nowhere to be seen, and no answer came to our calls. At last two of our students swam across and fastened the end of a long rope to the boat, by which it was hauled to our side. Several volunteered to be oarsmen, and when we had all crouched on the bottom they shoved out from shore. But they were powerless in such a current. In spite of all their efforts the boat was carried down the stream and dashed to pieces on the stones of a dam a short distance below. Beyond a few bruises and a thorough wetting we were none the worse. We never thought of kindling a fire to dry our clothes, for we knew that another stream and another had to be crossed, and a similar experience might await us at each. Travelers are not always in " perils of waters," for during fine weather in some districts the roads are good and the streams bridged or easily forded ; but in other parts and at other seasons an unexpected bath is of frequent occurrence.

On most of the larger rivers are numerous boats which carry passengers up or down stream. These boats are made of camphor-wood planks, wide, flat-bottomed, and light. They are built to run the rapids, and are called "rapid boats." Going downstream the steersman stands in the bow with a long oar, and the trip is generally pleasant. The trip upstream is very tedious ; the boatmen, wading through the water, grasping a pole tied across the bow, haul the boat slowly along.

The sedan-chair is another vehicle of travel. It is carried by two or four coolies, who can go twenty miles a day. The sedan-chair is sometimes a necessity; but to sit cooped up in such a box is to any foreigner who loves scenery and fresh air a great discomfort.

The rickshaw, a light covered gig drawn by a coolie, is very common, especially on the roads connecting Bang-kah, Toa-tiu-tia, and Tai-pe-fu. These cities are situated at the points of a triangle, each about three miles from the others; and the roads between are wide and good, having been built by that energetic and progressive governor, Liu Ming Chuan. About one hundred and fifty rickshaws run on these roads every day. An effort was made to establish a line of English carriages, but had to be abandoned because the horses could not compete with the coolies.

A line of railway runs between Kelung and Tek-chham, about fifty miles. The engines are all made in Germany or England, and the cars are fitted up in English style. The road is now owned and operated entirely by Chinese.

I am sometimes asked why we do not use a pony or donkey in traveling. I tried the donkey once, and am not enthusiastic over the experiment. There were no stables at the inns or chapels, and no provision for caring for the animal. And in the matter of time nothing was gained, as a coolie had to be employed to carry necessary food and clothing, and the time made by the donkey was lost by the coolie. The donkey was a present from the commissioner of customs, who was retiring from the island. We called him "Lu-a," and the students had considerable sport with him at Tamsui. One day we planned a trip to a chapel five miles away. Lu-a was brought to the door for my use, and as it was a great occasion I mounted and led the way. The students followed, greatly enjoying the sight of a foreign missionary astride a donkey. All went well, however, until we came to a narrow plank bridge crossing a ravine twelve or fifteen feet deep. The bridge was not more than three feet wide, and when Lu-a came he halted suddenly, planted his fore feet well forward, and set his ears back in a settled sort of way. Coaxing and urging both failed. I then dismounted and began to pull. The students took in the situation and thought to assist by pushing, one of them taking hold of Lu-a's rat-tail. But it was all in vain. Lu-a was "established." A consultation was then held and various plans discussed. Thinking that the donkey might have changed his opinion, I made another effort, and seizing the halter, began to pull with all my might. But he braced himself all the more firmly with his fore feet, and then began to kick. This had the effect of scattering the students in the rear, but I kept pulling in front. Lu-a then opened his mouth and brayed, making sounds such as the students never heard before, and as only a sulky donkey can make. The whole performance was so novel, and the donkey's heels went with such rapidity, that the students, shouting "Cheng-bi, cheng-bi!" ("He's pounding rice, he's pounding rice!"), lay down on the ground and laughed themselves nearly sick. But Lu-a conquered; and what made our defeat all the more humiliating was that one of us could almost have carried him across, he was so small, and that we lost an hour and a half of valuable time in the contest. Since then I have not experimented in this kind of locomotion.

Our experiences in traveling are never monotonous, as there is always change and incident enough to give interest; but to readers of the record one trip would appear much like another. Sometimes we take the chapels along the much-traveled public road, at other times the scattered savage villages, and at others the less frequented paths inland from the sea, where the Chinese pioneers are subduing nature's wildness and opening the way for the advancing settlements. In 1890 we traversed the entire length of the field from north to south without once approaching the public road. The narrow paths along which we went skirted and climbed the rugged mountains and wound through scenery of extraordinary beauty. The Chinese generally have but feeble sense of the sublime, and it was gratifying to observe the Chinese students gazing with wonder and admiration upon the picturesque scenery through which we passed. The truth of God had opened their eyes and touched to life their dormant senses.

We were accompanied on that occasion by a hillman, seventy-four years of age, who was my traveling-companion. He had nerves of steel and muscles of iron, and it was a pleasure to walk with one who had such powers of endurance. The others of our party were often far in the rear, and we had to sound an occasional hallo for their encouragement and guidance. After traveling a long distance in this way my companion began to show signs of fatigue, and at last, when we came to a large flat stone at the top of a particularly difficult piece of climbing, he sat down, perspiring and puffing, and said in a beseeching tone, "We move too fast."

As we walked along, this hillman spoke a great deal about the folly of idolatry, and offered me his god of the north pole, god of the kitchen, and god of war, before which he had been bowing himself for seventy long years. This offer was made good, and on our return we carried them with us as a contribution to my museum at Tamsui.

On the arrival of our party we set out again, all moving together. Our guide knew the way, and taking the lead, he rushed on ahead to a village near by to advise a school-teacher of our coming. We were welcomed at the school-room by the teacher, a particularly fine literary gentleman. Looking about the room, I was a little surprised to find on his table a copy of the Old Testament, a hymn-book, and a New Testament Catechism. He caught my glance, and laying his hand on the Bible, said, "Here I find what I longed to know. This Book tells me how this world was made." And he went on to speak of the delight and profit he found in studying the story of creation. The native preacher, himself one of the literary class, had given this teacher the Book, and as it was the opening chapters of Genesis that first arrested his own attention, he directed the mind of his inquiring friend to the same portion. The teacher became interested, and soon the new light began to dawn. There was a chapel not far from the school, and on the night we held service there he was present. During my address he would give expression to his consent and approval in emphatic exclamations, like the "Amen" of an old-time camp-meeting. At the close he rose and addressed the assembly : " I am sixty-four years of age, and have taught school for twenty-three years. I heard the gospel from the lips of the native preacher who is here to-night. He came to my schoolroom more than ten times. I believe this new doctrine with all my heart. It is good. I was a Confucianist, but Confucianism did not satisfy my soul. I read in the Bible how God created the heaven and the earth. I read, too, of eternal life after death. These things impressed me deeply. I kept pondering on them even in my school. Then an old friend came and brought Kai Bok-su, the foreign missionary. My old friend I found to be a Christian, and though he is over seventy years of age he is young again. He has fellowship with God. I have come now to understand. For many years I have not believed in idols. Now I am satisfied, and before all here I declare myself a believer in God and in Jesus. The gospel is good news to an old man like me." There was profound silence all the time, for this old disciple of Confucius was respected by all. His words were earnest, for in them was the reviving hope of an old man's life.

At Toa-kho-ham, a town near the mountains, we saw twenty-four savages imprisoned and condemned to punishment for the death of several Chinese camphor-workers in the border-land, whose heads were taken by the head-hunters of the tribe. The prisoners were secured with chains about their legs. Their tattooed women strolled about, unfettered and unconcerned, as if careless about the fate of their braves. But there was sympathy in their hearts, and although they loved the freedom of their forest retreats, that "touch of nature," love for their husbands and sons, bound them by invisible cords to the place of their imprisonment.

Our next night was spent at a village of Hak-ka Chinese, where we had to defend ourselves against the lances of the most blood-thirsty mosquitoes I ever encountered. They were regular warriors, and a smudge of weeds was but poor protection. Foreigners in Formosa invariably carry mosquito-curtains, but touring through inland settlements must be done without such luxuries.

At a chapel among the hillmen we were given a reception that, whatever might be said of its style, lacked nothing in the matter of heartiness. Guns and fire-crackers sounded out their glad welcome. A sumptuous feast of fowl and fish was prepared at the chapel, and the building was filled the entire day. Three hours were spent in listening to their recitations of psalms, hymns, and Bible selections, some in the Hak-ka dialect and others in the Hok-lo. Away yonder among the rugged hills a beacon-light is glowing, and those weary pioneers are finding their way back to God.

On our way toward the sea the first man to greet us was one who had been blind, but whose sight was restored. He had been treated some time previously, but when he caught sight of me that day, he rushed up, his eyes wide open, and exclaimed, "God did it; God did it! I can see now. God did it without medicine." Advocates of faith-cure might add this man to their number and regard his case as an unanswerable argument. There was faith and prayer, but there was work as well. The man had been suffering from anemia and granular ophthalmia. The treatment prescribed was for the toning up of his system, and a wash was prepared for his eyes. Reckless living was strictly forbidden and hygienic regulations enforced. Under the care of the native preacher he had made slow but sure progress, until his health was restored and his sight became clearer. When the supply of medicine was exhausted he no doubt prayed more earnestly and lived more consistently, and he thought that as his eyesight was restored when he was not taking drugs, his cure was exceptional and miraculous. " God did it," was his testimony, which, indeed, was true; but means were suited to ends, as must always be done if we would be blessed of God.

On returning from an inland tour we sought refuge for the night at Lam-kham, a day's journey southwest from Tamsui. There was no public inn, and no one would give us lodgings. We found a deserted cart-shed, in which we took shelter. A young man who was baptized at our first country station lived in that neighborhood, and when he found us out escorted us to his home. One evening a place was prepared and arrangements made for a service. I preached the gospel to the people, and set on the table eight idols which had been surrendered by their devotees. There is at Lam-kham a gnarled banian-tree twenty-five feet in circumference, said to have been planted by Koxinga. It is supposed to have in it the spirit of one of Koxinga's followers, and is reverenced, if not worshiped, by many of the people.

On my next visit to that place a man fifty-eight years of age came up and expressed great interest in us and our work. He followed us to Tamsui for the express purpose of overcoming the opium habit, which was fast ruining him. The pipe was placed in my museum, and then the struggle began. It was terrible beyond description. Those who have never experienced it cannot understand the power of the habit. When the craving came on, his body writhed in agony. Remedial measures were adopted, and by Christian fellowship and divine grace he held on, going from strength to strength, until the victory was won. He told me that it was he who, as head man of the village, led the people of Lam-kham in their opposition to us and in refusing us shelter. He spoke afterward at many of our large gatherings, and always made three points prominent: first, that he had been an opium-smoker and had been cured; second, that he had resisted our entrance and vilified us at Lam-kham; third, that he was now a follower of Jesus Christ, and by his grace feared neither men nor devils. He went back to his home and led his friends in constructing a thatched building for chapel purposes. After this building was destroyed by a typhoon a substantial and comfortable hall, roofed with tiles, was erected, at a cost of one hundred and fifty-six Mexican dollars, one hundred and twenty-six of which were given by the poor peasants themselves. Two poor old women, who walked four miles every Sabbath to attend the services, brought two fowls each as an offering. These were sold, and with the price five hundred tiles were purchased for the new chapel.

Looking over my journals, I find the record of many trips made in all directions. There are many brief entries of services held, churches opened, and sacraments dispensed. There is mention of interesting cases and encouraging experiences. The fidelity and affection of my students are recalled by incidents recorded. The journal of one trip of forty-six days, made with the Rev. Tan He, in the autumn of 1888, is crowded with interest. There were hardships, exposure, perils, and disappointment; but a glance at the record recalls not these things. To a stranger all would be meaningless, but to me the very names of the places awaken pleasant memories. There were Lun-a-teng, Toa-tiu-tia, Tho-a-hng, Ang-mng-kang, Au-lang, Lai-sia, Tiong-kang, and Tek-chham. As I write these names there rises before my inner vision picture after picture of eager congregations assembled in pleasant chapels, singing praise to

Jehovah-God, of whom until a few years ago they had never heard, listening with appreciative attention to the gospel message, sitting down together at the holy table and commemorating the dying love of the Man of Calvary, and coming with their little children, in response to Christ's gracious invitation, and covenanting in the ordinance of baptism to bring up their children "in the nurture and admonition of the Lord"; and then their heart-felt good-bys as we left them one by one, to preach the gospel and establish the church of Christ at other stations. It is easy to name over the chapels and to reckon up the statistics; and for all these marvelous tokens of God's blessing we are humbled into gratitude. But the real story cannot thus be told. It is not written in the records of ink, but in hearts that have learned to love the Saviour—hundreds of them now before him in the glory, hundreds more loyally serving him in the church upon earth. They are our epistles, and in their hearts and lives is written the record of our tours in North Formosa.

CHAPTER XIX

THE WAITING ISLES

The prophecy of the isles—Visiting Steep Island—On Pinnacle Island—
Sea-birds' island home—Agincourt Island—An old fort—Present-
day inhabitants—A tragedy—Adrift—Our last visit—Agincourt's
voice

THE isles shall wait for His law! That Old Testament
prophecy has been an inspiration in my life. I have seen
it fulfilled in Formosa. It has been fulfilled in the archipelago
of the South Sea. The islands of the frozen north will yet
sound his praises. It is not a poetic fancy. It is not a base-
less dream. He has spoken it whose words are sure. When
the continents shall have turned unto the Lord, and when their
kings shall have come to the brightness of his kingdom, surely
the waiting isles shall "fly as a cloud, and as doves to their
windows."

When Formosa had heard the gospel our eyes began to look
longingly east and north toward the lonely little islands beyond
the blue horizon-line. Off the northeast coast a few hours' sail
is Steep Island. We talked much about it because A Hoa's
mother was born there, and because upward of three hundred
Chinese dwelt there, many of whom had never heard the gospel. Passage for myself and several of the students on board
a junk loaded with planks was engaged from Tamsui. We set
out, but the winds were contrary, and after two days of tossing
and seasickness we rounded the northern point of Formosa

and ran into Kim-pau-li, on the northeast. Here we got water and food, for our supply was well-nigh exhausted. Setting sail again, we were driven far out of our course, first eastward and then to the north. For five days and nights we were carried hither and thither by the merciless waves. On the fifth day, scarcely knowing where we were, having been driven back over our track, we sighted land. What was our delight when we found that we were on the lee side of Steep Island, and right grateful were we for the welcome of the islanders.

The Chinese call Steep Island Ku-soa ("Turtle Mountain"), and from certain points of view the island does resemble a huge turtle standing on guard with head erect. One side is almost perpendicular, fully twelve hundred feet high. The rock formation is a laminated kind of slate, argillaceous sandstone, and igneous rocks. On sailing around the island we noticed sulphur steam ascending its sides, and near the sea-line were whitish cinders and hot water. The whole is evidently an oozing, seething mass of sulphur.

The inhabitants are nearly all fishermen. They grow on the island sweet potatoes, Indian corn, and several kinds of vegetables. There is only one village, and on the occasion of our visit the people were suffering from the effects of a fire which left forty families homeless. Near the village there is a natural pond, with no visible outlet, but having some underground communication with the sea. At low tide the water is fresh, but at high tide it is brackish. During certain seasons hundreds of wild ducks make this pond their rendezvous. The only spring of fresh water sends a stream trickling down an irregular ledge into the pond. Near it stands a solitary ebony-tree, the last, no doubt, of a numerous family.

The poor people were very hearty in their welcome, and gave us the best of what little they had. They brought their sick and suffering, and we sought to give them relief. With glad hearts they listened to the gospel message, and their destitution gave point and pathos to their pleading for a native preacher. When we left them the whole village accompanied us to the shore, and with many words of gratitude, and begging us to return, they watched us sail out of their life again. Five hours in an open boat rowed by a crew of their stalwart fishermen against a heavy sea, and we were landed on the shore of Formosa opposite Steep Island, and near to one of our chapels, where we found rest and food.

Away to the northeast of Formosa, more than a hundred miles from Kelung, are three islands, called Pinnacle, Craig, and Agincourt. The Chinese names, Flower-pot, Bird, and Large, are descriptive and singularly appropriate. These islands belong to Formosa, but are self-governing and practically independent.

Pinnacle Island is an irregular bare rock, upon which nothing grows and where no land animal could live. It stands one hundred and seventy feet out of the water, and serves only as a resting-place for sea-birds wearied with their long flight.

Craig is also unfit for man's abode, but was surely heaved up to be the home of the seafaring birds that gather there in flocks that at times literally darken the sky. On one side the island is a rugged and perpendicular wall of rock two hundred feet high. From that side it slopes down to the water's edge, forming a surface of two or three acres, which is smooth, without trees or shrubs, but completely covered with soft grass, in which the birds lay their eggs without making any kind of nest. I discovered twelve different kinds of grasses, but no flowers. Insects, including the dreaded centipede and several species of beetle, abounded. But the characteristic of the island is its bird-life. Gulls and terns gather there in millions. As they return homeward they hover over the island for a little, and then settle down like a wide-spreading mantle of wings. The whole sloping surface is covered, and the sight is worth the voyage to see. But the cruelty of man destroyed for us the beauty of the scene. On one occasion while we camped there a dozen or a score of men came from Agincourt to gather the eggs, and their large baskets were soon filled. When the birds came home in the evening and settled down in the grass, the men, carrying lighted torches, caught them alive and crammed them into large sacks. They were then taken to a large stone near which a fire was kindled, and there, one by one, they were dashed to death and piled in heaps several feet high. The sight and the wailing screams of the poor birds were sickening. In the morning they were dressed, salted, and dried. After securing the birds the men hooked turtles of immense size. Our crew made purchases, and on our return trip we were surrounded by birds living and dead, eggs sound and unsound, whole and broken, and in one corner a huge turtle five feet long lay on its back, groaning all night like a human being. What a night !

Agincourt is much larger than Pinnacle or Craig, and stands out of the water five hundred and forty feet. It contains perhaps ten acres, and is the home of more than a hundred Chinese, who came originally from Kelung, Formosa. They live in low stone huts on one side of the island, and about their huts are trees, shrubs, grass, and flowers. Maize is cultivated and eaten in every form, but generally pounded in a mortar and made into porridge. Millet, pumpkins, cucumbers, and beans are grown, which, with their salted birds and shell-fish, constitute their food. Unlike the Chinese elsewhere, they care little for rice. Skipping from hillock to hillock I saw flocks of goats, but no other animals were seen.

On a high place above the huts I came upon an old fort like the Pictish remains seen in Sutherlandshire, Scotland. It looked to be very ancient, but who were its builders and what its purpose remained a mystery. The oldest inhabitant, a man past fourscore, could give no account of it. One wondered if it belonged to the Dutch régime, and if, when they fortified Palm Island, at the mouth of the Kelung harbor, they also planted their guns here. Or were mutineers from some passing vessel left ashore on this lonely isle? Or is it the work of some shipwrecked crew, some Robinson Crusoe or veritable Enoch Arden? Nothing is left to tell the tale. Certain it is, however, that anxious hands in the far-gone past put stone upon stone, and there they stand, marking the place where, perhaps centuries ago, their builders sat, waiting wearily for the sail that never came, listening nightly to

" The myriad shriek of wheeling ocean-fowl,
The league-long roller thundering on the reef."

The present-day inhabitants of Agincourt we found to be bright and kindly in their disposition. On our first visit, in 1879, our party was made up of myself and wife, a friend from Scotland, and several students. When the people sighted us they watched us from the rocks along the shore until we were within speaking distance, when they warned us not to try to land, as the shore was dangerous. One of their men plunged into the water and swam out to our junk, having fastened round his waist a rope, the other end of which was secured to a rock. When he was taken on board and the rope fastened to our junk, we were hauled to shore. The ledge was very rugged, and as the waves carried the junk near enough, each one had to be ready and jump to shore, there to be caught by our new-found friends. It was a perilous landing, and were it not for the strength and bravery of those fishermen one of our number would not have returned. Our stay was made pleasant by the unfailing kindness of the people, who, though poor and ignorant, received us graciously, and listened with interest to the gospel we preached.

A few years ago an American sailing-vessel was becalmed near Agincourt, and the captain's son and a traveling-companion rowed to shore in search of game. Before their return a gale arose, and the ship was driven before the storm until it found shelter in Kelung harbor. The captain reported the catastrophe, and a steamer was sent in search of the missing men, but no trace of them was ever found. The islanders may have been blamed, but I am confident that in their hands the young men would have been kindly treated. It was not the poor islanders that did the deed, but the merciless, hungry sea.

I set out a third time to visit Agincourt. This time our junk was a small coal-boat that had been cleaned and ballasted with sand. With a good supply of food and fresh water, we set sail at dark. Our course lay in a northerly direction, but when morning dawned we were far down the east coast of Formosa, opposite So Bay. Putting about, we had to fight our way back against wind and wave. We were carried eastward until land was out of sight and night came down. Dense fogs had settled on the Formosa hills, and the crew were terrified and almost helpless. There was no compass on board except a small one attached to my watch-guard. The helmsman had completely lost his bearings, and our boat began to drift. The seamen were horror-stricken, but the students were calm and undismayed. In such circumstances nothing but a real trust in the living God can stand the stress and strain. Meanwhile I watched the scudding clouds, on the lookout for the beacon-lights of heaven. At last there was a rift and the glorious stars were seen, steady and true as of old. The helmsman was changed, the boat's course altered, and next day we sailed into Kelung harbor and found shelter at the mission-house there.

Our boat was repaired, a new crew secured, and we put out again. This trip winds and waves were favorable, and in due time the three islands were sighted. Craig was passed and we steered for Agincourt. The people went wild with joy, and not in vain did we tell " the old, old story." Their lot is hard, like life in St. Kilda, and their island is one of " the loneliest in a lonely sea"; but the gospel is for them, and the word spoken on those journeys will not return void. For He said, " Surely the isles shall wait for me;" and the voice of storm-swept Agincourt will be heard when

" 'Midst the streams of distant lands
The islands sound his praise;
And, all combined, with one accord
Jehovah's glories raise."

CHAPTER XX

IN 1884 a black cloud began to shape itself on our horizon, and soon the heavens were overcast and threatening. Those were days of darkness in North Formosa. China had become involved in a dispute with France about a boundary-line in Tonquin. It was not settled satisfactorily, and France, without declaring war, sent a fleet to the China Sea and bombarded the forts at Foo-chow and other places. As Formosa was under the jurisdiction of China it became one of the centers of attack, as was the case more recently in the war with Japan. In the summer of 1884 several French war-ships appeared, and very soon the news spread throughout North Formosa that the French were coming. The people were both alarmed and enraged. Their animosity was aroused against all foreigners and those associated with them. The missionary was at once suspected, and the native Christians were accused of being in league with France. Torture and death were threatened against all our converts. Chinese soldiers ground their long knives in the presence of the Christians, and sometimes caught the children, brandished their sharpened knives over their heads, and swore that they would all be cut to pieces when the first barbarian shot should be fired.

Letters from preachers and converts in different parts of the field were brought to me at Tamsui at all hours of the day and night. A cloud hung over our entire mission work. In July I was on Palm Island, at the mouth of Kelung harbor, teaching the students in the mission-house there. Chinese soldiers paraded in front of the building, sometimes, indeed, strutting into our study-room, jeering and vilifying us all the while, and threatening to kill us all on the spot should the French, then in the harbor, take action. One day a movement was seen among the French fleet. One large man-of-war weighed anchor and took position near the Chinese fort. The guns were directed and ready. The Chinese in the fort were in readiness for attack and would have answered the first charge. We watched every movement, awaiting anxiously the opening shot. But all remained quiet that day.

Shortly afterward a letter came from a native preacher requesting me to visit a Christian family, ten miles from Kelung, where there was sickness. We left Palm Island on this errand, but our departure was none too soon, for on August 5th five French war-ships bombarded and destroyed the Chinese fort. Four days after the bombardment, in company with an Englishman, I went around the coast in a steamship, and was allowed to go on shore to examine the smoking fortifications. Soldiers were lying on their faces, with bodies shattered. Evidently they had been fleeing when exploded shells ended their lives. These shells were sent with such terrific force as to cut off branches of a tree that were half a foot in diameter. A magazine that had exploded hurled masses of concrete to an incredible distance. The Englishman and myself, with one of my students, were invited on board the flag-ship " La Galissonair " and taken through every part of the vessel. When we went down below our attention was directed to three holes, nearly a foot in diameter, just above the surface of the water, made by shells from the Chinese fort. The vice-admiral spoke in the highest terms of the gunners who aimed so truly. Though he was a man of war, this officer was also a man of sympathy; for when my student looked afraid as the soldiers under drill and their officers dashed to and fro with swords dangling at their sides, he said, " Poor fellow! Tell him not to be afraid; we have no pleasure in killing people."

Now that the first shot had been fired and hostilities really begun, the joy of the ever-enlarging mobs of looters knew no bounds. They had nothing to lose in the war, but everything to gain. It was a rare opportunity for plunder and vengeance. They hoisted and carried black flags, butchered swine, drank *sam-shu* (liquor), and carried on their work quite methodically. It seemed as if there would be wholesale bloodshed. The Christians were their first and special object of attack. Seven of the best of our churches were utterly destroyed, and others were greatly impaired. At Toa-liong-pong, near the home of Koa Kau, the mob tore down the chapel, and, having made on the site a huge mound, they erected beside it, out of the bricks of the ruined chapel, a pile eight feet high, and, after plastering it over with black mud, they inscribed on the side facing the road, in large Chinese characters, the epitaph: " MacKay, the black-bearded devil, lies here. His work is ended."

At Sin-tiam the mob entered the chapel, took the communion-roll, which was in the drawer of the desk on the platform, and beginning with the first name, they marked every member as a victim. The name of the first having been announced, forty or fifty were despatched to set fire to his dwelling, plunder his property, beat his family, and destroy all their belongings. So suddenly was the attack made on the mission buildings that the native pastor's wife and family narrowly escaped with their lives. A man and his wife, each over sixty years of age, were taken to the water's edge in front of the church and given their choice between denying their God and death by drowning. They spurned the threat and would not recant. Then they were taken into the water knee-deep and the alternatives again presented, this time money being offered if they would renounce their faith. A second time they refused. Then in mad rage they were dragged still further into the flowing Sintiam, and a third chance given, to be a third time refused. There they suffered, martyrs for the faith, to whom death was nothing compared with dishonoring their Lord.

Another man, belonging to the same church, had splits of bamboo placed between the fingers, and these then tightly bound with cords. He was entreated to return to the religion of his fathers, but he remained steadfast. The cords were pulled tighter, and yet more tightly, until the blood oozed out at the finger-tips. Still he refused to surrender. He was then knocked senseless, and his assailants rushed off, in answer to the call of hundreds with the black flag, to destroy the property and torture the members of other Christian families. He recovered consciousness, survived the injuries received, and became more devoted to the cause of Christ than ever before.

The brothers of one man closed the door on him when he was flying for his life, because he was a Christian, and they tauntingly asked him, "Where is your God now? Why cannot your God protect you?"

Another was seized, hoops of bamboo bound around his head, and splits of wood tied around his legs, until he swooned away. Kicked and beaten, he was left for dead; but he survived, and harsh treatment was unavailing, for he did not forsake the true God.

The infuriated persecutors seized a young man, dragged him to a tree, and then, throwing his cue over a branch, they pulled it until his toes could scarcely touch the ground. Even this atrocity did not satisfy their malignant rage, for, while spitting upon him and jeering at him, they sneered, "This is one who joined the barbarian's church."

An elder and his family escaped to a coal-mine in the neighborhood, and for ten days they continued there, going out at night into the fields in search of potatoes to keep themselves alive. It was impossible to cook food, for the smoke would have betrayed their hiding-place. Thirty-six families at that once prosperous station were left homeless, houseless, penniless.

Three years afterward the Sin-tiam Christians sent me a letter to the effect that, though they had to begin life, as it were, anew, after the days of trial, they were in as good circumstances, and some of them in even better, than previously. Thus the true and loving God vindicates his own cause. Their enemies perished miserably; several of the ringleaders were murdered by the savages, others died of fever, and others were imprisoned by officials. "For evil-doers shall be cut off: but those that wait upon the Lord, they shall inherit the earth."

At Kelung the entire town was deserted by the Chinese. There was there an elderly female convert who owned a small house and some property. Wrapping the deed in a handkerchief, she placed it between her shoulders under her garments. Having bound feet, she could only hobble along with the aid of a staff, but still she hoped to evade the searching eyes of the persecutors. Unfortunately, however, they caught her, stripped her of her upper garments, found the deed, took possession of it, beat her with the sides of their long knives until she was horribly bruised from head to foot, and then they let her go. After peace was restored she returned to Kelung, and continued one of the most zealous followers of Jesus at that station.

These are only a few examples of the trials and sufferings endured by Christians in North Formosa as the result of the French attack.

In October the French war-ships were in position before the

Tamsui forts. An English man-of-war was by this time in the harbor to protect foreigners, and I was asked to go on board with my family and to take my valuables with me. I told the good friends that my valuables were in and around the college, and that I knew they could not go on board. Valuables! The men who were my children in the Lord, who journeyed with me, ministering to me in sickness, wading streams, scaling mountains, facing danger by sea and by land, never once flinching before any foe—they were my valuables ! While they were on shore I would not go on board. If they were to suffer we would suffer together.

When the bombarding began we put our little children under the floor of the house, that they might not be alarmed. My wife went out and in during these trying hours. I paced the front of the house with A Hoa, while shot and shell whizzed and burst around us. One shell struck a part of Oxford College, another a corner of the Girls' School, and still another a stone in front of us, and sent it into mid-air in a thousand atoms. A little to the west of us another went into the ground, gouging a great hole and sending up a cloud of dust and stones. The suction of one, as it passed, was like a sudden gust of wind. Amid the smoke from forts and ships, and the roar and thunder of shot and shell, we walked to and fro, feeling that our God was round about us. "Thou shalt not be afraid for the terror by night, nor for the arrow that flieth by day."

When the firing ceased, six unexploded shells, weighing forty pounds each, were found within a hundred feet of our door. With great care we had them conveyed to the river, placed in a boat, and sunk.

One poor heathen, not far from the college, found a shell, sat astride it, and began to work with chisel and hammer to extract the powder. It burst, carrying off both his limbs into the branches of a tree under which he was sitting. He lived for a few minutes, the explosion having so twisted the flesh and arteries that the escape of blood was somewhat interfered with. But for that last moment, with half his body blown away, his mind was still on the treasures of earth. Seeing the contents of his pocket on the ground, he said with his last breath, " Pick up that dollar." Poor, dark, hopeless heathenism!

From the commencement of hostilities until that date I had no rest night or day. After the bombardment I was ill and unconscious for some time. Here is the written statement of C. H. Johansen, M.D., who attended me at the time : " I have been the medical attendant of Rev. Dr. MacKay, who in the beginning of the war was overburdened with work, and in anxiety about the Christian people of the stations. This, combined with the pernicious influence of the hot Tamsui climate, brought on inflammation of the brain (meningitis cerebralis acute). During many days he was without sleep, and this brought on utter exhaustion of his system. The fever was never less than one hundred and two degrees during those days. One day a crisis seemed to approach ; everybody's opinion was that the result would be fatal, all medicines having failed to produce sleep. Fortunately I heard that the steamship ' Hailoong ' had brought ice to Tamsui for Mr. John Dodd. At my request, Mr. Dodd gave all the ice he had to cool Dr. MacKay's burning head. Almost immediately after the application of the ice he fell into a sound sleep, which lasted for thirty-six hours. Then the ice was finished, but he awoke saved."

The second week of October, my wife, children, and the Jamiesons left Tamsui for Hong Kong in accordance with the orders of the British consul. On the 21st I was induced to board the steamship " Fu-kien " to make a round trip and return to Tamsui. Four days afterward, as we entered the Hong Kong harbor, we heard that Tamsui was blockaded, and that we could not return. At length, hearing that the blockade had been raised, I left my family still at Hong Kong and went on board the steamship " Hai-loong." When half-way across the Formosa Channel we had to tack about and return to the mainland for shelter, because of a terrific storm and heavy sea. After some delay we again headed for Tamsui; but when in sight of that port we saw two large French men-of-war, one on either hand, guarding the entrance. We started as if to pass between them, and signaled, " Blockade raised." We were answered by a blank shot. Our captain signaled again. This time we were answered by a shell whizzing across our bow. Immediately the bugle sounded, and we saw guns run out, and men at their posts ready to give us two full broadsides. Our little merchant steamer moved slowly back, and when the captain boarded the French war-ship he was told that the report of the blockade being raised was false, and that if we had moved a foot farther forward the third shot would have sunk us. We then steered to Amoy, on the mainland, and after a delay of one hour there we steamed for the Pescadore Islands, not far from Formosa, where the French headquarters were. There the French admiral was interviewed, and after returning to Amoy we once more set sail for Tamsui. One day, at two o'clock in the afternoon, I stepped ashore, and was met by preachers, students, and converts, many of whom wept for joy.

After some time, desiring to visit the churches, I procured a pass, of which the following is a copy:

" BRITISH CONSULATE, TAMSUI,
" May 27, 1885.

"TO THE OFFICER IN CHIEF COMMAND OF THE FRENCH FORCES AT KELUNG:

" The bearer of this paper, the Rev. George Leslie MacKay, D.D., a British subject, missionary in Formosa, wishes to enter Kelung to visit his chapel and his house there, and to proceed through Kelung to Kap-tsu-lan, on the east coast of Formosa, to visit his converts there. Wherefore I, the undersigned, consul for Great Britain at Tamsui, do beg the officer in chief command of the French forces in Kelung to grant the said George Leslie MacKay entry into, and a free and safe passage through, Kelung. He will be accompanied by two Chinese followers belonging to his mission, named, respectively, Giam Chheng Hoa and Iap Sun.

" A. FRATER,

"*Her Britannic Majesty's Consul at Tamsui.*"

I took a bamboo pole, twenty feet in length, and tied thereon the old flag of Great Britain; and, with the two preachers mentioned in the pass, and a burden-bearer, proceeded up the river. Through Bang-kah we passed, the flag waving in the breeze. In a few hours we neared the Chinese encampment. Soldiers rushed out and shouted in their own dialect, "The British flag!" We marched right on. Soldiers opened right and left. We passed through thousands of them, and right up into the presence of the Chinese commander-in-chief, Liu Ming Chuan. A few words inspired mutual confidence, and I changed my flag for a flag of truce. The general stated that I would be treated with respect by all the soldiers under his command, but he advised me not to approach the French, lest I should be fired upon. An American was in the employ of this military official, and he drew up the soldiers under his command into two lines to present arms as we passed between. We were then escorted within sight of the boundary between the Chinese and the French, who were still in earthworks on the tops of the hills and peaks.

We crossed the river in a longboat, and went into a cleared spot of ground—a tea-plantation—planted our flagstaff, stood beside it, and waited for the French signals. We were observed immediately, and eight soldiers ran down the steep hillside to meet us. When within hailing distance one waved his hand. I understood that to mean that we should advance, and accordingly we moved forward. When in a winding path, where the reeds were in some places above our heads, marching single file, we came suddenly face to face with the soldiers. I was in advance of our party. Straightway four of the soldiers dropped on their knees, the other four stood still, and all leveled their rifles at my breast. Turning around, I pointed to my flag of truce, and signaled the bearer to step to my side. One of the soldiers advanced. I stepped forward, saluted him, and showed him my pass. He glanced at it, and after some altercation, in which one of the Frenchmen who knew a little English acted as interpreter, we were blindfolded with our pocket-handkerchiefs, and conducted by the soldiers, one on each side of me, and one with each of my followers. They led us through streams of water, among tall grass, under a burning sun, for seven long hours. Had we been taken in a straight course we could have covered the distance within an hour. About six o'clock in the evening we were brought into the presence of the French colonel in the Chinese custom-house, and there a number of impertinent questions were put to us. We were told that we could not remain ashore for the night, but would be sent on board a man-of-war in the harbor, as prisoners of war. We were then led away to the water's edge, taken into a boat, relieved of the blindfold, and in five minutes were alongside of the man-of-war. There was much sneering and laughing among the soldiers and sailors, for they supposed that in me they had captured a German spy. We were ordered upon deck, where the white-haired commander, after a short interview, gave orders that my party should be kindly treated. I was taken into his cabin, not as a prisoner of war, but as a guest. The good old Frenchman said he had heard about our mission work, for they had an English pilot in the fleet who was an old Formosan friend of mine. In the morning he went ashore with us himself, and the insolent colonel was much more civil. The old commander said he regretted that we would have to be blindfolded again in going back through the lines, but it was in accordance with the usages of war. In returning through the lines all were more respectful and friendly when they learned who we were. Soldiers were told off to take us within sight of the Chinese lines. They shook hands cordially, and watched us until we recrossed the stream in the same boat and went outside of their boundary-line.

Once more at liberty, we visited the Kap-tsu-lan plain, on the east coast, and found the chapels clean, and the converts cheerful and happy. The persecutions and hardships they endured only bound them more closely to the cause of Christ. There were no desertions from his standard, and everywhere the heathen marveled to see men and women prefer suffering and even death to peace, dollars, and life that could be theirs only by denying their Lord.

Leaving Tamsui in June, 1885, under a burning sun, we proceeded to Kelung, and boarded the French man-of-war commanded by Vice-Admiral Lespes. We were told we could get ashore anywhere, as the French would soon be away. I immediately rowed to Palm Island, and arrived in time to save our property from the mobs that were gathering in crowds to loot and plunder before the owners returned. I hoisted the British flag over the mission premises. In half an hour we heard the bugle sound, and there was commotion among the ironclads. A tremendous cheer rent the air, for the French sailors were glad the war was over. One ship steamed slowly up, followed by another and another, until eight were in line out at sea. One remained to pick up stragglers. I boarded her the following day, and the commander assured me that he was disgusted with the whole affair, as was also the admiral himself.

On shore I found not a vestige of the Kelung chapel save rubbish. The temples had been plundered, the carved work defaced, buildings overthrown, roofs torn from houses, and poor Kelung was lying silent and deserted. The Chinese were on the hills, waiting the departure of the French, when they would return to their desolated homes in the town.

When the French left, the heathen were jubilant. They thought Christianity was blotted out because the chapels had been destroyed. Everywhere the shout of derision was made to ring in our ears: "Long-tsong bo-khi!" the meaning of which is, "The mission is wiped out." We were not discouraged, however, and I prepared a statement of our losses in the destruction of mission property by looters, and submitted it to Liu Ming Chuan, the commander-in-chief of the Chinese forces. Without delay or argument, and without reference to Peking, he paid as indemnity the sum of ten thousand Mexican dollars.

When I received the indemnity money and planned the rebuilding of the chapels I had to decide whether to erect twenty-four fragile structures or twelve medium ones or six substantial, commodious buildings. Deciding on the last, I drew plans and made models. Standing on the site of the ruins at Sin-tiam, we lifted a song of praise to God. With our chapel in ruins, the townspeople and others looking on thought us crazy. But out of the ruins another building would rise, and so we sang with glad and hopeful hearts. I employed men to go into the neighboring hill and quarry sandstone; and others with their boats to bring poles, boards, and lime for building. Neither the workmen nor the overseers ever saw a building like the one we now planned to erect. I made some of the models out of turnips, others out of brick and mortar, and still others out of wood. We began work at three places simultaneously —at Sin-tiam, Bang-kah, and Sek-khau—and in twelve weeks we finished three splendid edifices. How imposing they looked, with their seventy or eighty feet of tower and spire of solid masonry! And how our spirits revived as we saw them rise in their splendid beauty on the site of our ruined churches!

But why use money in building spires? Was it for ornamental or for useful purposes? For both ornament and use, especially as a standing disproof of the Chinese superstition about feng-shuy, by which in a general way people mean "good luck," and which has reference to a thousand things. They suppose, for instance, that there is a sort of equilibrium, or indefinable something, in earth or air, which must not be recklessly interfered with. It is only necessary to continue the wall of a new chapel a few inches above the surrounding buildings to arouse neighbors into fury and consternation, for that would interfere with feng-shuy. Thousands of disturbances have been caused by foreigners carrying on their own work in their own way, but unwittingly running counter to this Chinese notion. Knowing that the governor was progressive in his ideas, that he was friendly to myself and the mission, and that he had no great affection for the Bang-kah people, who through all the French troubles had maligned and abused him, I thought it opportune, now that new churches were being built, to erect spires upon the chapels at Bang-kah, Sin-tiam, and Sek-khau, to show the heathen that their notion of good luck was vain superstition. We continued the tower above the gable of the roof seven feet, and then higher and higher. The people would stand and gaze for hours in wonder and amazement. But they made no disturbance, save that they quarreled among themselves. The point in dispute was whether it was the scaffold or the newly erected spire that was swaying in the wind, and once the contention almost ended in a hand-to-hand fight. We finished the spires. On the front of each, in stucco plaster, I put the burning bush, with the historic motto, "Nec tamen consumebatur," in Chinese characters.

The cry about the mission being wiped out now ceased to

be heard, and the people called themselves fools for tearing down the old chapels. "Look now," they said, "the chapel towers above our temple. It is larger than the one we destroyed. If we touch this one he will build another and a bigger one. We cannot stop the barbarian missionary."

While the work of rebuilding chapels went on, other departments were not neglected. Medicines were dispensed, the students were taught, the various fields were visited, and every night the gospel was preached.

New churches were erected in place of those destroyed. Repairs were made wherever needed. And that was not all. Not only had we our forty chapels, as before the coming of the French, but five new stations were opened, and at each a chapel was erected. Month by month and year by year the work prospered. Point after point was occupied. Chapel after chapel was built. The forty became fifty, and the fifty increased to sixty. That was how the mission was wiped out! The fire of God was indeed in the bush, but over it all was inscribed "Nec tamen consumebatur."

THE CONQUERED ABORIGINES

CHAPTER XXI

PE-PO-HOAN CHARACTERISTICS

Subduing the savages—Chinese and Pe-po-hoan—Original houses—
Frankness of Pe-po-hoan—Pe-po-hoan cruelty—Nature-worship—
Dislike of idolatry

AS has already been indicated, the Chinese in Formosa have
been gradually overcoming the various aboriginal tribes
and subduing them to their own modes of life and worship.
We have, therefore, on the island aborigines in all stages of
civilization. In the mountains are the wild, unconquered savages, who scorn the intruder's claim, and never lose an opportunity to wreak vengeance on some ill-fated Chinese head.
These the Chinese call Chhi-hoan ("raw barbarians"). But
the power and patience of the superior race are too much for
the unskilled and shiftless savage, and tribe after tribe is being
brought under subjection. We come now to speak of these
conquered aborigines, and of life and work among them. The
most important are the Pe-po-hoan, with whom are allied the
few settlements of Sek-hoan. The Lam-si-hoan, farther south,
are not far removed from savage, and have only recently submitted to Chinese authority.

The Pe-po-hoan are found in many parts of the island; but
their home in North Formosa is in the Kap-tsu-lan plain, a
rich, low-lying tract on the east coast, between the mountains
and the sea. This plain is of recent geological date, and was
formed by the filling up of a large bay by sand and debris

washed down by mountain streams. The soil is admirably adapted for rice-culture, which is, indeed, carried on very extensively by the inhabitants. The atmosphere, however, is very damp ; heavy vapors driven in from the sea, and floating clouds tapped by the mountain-peaks, not only make traveling uncomfortable and at times well-nigh impossible, but make life itself, to both native and foreigner, a burden too heavy to be borne. The dread malaria works havoc in every home. Prior to their subjugation by the Chinese the Pe-po-hoan lived in houses very different in style and very much superior to those they now inhabit. Their raised floors were much more conducive to health than the damp mud-floors of the Chinese dwellings now to be seen everywhere in the plain. In this respect, at least, the change has been for the worse. The Pe-po-hoan is by nature simple, easily imposed upon, thriftless, and improvident. He has still a streak of the savage, and in those qualities that go to insure success he is distinctly inferior to his Chinese conqueror. There were at one time thirty-six thriving villages in the Kap-tsu-lan plain. The Chinese settlers came in, enterprising, aggressive, and not overscrupulous, and little by little the weaker went to the wall. The Pe-po-hoan were crowded out of the cultivated land, many of their villages were scattered, and they had to begin life anew in the waste jungle. And very often, when they had succeeded in reclaiming land to grow rice and vegetables enough to supply their meager wants, the greedy Chinese would again appear, and, either by winning their confidence or by engaging them in dispute, would gain a foothold and in the end rob them of their lands. Being unable to read and being ignorant of law, they are almost entirely at the mercy of their enemies. It sometimes makes one's blood boil to see the iniquities practised upon these simple-minded creatures by Chinese officials, speculators, and traders.

When foreigners first come in contact with the Pe-po-hoan

they are delighted with their frankness of manner and warmth of emotion, and forthwith express the opinion that this race is superior to the Chinese. I never shared that view. The longer my experience among them the plainer appears to me the inferiority of the Malayan. For downright cruelty and cut-throat baseness the Pe-po-hoan far outdistance the Chinese, and with all their easy good nature they manifest the revengeful spirit of the race to which they belong. One example will illustrate Pe-po-hoan cruelty. A girl was engaged to be married to a young man. One night, when the whole village was staggering in a drunken carousal, the girl was lost. Her dead body was found by a search-party, stripped of its clothes. Suspicion fell on her lover. He tried to escape, but was seized and placed in the stocks, a rude construction of logs extemporized for the occasion, capable of inflicting great agony. His hands were stretched out above his head and tied. In a few days he was removed to the sand-bank beside the sea. The father and mother of the maiden took an old knife, slashed his limbs, and cut portions of his body and put them into his mouth. He was left there on the burning sand with the blood oozing from his wounds and drying in the heat of the sun. His thirst became intolerable, and he cried piteously for some one to end his misery. But no; his sister was not allowed to go to him with one small "bamboo" of water to quench his thirst. There he perished, and his body was left to the ravenous dogs of the plain. Such is Pe-po-hoan vengeance.

Originally the Pe-po-hoan were nature-worshipers, like the savages in the mountains. They had no temple, idol, or priest. They had no idea of a personal God, but believed in the existence of innumerable spirits, whose favor and help it was to their interest to propitiate. They reverenced the spirits of their ancestors, who had gone away, as the American Indian would say, to the "happy hunting-ground." They had all the superstitions of the savage, and indulged in such feasts and orgies as still constitute the religious rites of the untamed mountain tribes.

But all this was changed when they bowed their necks to the yoke of civilization. Their conquerors forced upon them not only the cue and their style of dress, but also the whole paraphernalia of Chinese idolatry. Whenever a tribe submits, the first thing is to shave the head in token of allegiance, and then temples, idols, and tablets are introduced. At the present time the religion of the Pe-po-hoan is the potpourri of Confucian morality, Buddhistic idolatry, and Tauistic demonolatry, to which they have added relics of their own nature-worship and superstition. Some of the younger devotees are the most bigoted idolaters in China, but very many of the people hate the new order of things. Idolatry does not suit the average Pe-po-hoan, and it is only of necessity that he submits to even the formal observance of its rites and ceremonies. It is political rather than religious, and to the large majority is meaningless, except as a reminder of their enslavement to an alien race.

CHAPTER XXII

RICE-FARMING IN FORMOSA

The honored farmer—A Formosa farm—Irrigation—The water-buffalo
—Rice-culture—The farmer's lot

FORMOSA is essentially an agricultural country, and the farming class is both important and honorable. In all parts of China the place of honor is given to the literary man; but the farmer makes a good second, and is much more highly esteemed than either the mechanic or the merchant. The emperor pays honor to husbandry once a year by holding the plow. In Formosa the agricultural class is the mainstay of the country. They are, on the whole, hard-working, honest, and free from many of the vices that characterize city life. As the Kap-tsu-lan plain is one of the richest parts of the island, and as rice is the great staple of the land, special reference may now be made to this department of industry. A plain and brief account of rice-farming should find interested readers among other classes than those who themselves till the soil.

When we speak of a farm in Formosa one must not imagine broad fields inclosed in high fences, and each farmer the proud possessor of one hundred or one thousand acres. The entire farm of a family in Formosa would make but a garden for an agriculturist in America. The owner of eight or ten acres is looked upon as in easy circumstances. The farms are all small and are entirely without fences. A rice-farm is divided into little irregular plots for the purposes of irrigation. These plots are made by throwing up around each low mounds of earth, by which means the water is retained at the required depth.

Rice is grown in fields flooded with water, and the farmer exhibits great ingenuity in the various modes of conveying the water to where it is required. The most efficient is by a great watercourse constructed along the circuitous bank of the river near Sin-tiam, by which the whole of the Bang-kah plain is thoroughly irrigated by water taken from within the mountains. In the construction of this watercourse a tunnel eight feet by six was made through an extensive rock; an aqueduct fifty feet high carries the water over another river, and when it reaches the Bang-kah plain it is divided into innumerable drains and conveyed to all the farms. A clumsy contrivance like a treadmill is sometimes used for slight elevations; a windlass fixed in a box-trough, the lower end of which is in the stream, is operated by two men, and works an endless chain of carriers conveying the water up the trough and depositing it in a drain on the bank. Another method of irrigation is comparatively simple. On the uplands a circular reservoir is excavated and is supplied by the heavy rains. These reservoirs are exceedingly useful, not only for the purposes of irrigation, but also as bathing-places for the water-buffalo. By these methods every foot of rice-lands is adequately supplied with water.

For dry plowing the ox is used, but in rice-cultivation the water-buffalo is indispensable. He is, indeed, by far the most valuable animal to the farmer, and so highly prized that proclamations are often issued forbidding the people to slay him for food. He is more uncouth than the ox, and on account of his intractability of temper would seem to have been only recently domesticated. Large pools of water are absolutely necessary for this creature to wallow or bathe in; hence the name water-buffalo. As soon as released from the plow he will plunge into the pond and remain there a considerable time, with only part of his head, his nostrils, and his horns above water. The implements required by the farmer are few and simple, and are no improvement on those used centuries ago. A broad hoe, a wooden plow with an iron share, a heavy wooden harrow or " drag," and a harvest-sickle are all that he requires.

The rice grown in Formosa must be distinguished from the rice (*Zizania aquatica*) found growing wild in Rice Lake, Ontario, and other parts of America. It is a distinct variety (*Oryza sativa*) and of superior quality. A mountain-rice is grown on the dry uplands, and does not require irrigation, but it is quite inferior.

Rice is not sown broadcast in the open field, like wheat and other cereals, but requires to be transplanted. The seeds are first steeped in water and spread out in large baskets under cover till they have begun to sprout. They are then sown thickly in a small bed, which is protected from winds and birds and watered with a liquid fertilizer. At the expiration of three months the crop is about six inches high and is ready for transplanting.

Meanwhile the large rice-field has been plowed, harrowed, and prepared for the plants. The field slopes down to one side, and the plots already referred to are submerged in about three inches of water. The water from the reservoir or aqueduct is first run into the plot farthest up the slope, from which it is let into the others, one by one, by opening a place in the dividing mounds or dikes. The entire field must be kept under water from before the transplanting until the grain is ready to harvest.

Transplanting rice is a very arduous and wearisome task. The farmer digs up the plants from the bed in spadefuls, leaving a liberal supply of mould about the roots. With a large flat basket of these seedling plants he goes into the miry field, where the mud and water reach his knees. The basket floats on the water. Carrying a supply of the plants in his left hand, the farmer wades backward from end to end of the row, and breaking off tufts, he sinks them in the soft mud beneath the water at intervals of about eighteen inches. The rows are about two feet apart. Then a fortnight later he goes over the whole field again on his bare knees, removing the duckweed and other obnoxious growths. This is perhaps the most distasteful part of the farmer's work, and is a fruitful source of rheumatism. Before the grain is ripe he may possibly go through once more, bending the bunches down to protect them from sweeping winds.

Three months after the transplanting comes the harvest. This is a busy season with the husbandman. The water is drained off; the rice is cut rapidly by a reaper with the sickle or bill-hook, and made into bunches large enough to be held conveniently between the hands. The reaper is followed immediately by a thresher, who draws after him a portable tub. This tub has poles set up around almost the entire mouth, to which is fastened a canvas screen to prevent the rice-grains from flying away. At the open space the thresher stands, and taking a bunch of rice, he gives it two smart strokes on a ladder-like framework placed within the tub after the fashion of a wash-board. The straw is then bound into sheaves, and when dry is stacked away to be used as fodder for the water-buffalo. The grain is carried home in large baskets and placed on a winnowing-floor in front of the house. There it is cared for, heaped up, and covered every night with rice-straw, and spread out in the morning with wooden hoes. It is then winnowed in a fanning-mill similar to that used by Western farmers, and is stowed away in granaries. The next process is the hulling, which is done in a hand-mill constructed on the principle of the millstone. This removes the chaff. The bran-like shell is removed by pounding the grain in a mortar. The rice is then ready for the pot.

The sheaves are no sooner removed from the field than the plowman is once more in the mud and water, a second crop, which is now ready for transplanting, is immediately "set," and the second harvest is reaped in September or October. After the second crop is removed, some plant sweet potatoes, others mustard or rape for fertilizing. Three crops can thus be secured in the course of a year.

As two crops, and sometimes three, are reaped every year, the farmer is kept busy from spring to autumn. During seed-time and harvest his wife rises at three o'clock in the morning, cooks rice and salted vegetables, prepares hot water for the men to wash with, and about four calls them up to breakfast. The men are in the field about five o'clock and work till ten, when a lunch of boiled rice and some salted vegetable is carried out to them. At noon they return home for dinner, and rest for an hour and a half. In the afternoon the same kind of lunch is taken to the field. At seven o'clock they return, wash their breasts and limbs, and sit down to a better meal, generally consisting of a tiny cup of hot liquor, pork, and fresh vegetables boiled with rice. At nine they retire.

The farmer's lot in North Formosa is not altogether an unhappy one. He works hard and is generally thrifty and economical. His wants are few and easily supplied. There is monotony, perhaps, but then he knows nothing of the "nameless longing" that fills the breasts of much-read farmers in the restless West. He has no high ideals, and if he succeeds in providing himself and his family with rice and vegetables he does not object to the drudgery of his lot. The Pe-po-hoan farmer in the Kap-tsu-lan plain would be tolerably comfortable were it not for the oppression of the Chinese landowners and yamen men, who often rob him of his hard-earned *cash* and evict him from his land.   Under the Japanese régime all this is likely to be changed, and the various aboriginal tribes may look forward to a brighter day under the flag of the " Rising Sun."

CHAPTER XXIII

MISSION WORK AMONG THE PE-PO-HOAN

Beginnings—Traveling—Night in a rice-field—" Discouraging "—The first chapel—Results—" No room for barbarians "—Night in an ox-stable—An old feud—Savage craft—A surgical operation—At Sin-sia—Service at Pak-tau—Dr. Warburg

HAVING gained a foothold for the gospel and established churches among the Chinese in the north and west, our attention began to be directed toward the civilized aborigines in the Kap-tsu-lan plain on the east. I had already learned something of the Pe-po-hoan character, and was prepared to find them more emotional, approachable, and responsive than the Chinese, although, perhaps, less solid and stable. The obstacles to the gospel among them were not different from those meeting us everywhere. They were all heathen, blinded by superstition, degraded by idolatry, and with few and weak aspirations after higher things. Many of them are poor, and are kept in poverty partly by their own indolence, partly by untoward circumstances, and mainly by Chinese exactions and oppression. They are warm-hearted, and, notwithstanding many weaknesses and failures, work among them has been full of inspiration and encouragement.

Setting out from Tamsui with a party of students, we made our way over the mountain-ranges south of Kelung and entered the Kap-tsu-lan plain. As this plain is but a few feet above the sea-level, and as the rainfall is very much greater than in

other parts of the island, traveling is always attended with
discomfort and difficulty. By keeping near the sea one can
find a rather dry path, but inland, during the rainy days, one
has to wade through sticky mud, sometimes a foot and a half
in depth. The paths through the rice-fields are narrow and
winding, and when the fields are irrigated are at times completely submerged. Traveling near the base of the mountain,
we passed by the mouth of a ravine, and there we heard yells
and screams. Immediately a Chinese came up, breathless, and
reported that four of his companions had just been speared
and beheaded by the savages, and that he escaped by dodg-
ing. On entering again on the steep brow of a hill overlooking the sea, I was in advance, and was just past the mouth of
the gorge when three savages with spears rushed out and attacked several elders who were a little way in the rear. The
elders, with great presence of mind, threw themselves into the
water and got out of reach of the deadly thrust.

Once, overtaken by night, we got astray and went miles out
of our way. The night was dark, and we were wet, hungry,
and absolutely without our bearings. We staggered round
and round the plats of a rice-field, stumbling into the mud
and water, until we stood still and thought awhile. It was a
moment for serious thought. We were lost and in a strange
territory. No light could be seen near or far. But we remembered that we were on our Master's business. My students uttered no word of complaint; indeed, they were posi-
tively cheerful. We thought of God in front, God in the rear,
God on the right, God on the left, God within, God above,
and underneath the everlasting arms. So we plodded along,
tumbling into mud-pools, scrambling out, and pushing on
again. The first object with which we came in contact I
knew by touch to be a rice-stack, and we passed the night
under its bulging sides.

The next night was spent in a grass-covered hut. Its sides

were of reeds, but the mud had been washed from the inter-stices and now the rain was driven in on the black floor. Going right to one of the villages of about three hundred in-habitants, we were received with disdain. The men grunted, and calling out " Barbarian!" and " Foreign devil!" walked away. Women and children ran into their houses, and then urged wolfish-looking dogs upon us. We stood listening to the yelping of these hungry creatures, and were obliged to leave, for not a soul in the village would hear our words. We visited another village and received similar treatment. This experience was repeated in a third village. Up and down through that plain we labored, tour after tour, and still no one came forward to accept our message of salvation. " How discouraging! " I hear some one say. Who calls such experi-ences discouraging? I do not. I never did. Our business is to do our duty, and to do it independently of what men call encouragement and discouragement. I never saw anything to discourage in twenty-three long years in North Formosa.

At length three men from a fishing-village by the sea came and said : "You have been going through and through our plain, and no one has received you. Come to our village and we will listen to you." One was a very old man who was fittingly nick-named "Black-face." A second was middle-aged and had once been an actor on the stage. The third was a young man. On arriving at their village we sat on large stones in front of the head man's house. We talked over matters with some of the influential men, and partook of rice and fish. When evening came on a tent was constructed out of poles and sails from their boats on the beach. Several stones were placed at one end and a plank laid upon them for a platform. At dark a man took a marine shell with the end broken off, such as they used in days gone by when setting out on the war-path, and with this "trumpet" he summoned an assembly. Families brought benches out of their huts and arranged them in rows.

These preparations completed, they invited us to proceed with our service. We sang, preached, conversed, discussed, answered questions, till the small hours of the morning. The following day the inhabitants decided to have a house in which to worship the true God. They sailed down the coast into savage country for poles, and although they were attacked and wounded, returned with their load. Bricks were made out of mud mixed with rice-chaff, moulded into shape, and dried in the sun. We erected the walls, covered the roof with grass, and built a platform of mud. Then every evening, at the blowing of the " conch," the whole village turned out. They continued to carry their old benches till we procured new ones, and there they sat to be taught the everlasting gospel of our Redeemer. In several weeks—not months—boys and girls learned many of our psalms and hymns, while the elder people acquired more or less Christian knowledge.

After laboring there day and night for six or eight weeks I came to be much impressed by three different classes who attended our services. There were poor old toothless women, who had wrought hard in the constant struggle for existence, squatted on the bare earth, weaving, and as they threw the thread they crooned in a low voice :

> " There is a happy land
> Far, far away."

That land was very real to them—just as real as to their sisters in Christendom—and they came to look wistfully for the sign that would call them, not to the grass-thatched chapel out in the narrow street, but away to the temple not made with hands, in the land where the weary rest. Then there were the boys, with their bright young faces, into whose lives our songs brought something of hope ; and all day long they sang in their own tongue our children's hymn :

> " Jesus loves me, this I know,
> For the Bible tells me so."

And not the least attractive were the hardy, bold, brave fishermen going out in the mornings through the surf, standing—
not sitting—in their boats, and as they pushed their long oars,
kept time to the stroke, singing the old Scotch paraphrase:

> " I'm not ashamed to own my Lord,
>   Or to defend his cause."

It was grand. Standing away yonder on the sandy beach
looking at them and listening to their voices, I wished that it
were possible for the critics of foreign mission work to drop
down and, just for once, see for themselves that the gospel of
Christ is still "the power of God unto salvation to every one
that believeth; to the Jew first, and also to the Greek."

Despite many weaknesses and imperfections in these poor
aborigines, quite a number of that first village remained constant to the end, and have gone home to God. The village
became nominally Christian. My apartment during those
weeks was a low, musty room, where I slept on a box at night.
To that place the cast-off machinery of idolatry was brought,
and more than once I dried my clothes before fires made of
idolatrous paper, idols, and ancestral tablets. Three men were
employed to carry other paraphernalia of idol-worship to the
museum in Tamsui.

A deputation from another village came to make inquiries.
I detained them, that they might be present at an evening
service. They heard fully two hundred voices ring out the
praises of Almighty God, and they were so charmed that they
at once invited us to visit their village. I do not know what
others would have done, but I formed a procession, heading
it with A Hoa at my side, and arranging the converts in
double column behind. We marched slowly along the circuitous path, singing as we went. At the end of our short journey we drew up into a compact body, and another stirring
song of praise rose from our lips. With God's message sung

and preached we captured that village, and the people decided
to have a place of worship. Willing hands soon completed a
building, and a native preacher was left in charge of the work,
as another had been in the first village. We thus had five
hundred who had thrown away their idols and were nominally
Christian; and when they all assembled in the open air to sing
the songs of Zion I forgot the dark night in the rice-field, the
cruelty of our first reception, and the many weary hours at
night, among old baskets, ropes, and nets in a damp room, a
stranger and alone. Oh, it was soul-inspiring, refreshing, glorious! We visited other villages and preached the gospel year
after year to those dark-skinned aborigines. A third chapel
was erected, a fourth, fifth, sixth, seventh, eighth, yes, even a
nineteenth chapel in that Kap-tsu-lan plain, and over each a
native preacher was placed.

The most southerly village in the plain is Lam-hong-o
("South-wind Harbor"), on the south side of So Bay. It was
visited on a previous occasion, but we were scorned and our
message rejected. We resolved to revisit it. It was nearly
dark when we climbed the steep mountain near the sea, and
had yet to descend on the other side. Holding on to the
rocks with our hands, we slid down in safety and then followed
a long bend inward. When we reached the village the rain
was descending in torrents. Approaching a house, I asked if
we could remain overnight. "No room for barbarians," was
the curt reply. We went to a second house and received a
similar rebuff. The door of the third was slammed in my face.
It was hopeless. The night was so dark and the Pacific Ocean
so tempestuous that we could not go east; mountains stood.
to the south; on the north was the harbor, and on the west
savage territory. We thought of one Chinese family in the
corner back of the village, and hoped for better things than
from the Pe-po-hoan. We set out, making our way now over
seaweed, now thumping against a boat, and now caught by

the prickly screw-pine. When we reached the door I called out, "Can we get any accommodation here for the night?" A white-haired man slowly opened the door and drawled out, "No room here for barbarians," and slowly closed the door. We stood there in the dark and rain, not knowing what to do. Then the door opened again and the old head reappeared. Man's better nature triumphed, and it was with gratitude we heard the Chinese drawl once more: "It is very stormy. You can go into the ox-stable if you like." I see it still, there on the left, with its bars across like an old-fashioned farm gate. We crawled through. The old man held a light until we could see the one empty stall, and then all was dark. We secured rice-straw and prepared to spend the night with the water-buffaloes. In about half an hour a dim light appeared at the door, and there stood the Chinese with a bowl of warm rice for each on a tray. And what was strangest of all was his refusal to accept *cash* for either the lodgings or the rice. We had with us Ko Chin, an elder, who, though born in Formosa, had never spent a night in an ox-stable before. He told me afterward that the thought that I was so far from my native land, and in such a place, exercised him greatly. It made that night memorable in his life, for, though he was a good Christian before, he was more determined, more devoted, more self-sacrificing ever after.

On the morning after the night in the ox-stable we went up the mountain to the site of a Pe-po-hoan village called Kau-kau-a. There oranges now grow, and peaches, pumelos, persimmons, plums, and bread-fruit. It is almost within savage territory, and the savages had been friendly until some of the villagers gave them dog's flesh for venison. When the truth came to be known the savages swore vengeance and began hostilities. The Kau-kau-a people had to leave the place. They moved three miles north to So Bay. There many died of malarial and other forms of fever. Those who survived chose

another site and founded the village of Lam-hong-o. There
are now eleven families descended from the Kau-kau-a villagers. Fifty years have elapsed since the feud began, but
no reconciliation has ever been effected, and the savages are
still their sworn enemies.

A chapel was in due time erected at Lam-hong-o, and,
despite my protestation, was named "MacKay Church," in
memory of my father. Many evenings, when I was addressing them, bitter, burning tears rolled down their cheeks as they
thought of the cold-hearted manner in which they received us
at first. The chapel came to be a place of safety as well as
of worship. Many nights the women and children, for fear of
the savages, slept on the tiled floor, while their husbands and
fathers were out on the sea in their fishing-smacks. The
savages were very artful and daring. Sometimes they would
make marks in the sand in imitation of turtle tracks, so that
when any villager went hunting the turtles they would spring
from their ambush and run him through with their long lances.
One evening, on going toward the gate, I heard in the hedge
a whistling noise. Hastily stepping back, I learned that a
dozen savages were outside ; but my sudden movement made
them think they were discovered, and so they decamped.

In 1884, at one village near the sea where we had a teacher,
but as yet no chapel, the people had to guard their families
nightly with loaded guns. On the occasion of one of our visits the savages were out on a head-hunting expedition, and
the converts, men, women, and children, sat up till daybreak,
and at intervals made the hills ring with our sweet hymns, sung
to their wild mountain airs. The savages prowled around and
occasionally threw stones and other missiles. While there I
cut out of a man's thigh an iron arrow-head that had been
shot from the bow of a savage. It was embedded nearly five
inches in the flesh, and as it had been there for four months it
was an ugly sight. The poor fellow sat day after day watch-

ing it slowly corrupting, and suffering increasing pain. I had surgical instruments with me, and, after two hours, succeeded in performing the operation. When the arrow-head was removed and laid on the man's hand his gratitude knew no bounds. He was at that time a heathen, but he listened to the message of a Saviour who "healeth all our diseases, and bindeth up our wounds," and it was delightful in after-years to hear him tell the heathen around how he was led to forsake idolatry and worship the living and true God.

Sin-sia is a Pe-po-hoan village with quite a percentage of Chinese. On the bank of a clear mountain stream stands our chapel, called "Burns's Church." Beautiful is the situation, and the structure is worthy of the site. It is built of stone, plastered, and well lighted with glass windows. I drew the plans, but the construction was superintended by a native preacher, Tan He. It is extremely difficult to get a building erected in Formosa for the sum specified in the contract; but so shrewdly did Tan He do his work that there were no extras. The splendid donation from Mrs. MacKay, of Detroit, sufficed to complete the building in memory of one of the world's greatest evangelists and missionaries. The preacher is Pe-po-hoan, and both aborigines and Chinese meet for the worship of the God of all the earth.

Nearly south of Tai-tun Mountain, and nestling at its base, is Pak-tau, a Pe-po-hoan village, with upward of a hundred aborigines in the homesteads around. It is two hours' brisk walk from Tamsui, three from Bang-kah, and four from Sek-khau. We secured a place of worship there in 1891. Sulphur-springs hiss and roar in the vicinity, and a warm medicinal stream runs within five minutes' walk from our chapel. I had in view the establishing of a church there fully fifteen years ago, for we knew something of the value of the springs. Scabies can be completely cured by bathing in these waters; and tinea, in various forms, can be so far removed that other medicines eradicate the fungi or bacilli with greater efficiency.

In conducting a mission few things require more attention than the placing of the right man in the right place. Who, then, should be sent to Pak-tau? Why, an able, earnest Chinese preacher whose wife was a Pe-po-hoan, whom we brought up from childhood, and who received careful Christian instruction. Success attended the young preacher's mission work. One Sabbath, my wife, three children, women from the Girls' School, and students from the college attended service at Paktau. They found the building literally packed, and scores in the branches of a tree where they could both see and hear. It was a great day, and the speakers were carefully selected. First came one who had been a Tauist priest, because many of his old associates were present; then a Pe-po-hoan from the east coast and another from one of our southern stations, because their relatives were among the hearers; then four Pe-po-hoan women whose homes were in Kap-tsu-lan rose and sang "Jesus loves me," because their Malayan sisters were sitting near by; six Chinese Bible-women sang another hymn, because Mongolians were listening. Such a variety made the services both interesting and profitable. Each hearer got a suitable portion of the bread of life. I addressed them on Joshua xxiv. 15: "Choose you this day whom ye will serve," and called on them to decide for or against the world's mighty Redeemer. A few weeks afterward ten young Pe-po-hoan women who became interested in the way of salvation went out to Tamsui to see the Girls' School, Oxford College, and the museum. Agreeable and intelligent, they showed a lively interest in all that they saw. The work at Pak-tau goes on prosperously.

Touring in the Kap-tsu-lan plain is full of interest, but one trip is much like another. Variety is sometimes given by the company of some European traveler or scientist. In 1888,

Dr. Warburg, from Hamburg, Germany, joined us at Kelung for a tour. He was a young naturalist collecting specimens for his college, and he procured many plants and flowers, and many relics and weapons belonging to the aborigines. He had an open eye for mission work, and was greatly interested when more than three hundred assembled for worship. As we marched inward to newly reclaimed valleys, upward of thirty tattooed savages from the mountains presented themselves and were photographed. At one aboriginal village, near a mountain-spur, fully five hundred of our converts met, and we had a glorious gathering. When we were parting the doctor said :

" I have seen sixteen chapels, and people in them worshiping God. I have also seen native preachers standing on platforms preaching the truths of Christianity. I never saw anything like it before. If people in Hamburg saw what I have seen they would contribute for foreign missions. If scientific skeptics had traveled with a missionary as I have, and witnessed what I have witnessed on this plain, they would assume a different attitude toward the heralds of the cross."

CHAPTER XXIV

A TRIP DOWN THE EAST COAST

Setting out—Eager for a chapel—Ordinances and sacraments—Afloat—
Beauties of the ocean—In sight of savages—In Ki-lai—The cook-
preacher—Burning the idols—Five hundred—A perilous pull—A
sample program—Edification—Glengarry Chapel—In a new plain—
Home again

ON August 27, 1890, at 8 A.M., I set out from Tamsui, with
Tan He, Sun-a, and Koa Kau, on a trip far down the
east coast of Formosa. The reason for never traveling without several students or preachers is that they may become
practically acquainted with all departments of mission work,
efficient in service, and prepared for all emergencies. The
work is divided, and each has his allotted task. Our purpose
on this trip was to visit chapels in the Kap-tsu-lan plain, and
to go farther south to another plain, where a number of Pe-po-
hoan families have settled. That south district is the Ki-lai
plain, and is the home of about four thousand semi-civilized
aborigines called Lam-si-hoan. Of life among that people we
will speak in another chapter. In this attention will be directed
to the Pe-po-hoan villages.

We took a steam-launch up the river to Bang-kah, railway-
train to Tsui-tng-kha, and walked the rest of the distance to
Kelung. Sun-a, who is a most dexterous tooth-extractor,
practised his profession on a number of patients by the way.
At Kelung a service was held. Next morning we passed
Ki-a-liau, with Chhim-o Mountain rising twenty-eight hun-

dred feet high, and extending its base, rough with recently fallen boulders, to the water's edge. Traveling was very dangerous, owing to the loosened rocks overhead and the wet and slippery stones beneath. Once I disturbed a mass by leaping over a chasm, and it came tumbling down at my heels. Toward evening we turned a point and were in full view of Lam-a-lin, a fishing-village with thirty or forty families. Lim Kau Pau, the head man and owner of the entire range of hills around, came out to welcome us. There was no chapel there, but we sang and preached. In the morning Mr. Lim took us over his estate, and, pointing to one place here and another there, he would say, "That would be a nice site for a chapel." It meant something for that Chinese landowner to make such an offer, for he knew what a chapel meant. He knew that idols and tablets would be cast away. When we were leaving the village he ordered out two boats to carry us down the coast past a difficult and dangerous promontory. On returning from this trip, as we neared his homestead, his servants came out yelling, running, and beckoning to us, followed by his son, who begged us to remain overnight. We could not wait, but that evening the son and the servants followed us to the Teng-siang-khoe chapel. Is there not an "open door" at Lam-a-lin?

That day at Phi-thau the villagers pleaded for a chapel. Before leaving, medicines were dispensed, teeth extracted, and then the gospel was preached to a large crowd. Off again through bamboo-groves, across "the point" to Na-tang. We reached "Burns's Church," Sin-sia, about dark, and spent an hour singing, speaking, and examining inquirers. The next day being the Sabbath, we held three evangelistic services, had a Sabbath-school, and dispensed the Lord's Supper. Another day's tramp brought us to Ta-ma-ien, a Pe-po-hoan village, where thirty-nine communed, four infants were baptized, and an elder and deacon were ordained.

A river-boat took us near Hoan-sia-thau on Tuesday, September 2, 1890, at 10 A.M. Beating of the drum brought men from their nets, women from their looms, and children from their play. At once we attended to the suffering, examined inquirers, listened to recitations, ordained two office-bearers, addressed hearers, and administered the sacrament to forty-one communicants. After dinner we crossed a narrow strip of sand to the sea and entered a fishing-boat with eight rowers. They pulled with great energy, and by sundown entered the mouth of a mountain stream, then rowed on the fresh water till 8 P.M., when we landed at the Lau-lau-a chapel. Services soon began, and at the close a young couple stood up, attended by two others, and by the ceremony of Christian marriage were made husband and wife. This event was unexpected, for the bride arrived only an hour before from another Pe-po-hoan village. At daybreak a fishing-outfit was engaged. We put out in the face of a heavy sea and brisk gale. We were tossed about all day, and could not enter So Bay harbor till 4 P.M. Once there no time was lost in addressing our people at Lam-hong-o church, and in securing a boat suitable for our trip beyond. The only available one was about twelve feet long and quite open. This little craft we manned with six Pe-po-hoan rowers, all Christians, and pushed away at 5 P.M., singing a hymn, while preacher and converts stood on the shore waving us God-speed.

Once round the point, away down the coast the rowers pulled, hugging the shore. Night came on, but no one thought of sleep. Each selected a spot in which to sit or crouch, and be out of the rowers' way. I sat in the stern beside the helmsman—a good position for surveying the scene. It is grand at any time, but that night it was sublime. Long and high ranges of forest-clad mountains stood like dark perpendicular walls on the right. On the left lay a broad and boundless expanse of water. Stars were twinkling brilliantly above;

Medusæ, Nereidæ, and *Infusoria,* children of the ocean, were blazing below. I have seen many wonderful sights in the steamer's track in the Bay of Bengal and the Arabian Sea, but never before witnessed anything comparable to the phosphorescent glory of that night. Sitting low in the boat, on a level with the surface, I scooped out handfuls of jelly-like globules, my fingers like so many rods of red-hot iron, dropping balls of molten fire. Countless millions of *Noctiluca miliaris* rose to the surface with lightning speed, then darted hither and thither, like sparks from a blacksmith's anvil. Oars scattered jets of light at very stroke, and our little craft seemed gliding on a glittering surface and through flames of amber and gold.

> " Within the shadow of the ship
> I watched their rich attire—
> Blue, glossy green, and velvet black ;
> They coiled and swam, and every track
> Was a flash of golden fire."

Now and then westerly winds blew between long ranges and filled our little sail. By dawn we were close to the shore, where stretches a long level piece of ground. Savages were at the beach, and their houses could be seen a short distance up the mountain-side. Our boat was quickly headed seaward. I recognized the place at once—the "spur," the creek, the rocks. It was the spot where, on June 4, 1876, H. B. M. man-of-war "Lapwing" dropped anchor on the rough sea, while her commander, chief officer, and myself got into one of her lifeboats, manned by six "blue-jackets," without any weapon of defense, and were rowed toward the shore. Several hundred savages came down the spur of the mountain and watched us. Our boat tried hard to land, but the surf was against us. We hailed, beckoned, and threw several shining silver dollars toward them. They were naked and vicious-looking, but no one dreamed of danger—only to land and see them. The surf saved us. Had we succeeded in landing no one would have returned. Many an unsuspecting explorer has been murdered there by that tribe. God holds the winds and the waves in his hand, and was behind the surf that day.

We pulled away, and at noon, under the scorching sun, thermometer 120 in the open boat, we drew up at Hoe-lien-kang, a trading-post at the sea in the Ki-lai plain. This is the plain I longed to visit during the past, where Kap-tsu-lan people moved, and where a cook from Oxford College went of his own accord, and began to teach and preach to the Pe-po-hoan. Hoe-lien-kang lies on a sea-washed sand-bank, and has two rows of thatched houses, with a street two hundred feet wide. Its inhabitants are mostly Chinese, with a few Pe-po-hoan families in the outskirts, engaged in trade with the aborigines. Close at hand is an encampment of Chinese soldiers under a military official.

Our boat was no sooner hauled on the pebbly beach than a Chinese officer, the head man, sent an invitation to have dinner with him, and showed us other attentions. I was surprised to hear my name on every hand. We were never there before, but some of them knew about our work in the north. Our new friend ordered his hostler to saddle a pony, and of course put on the string of bells. Thus the unexpected did happen, for I rode a fine, plump, if not fiery steed, preceded by a groom. About dark we entered Ka-le-oan, the Pe-po-hoan settlement I longed to visit for upward of a dozen years. We found the cook who turned out preacher in a small grass-covered bamboo dwelling that had been erected for him. As they had been writing and waiting for us a long time, the warmth of their welcome can hardly be imagined. The room was soon packed and a large crowd stood in front of the door. Instead of continued preaching, we tried to grasp the state of affairs. Really good work had been done by the cook-preacher. Not a few had a clear idea of the gospel message, while many more were evidently weary of idol-worship. They seemed ripe for decisive action. Being told that the military mandarin declared that they must continue idolatry as being a token of subjection to China, I rode up to the encampment, had an interview, and got a gracious reception. Whatever was said or done in the past, it was all right now. Soldiers began to praise our mission: one had got medicine from me at Tamsui, one from a preacher at Kelung, and another knew the Bangkah preacher. Yamen men joined, praising the men, the museum, etc. There was only one opinion, and the officer wished me "peace." I galloped back, and asked all who were for the true God to clean their houses of idols and take a decided stand. A council was held at dark in an open space; it turned out to be a noisy and boisterous meeting. The chiefs were declaiming aloud in their native tongue. I stepped among them and asked an explanation, and if there were difference of opinion. An answer came quickly. The five villages were unanimous to a man. They wanted to worship the Jehovah-God. They went further. An idol-temple built for themselves at a cost of two thousand dollars was handed over for chapel services. The following was a joyous day. No one went to work. The head man invited our party to join him, and ordered four boys to follow, carrying eight baskets, one on either end of a pole. We then went from house to house and from village to village, until the idolatrous paraphernalia of all were collected into the baskets and carried to a yard near the temple. There was a large pile of mockmoney, idols, tablets, incense-sticks, and flags. A great crowd assembled, and several vied with one another in firing the heap. Many showed their contempt for the dirty, dusty, greasy old idols. One chief took special delight in poking the burning objects of worship, while roars of derisive laughter followed the pulling out and holding up of a blazing "goddess of mercy." The temple was lighted up long before

dark, and the people crowded in.   I called on all to join in
singing:

> " All people that on earth do dwell,
> Sing to the Lord with cheerful voice."

Precision of attack may have been wanting, some voices may
have been off the key and out of tune, but they sang with
heart and soul, and never was the old Hundredth Psalm more
fittingly sung than on that night when it signalized the conse-
cration of an idol-temple to the honor and glory of the eternal
God.

Ka-le-oan is the name given to the settlement, no doubt
after one of the same name in Kap-tsu-lan, whence most of
the people hail.   There are five villages : Toa-sia, which means
"large village," where the church now stands ; Tek-a-na, Bu-
loan, Ian-ko, and Chhit-kiet—in all about five hundred.   This
is the entry in the record of our trip to that settlement :

" Nearly five hundred idolaters cleaned their houses of idols
in our presence.

" They declared themselves anxious to worship the Lord
and Redeemer.

" They gave a temple built for idols as a house in which
to meet and worship the only living and true God.   Are
missions a failure? "

For an entire week the pony and groom were at my dis-
posal, without charge, and I went this way and that through
the Ki-lai plain, preaching, dispensing, tooth-extracting, and
studying the rude life and manners of the Lam-si-hoan.   On
Wednesday, September 10th, we made ready to return northward.   We gave medicines in the military encampment, by
permission of the official.   The mandarin himself threw off all
mandarin ceremony, and talked, laughed, handled the forceps,
and had his teeth examined.   He even stood at our backs to
see us attending to the sick and suffering among the soldiers.

There were not a few malaria patients among them, and I am quite sure we left the soldiers and their general all wishing for our speedy return.

A crowd followed us to the seaside and shoved our craft afloat. The rowers had to pull hard against a northeaster. At dark we were skirting the shore near the steep mountains. Here and there, like flaming beacons along the shore, the night fires of savages burned holes in the darkness of tangled foliage and forest. All night long the rowers struggled against wind and wave, afraid to go too near the shore, for the rocks were sharp and the savages cruel; afraid to launch out into the deep, for our craft was light and the sea was wild. Morning came, and, drenched and weary, we were still amid white billows. All that day we pulled almost in vain, thankful that we were not dashed on the rocky ledges. No one had tasted food since the previous morning, for though we had a supply of rice we could not land to have it cooked. The weary rowers were fast becoming weak. Eyes brightened when at 3 P.M. we turned a point and ran into a basin three hundred feet wide, one hundred feet deep, with fifty feet of a pebbly beach, and a perpendicular wall several hundred feet high standing at the back and sides. There was a veritable security from storms and savages. A sweet spring of water tumbled over the high cliff above, forming a stream of fresh water, which ran into the bitter sea. Rice was cooked in the water-jar I was carrying back as a sample of Lam-si-hoan pottery, and with a condiment of salted venison it was a delicious meal. By 7 P.M. the sea calmed somewhat, and we struck out again. Toward cock-crowing So Bay was entered, and a breath carried us to Lam-hong-o. Soon preacher and people were astir, and all day was spent in the chapel. Children were examined, three were baptized, and sixty-five sat down around the Lord's table. By sea-boat we ran to Ka-le-oan, there gave medicines to the sick, inquired after members, arranged matters with elders and deacons, and walked over to Lau-lau-a, where similar work was done and the night spent.

Leaving Lau-lau-a, we visited every station in the Kap-tsu-lan plain, spent a night at each of the twenty chapels, and inspected work at six other points. We never traveled there before as on this occasion. Taking a river-boat, we rowed, where practicable, to each locality. Thus I had a fair chance of making a pretty accurate map. The streams rush rapidly near the mountains, but run sluggishly enough in the level plain. At many points they are so narrow that the boat had to be pushed along with two bamboo poles. On these narrow dark streams, with trees and bushes overhanging and meeting, charming spots could be seen through the foliage, and the sun shone at intervals through the clouds floating overhead.

Arriving at and leaving a Pe-po-hoan village was simply soul-inspiring. As our party would start a hymn, a crowd of men, women, and children would join and make the banks resound with joyful notes. I always enjoy this a thousand times more than singing in a chapel. It is so grand, so free from formality, thus to praise our God on the flowing water, among the trees, and within hearing of the birds he makes to sing. It would be wearisome to the reader to give the names of so many strange places and state what was done at each; but a sample of our program may be of interest.

1. On arrival we visited the sick in their homes; then, taking our stand outside in an open space, we gave medicines and extracted teeth. The filthy betel-nut gives tooth-extracting prominence. The four of us worked, but each patient passed through my hands for diagnosis.

2. We wrote the names of all the families, with their worldly possessions, in a book. This was necessary on account of removals to new settlements. I think we know the circumstances of every family, and what the stations are able to do toward self-support.

3. We held meetings with the elders and deacons concerning contributions, chapel repairs, Sabbath attendance, etc. Here is progress. Every chapel in the plain was either re-roofed, plastered, and otherwise repaired, or materials were on the ground; and only in one village did an elder ask for assistance.

4. Children, young men and women, were examined in presence of all on subjects previously assigned, and other subjects to be studied were selected.

5. Singing practised for an hour by the people in divisions, such as old men, women, young men, girls, and children.

6. We preached in turn, short addresses being most profitable, and I immediately questioned them on what was spoken.

7. Office-bearers elected by the congregations, and I ordained them.

8. Baptized infants and adults, though the reception of many adults was delayed for further instruction.

9. Observed the Lord's Supper, having not a few refreshing communions.

The above labor was accomplished, and much more. The effect at every station was marked. Converts were stirred up, and the contrast in their condition and demeanor on our arrival and at our departure was very marked, especially where we remained overnight and had opportunity for meetings, afternoon, evening, and morning. There is a world of meaning in the words " edification," " building up," " grow up into Him in all things," "for the perfecting of the saints." I have stated that at one place nearly five hundred cast their idols away. Some good people may think the work among them was about done then. If I know anything about it, if twenty-three years' experience be of value, then I should say the work was only begun. Paul knows best, and says they must be built up. I do not believe in perfection on this side of the " river," but such converts as we have in Formosa, like some we have in America, are a long way from what is attainable here. Many things are needed in leading them on. One thing before all things else is needful, viz., patience.

One of the churches visited was " Glengarry Chapel," at Tang-mng-thau, where a spreading gourd served as a dispensing-room. At the service all were orderly and reverent. We sang many hymns, and I told them about Glengarry in Canada, and the kind young friends there who raised the money for the building of that chapel. They were greatly interested, and the thought that people at home would deny themselves for poor heathen in far Formosa was not without its influence.

Leaving Kap-tsu-lan, we entered the plain of Toa-o, which is a triangular extension running far inland from Kap-tsu-lan, flanked on two sides by high, steep, densely wooded mountains. It is new ground, only now being reclaimed from the jungle. The reeds are cut with knives, then the whole set on fire, large hoes dig the roots, farmers sow or plant their grain, and in this way much is cleared. Houses are built in a few days. Poles are put in the ground, a thatched roof put on, sides closed in with reeds, plastered with mud, a door of split bamboo tied to one side, holes left instead of windows, and the family move in. At times it is dangerous to travel in any part of that plain, on account of savages who have been driven to desperation by Chinese soldiers. On arrival at the east end we called on one Colonel Tan, an old friend, who persisted in sending a number of men with spears to escort us by the way. The night was spent at Phoa-po-o, where one hundred assembled and we preached the gospel. The morning following was lovely, and, according to every day's work, men were armed to lead the way to a new village through reeds and grasses. No one goes out to work without weapons at his side. Forty odd-looking fellows went along with us, several of whom had Martini-Henry or Remington rifles, some carried old American muskets, the most swung over their shoulders Chinese matchlocks, and others held long spears in readiness. Four times the number of savages would have had to flee before them that day. The Pe-po-hoan welcomed us at Teng-phoa-po-o. We followed our usual program and set off with half the village at our heels. At length we came to Thien-sang-pi, the most inland settlement in all that region. People are only beginning to test the virgin soil and erect huts.

We walked half a mile farther, mostly through wet grass, to the rather sharp curve in the mountain. There I got up into a tallow-tree out of the wet rushes and sat on a large branch, admiring a pool of water in the bend which no foreigner ever gazed upon before. Crescent Pool is an appropriate name for it. It is full of nearly a dozen varieties of fish, and the marshy land around has eels thirty and forty pounds in weight. Two savage villages were visited, one at the base and the other on the spur of the mountain. Old and young looked dissipated and haggard.

At Cheng-kui-sia upward of one hundred met outside, and we had an open-air service, then crossed several streams, and walked through rice-fields to Ang-chha-na, where three times the bricks were made for a chapel and destroyed by the rain. Being quite within the mountains, they have very few dry days. At dark oil was put into bamboo poles six feet long, stuck in an open space, and in that flickering light we proclaimed the message of salvation to a crowd of poor toil-worn aborigines.

Thus we labored in that plain, taking all the chapels in order, then back over the hills to Kelung, Tsui-tng-kha, Bang-kah, Toa-tiu-tia, and out again to Tamsui, after an absence of forty days. It was one of many such tours, not much different in experiences and results from others. If the reader has gained a more accurate idea of the lights and shadows of missionary life, and if hearts are stirred up to more earnest prayer and more consecrated service, the recital will not have been in vain.

CHAPTER XXV

A SEK-HOAN MISSION

Refused accommodation—Ordered out—Invited back—A plot—The traitor—Building a chapel

ON the west coast are settlements of aborigines that have
made considerable progress in Chinese civilization. They
are called Sek-hoan ("ripe barbarians "). On one of our visits
to Sin-kang, a village of these civilized aborigines in the Biau-
lek district, on the west coast, three days' walk from Tamsui,
and as many miles from the sea, the people refused us accommodation for the night. At dark, however, a stalwart-looking
native made provision for myself and students under his
thatched roof. On inquiry we learned that preparations were
being made for worshiping the spirits of their ancestors. Their
own savage customs and superstitions had been mingled with
those of the Chinese, with the result that no outsider could be
allowed within the precincts for three days. Accordingly our
host was urged to expel us; but though he stood alone he refused. Later on a letter was handed me from the head man.
It read thus:

"You black-bearded barbarian, with your Chinese disciples,
must either leave in the morning or stay in the house for three
days."

After a while I sent this reply:

"We the servants of the Lord Jesus Christ will neither
leave in the morning nor stay in the house, but by the power

of our God we will preach his gospel in your streets on the morrow and following days."

Immediately the whole village was greatly excited, and many gathered around the place where we were. Some were for killing, some for beating, and others for leaving us alone. The counsel of the last prevailed. Morning dawned, and I told my students to choose between remaining or going back to the north. In a moment they were at my side, ready to abide all consequences. We walked into the streets and found villagers in groups, squatted on the ground, with stones and other missiles in readiness. They were true pictures of men with pent-up rage, and with vehement grunts did they denounce us. A stone thrown by a young man passed the shoulder of a student and grazed my head. We sang several hymns and then returned to the house. On the second day we were out again, and on the third. On the fourth day a number came near us and spoke somewhat friendly. They felt not a little ashamed of their conduct, which feeling was never overcome; for not once in subsequent years did they refer to our first reception. Once converted to the religion of Jesus, the man who threw that stone became a student, traveling over mountain and valley with us, acquiring knowledge, and later a preacher laboring in Kap-tsu-lan, till he fell a victim while bravely nursing suffering ones during an epidemic.

Weeks rolled by, and I was approached at Tamsui by two men from Sin-kang, with an earnest request to visit them and preach the gospel. We accompanied them back, and ere long had a chapel in course of erection. When the walls, which were built of sun-dried bricks, were five feet high, a rumbling noise was heard and the earth shook with convulsions. The earthquake left the building leaning over. Unfortunate omen! "The earth is against them, and the spirits opposed," shouted some, and all resolved to unite to quash our proceedings at once. Every hamlet and town within miles joined in the cry, and excitement ran so high that danger and death threatened us every moment. We maintained our position, however, finished the thatched chapel, and proclaimed Christ, and him crucified, night after night to upward of a hundred hearers.

One Sabbath afternoon, when engaged in service, a letter was put on the table before me. I was therein warned not to enter savage territory again or death would be the result. Our plans were previously arranged to enter the next day. At cock-crowing we were on the march. When on the top of the first mountain-range a piercing yell told of savages at hand, and at a stream in the valley below we met more than fifty of them. Salutations were exchanged. The wild mountaineers pointed their guns upward, fired a volley, and bade us follow them. They welcomed us to their mountain retreat, where we spent the night, and they were entirely friendly. The origin of the letter warning us against the savages remained a mystery for years. But when on my last visit to that village, before returning to Canada in 1893, the mystery was solved. A man of eighty years of age, Ap Hoan, confessed that he wrote it, and that he urged to the utmost the savages to waylay and kill us. They not only refused, but in time forced him and his family beyond the domain of their tribe. There being evidence of his conversion, I baptized him at his own request, and along with him two others who, like him, had passed the limit of fourscore years.

This uncultivated valley was gradually transformed into rice and potato fields. A chapel was built, and has served as a center for work in that region. From that village trips are made into savage territory. There are about one thousand Sek-hoan at Sin-kang, and in all points work there is similar to work among other semi-civilized aborigines.

CHAPTER XXVI

LIFE AMONG THE LAM-SI-HOAN

The Ki-lai plain—A tropical scene—Racial marks—Government—Agriculture—Pottery-making—The village well—Architecture—A simple costume—A novel shade—Tobacco and betel—A public bath—Morals and manners—Forecast

THE Ki-lai plain, far down the east coast of Formosa, is the home of about four thousand aborigines who have been subdued by the Chinese, but who are scarcely started on the road to civilization. To this plain I have made several trips, and have learned not a little about the people. On my first visit I had the use of the pony already referred to, and enjoyed many a ride over the broad, clean, winding roads.

The plain is about thirty miles long from north to south, and about six miles in width between the mountains and the sea. It was formed out of mountain debris carried down by the streams, and sands washed up by the waves. Along the shore is a stretch of sand, and back of this an upland, upon which more than a thousand water-buffaloes find pasture. Farther inland the soil is light, and in places stony, but suitable for grazing purposes. The land nearer the mountains is a rich, deep black loam, mostly of decomposed vegetable matter washed down from the densely wooded mountains. The beds of the mountain torrents reveal that up in the country of the savages, where the explorer dare not go, there are granite, coal, slate, and mica.

This plain is by far the most tropical-looking place I have ever seen on the island. The roads are remarkably good and evidently receive not a little care. On either side large ever-green shade-trees sometimes grow, and every mile or so rest-ing-places are made of bamboo sticks, upon which burdens are laid while the carriers sit down, eat betel-nut, and rest. The scenery is refreshing after the narrow paths, paddy-fields, and inevitable water-buffaloes of the north. There is an acre of mountain-rice that needs no artificial irrigation; next is a patch of taro, then wild indigo, watermelons, sweet potatoes, golden pumpkins, the climbing bean, and, not least welcome, beautiful green grass. In the fields grow rows of pride-of-India trees, and at intervals are erected small square shade-huts. The birds sing among the branches, the sun shines overhead, and one feels "the wild joys of living."

The inhabitants of this plain, where "every prospect pleases," are perhaps the latest arrivals of the aborigines of Formosa. Like the other tribes, both civilized and savage, they are allied to the Malayan race, and in some respects show even more strongly marked likeness to the present-day islanders in the Archipelago. Their dialect is peculiar, and quite distinct from the Pe-po-hoan and the mountain savages. They are entirely ignorant of the Chinese language, and have themselves no lit-erature of any sort. Chinese authority is acknowledged, and an encampment of Chinese soldiers under a military mandarin is stationed in the plain; but the people do not shave their heads or wear the cue. The old men have their hair short; but some of the younger generation are imbibing other notions, and are quite proud of their long black locks parted in the middle.

Their government is tribal, or perhaps their companies might be called clans. All the men are divided into ranks, on the principle of seniority. There are nine such companies: the first being composed of all the men from fifty-five to sixty years of age; the second of those from fifty to fifty-five; and so on down to the ninth company, made up of the youths from fifteen to twenty. Every five years the senior company is retired and a new one formed. On a day appointed a contest of running a mile and back decides who is to be chief of the new company. The chief of the whole tribe is chosen in a contest among the chiefs of the several companies. Each company is subject to the one above it in rank, and to each some special task is assigned. One company makes roads, another tills the soil, a third attends to the wicker-work, and other departments have each a company to carry them on. When any special work has to be done, such as hunting, harvesting, fighting, several companies may combine. Inferiors in age and rank are all under control of superiors. In case of an offense being committed superiors drive the offenders out of the village, and they dare not return until after six days, on pain of being beaten, having their property destroyed and family driven out, and they themselves exiled from the village until called back. One evening at Ka-le-oan a dozen fine, strong fellows were performing tricks and feats for their own and my entertainment, when three of their superiors appeared, and the young men bounded out of sight in a moment, thus signifying ready obedience and fear. The inferior company was out on a hunting-expedition, and when the superiors saw these young fellows taking it easy instead of sharing with their comrades the trials of the chase, they were very angry and drove them from the village in punishment. A day or two afterward word came that three of the tribe had been killed by the savages, and then the young men were summoned back to go on the war-path.

The rich soil is pretty thoroughly worked, the farmers being hard-working and industrious. Mountain-rice, millet, and taro are grown extensively, and fine sweet potatoes, Indian corn, beans, watermelons, and small pumpkins. The short-handled hoe is the chief implement, and is used in the fields very dexterously. Wherever they learned the art, there are in that tribe blacksmiths able to do all the making and mending required.

Pottery is manufactured, both the mixing and moulding being done by the hand. At Sa-ka-eng, in the north, the Chinese potters use a horizontal wheel, like the people in Palestine; and Thomson's description in "The Land and the Book" accurately describes the Chinese process. But these Lam-si-hoan pottery-makers do not belong to that school; they use neither mould nor wheel. The clay is dug up, pounded in a wooden trough with a stone, and mixed with water. A lump is then taken and bit by bit added, made into the required shape, and then smoothed with the hand and water. The jars are similar in shape to those made in Syria and Judea, but not so high, and have an "ear" on each side for the hand. They are always carried on the head; if empty they are inverted, the mouth, which is about six inches across, fitting like a cap. Twenty or thirty women returning along the road from the village well, talking, laughing, singing, their figures well developed, their carriage erect, their hands hanging at their sides, each with a filled water-jar on her head, make a picture that even a weary-eyed globe-trotter turns to see.

The people live mainly in villages. Each village is surrounded by stately bamboo-trees, and inclosing all is a deep moat or ditch. On entering the large gate into the village there, on one side, stands a long open shed of bamboo, in which a number of men sit, making various kinds of wicker-work and discussing questions of the day. Near at hand, shaded by large trees, is the village well, a circular hole twenty feet deep, fully a hundred feet in diameter at the mouth, and narrowing down to two or three at the bottom. At one point the side is cut down, making a more gradual slope, up which the earth had been carried, and which now serves as a path down to the water. Around the mouth of the well and down this incline a railing of bamboo is run. All day long the women come and go with their water-jars on their heads, getting their supply from this general reservoir.

The houses are all after one design, entirely different from the Chinese, and in the matter of floor distinctly superior. Each house is about fifty feet long, twenty feet wide, twelve feet high at the ridge, and sloping down to about four feet at the eaves. Boards are lashed with rattan to a sort of balloon frame. The grass roof is fully two feet thick, and projects over the eaves three or four feet, making a kind of low veranda. The building is constructed with regard not so much to the comfort and convenience of the inhabitants as to the power and destructiveness of the typhoons, which sweep over the plain every year. Every house is floored with rattan about an inch thick, laid close together and bound or laced with rattan splits. This makes a strong, neat, and clean floor, and, being raised a foot above the ground, is much healthier than the mud-floors of Chinese houses. Indeed, it makes a very comfortable bed, and is generally put to that use. At one end of the room a space is built up with earth, making the "fireplace." There are two doors to the house, one on each side, made of bamboo. The houses are not arranged in any particular order, each one being quite independent of every other and of any general plan or survey. At every door there is at least one ugly dog, always lean and hungry.

A typical Lam-si-hoan costume is simply made and easily kept in repair. The women all wear earrings made of bamboo, and generally a kind of waist-cloth. The men are content with the earrings, and do not worry if even that suggestion of clothing be lacking. The women have a fondness for necklaces made of shells an inch square, tied together with thread and beads. The more extravagant of the young women set their hearts on bracelets of brass and other ornaments, which they keep bright and shining. Tattooing is not practised by any of the tribe, and they are unable to explain the origin of the custom among their kinsmen in the mountains, or its disuse among themselves.

The tropical sun is very hot and the rain heavy, and as a protection they have devised a simple but effective shade. A frame of light wood is made, three feet long and eighteen inches wide, across which the fine tops of reeds are laid, and secured close together with rattan bands. A thin piece of board across the middle acts as a support, and to it strings are attached, with which the shade is tied around the neck; and in this way it is worn on their shoulders by the workers bending over their task in the sun or rain, without interfering with their movements or the freedom of their hands.

Rice is the staple food, and at meal-time the whole family squat around a large plate set on the floor, and, not with spoons or chopsticks, but with two fingers and the thumb, each " takes rice." A piece of raw meat is relished as a sweet morsel, and is not cut with a knife, but torn with fingers and teeth.

Tobacco is grown very largely, and the dried leaves are rolled as required into huge cigars six or eight inches long and about an inch and a half thick. Cigar-smoking and betel-nut eating are universal with both sexes. Under the shade of the trees, in their houses, by the roadside—everywhere—men and women may be seen, singly or in groups, each with a small gourd full of lime made from burned sea-shells and coral, and bags of tobacco-leaves and betel-nut. Their mouths are dirty, disfigured, and seemingly tireless. When walking or resting the whole time is employed in preparing or using the betel and cigar. The habit is not only unspeakably filthy, but degrading and ruinous to their health.

But lest one might think them indifferent in the matter of cleanliness, one will be taken to see the public baths with which some of these villages are provided. I was invited to inspect

the one at Chhit-kha-chhoan, a village of more than a thousand people, gathered together at the base of a high, steep
mountain. A clear, cool stream from a mountain spring issued from the side of a rock and supplied water for the inhabitants of the village. The bathing arrangements are very simple. Two sets of split-bamboo spouts, one four feet long, the
other eight, are erected seven feet high, and convey the water
out from the side of the rock. From these spouts the pure,
fresh water is pouring all the year round, and there, with nothing but the sky or clouds for walls or covering, is the public
bath. But even in that primitive state of society there are
rules and regulations, and the fixed law at that bathing-place
is that the men stand under the outer streams and the women
under the inner. At all hours of the day they are coming and
going; the women with their jars, which they first fill and set
aside; then they stand, sit, or crouch under the water-streams,
chuckling and grunting with delight as the cool water falls upon
them; and when they have exhausted that pleasure, or other
duties call, the jars are raised again, and with heads erect they
march homeward, singing, it may be, some snatch of song.

In society constituted as it is among the Lam-si-hoan, neither
refinement of life nor elegance of manners need be looked for.
Their lives have not been touched by those great movements
that have fixed the standard of manners in Christian civilization, and they never indulge those habits of thought and intro-
spection that awaken self-consciousness and a sense of shame.
They never heard the name of God, and have no knowledge
of his grace and truth. The life they live is full of toil and
hardship, and their nature-worship is powerless to redeem or
sanctify. To their minds, darkened by innumerable superstitions, the thought of anything unseen that is not to be dreaded
is hard to grasp. The spirits they believe in are vengeful and
cruel, and were it not for their direful power would be neglected
altogether. Without priest or idol or temple, they live in

bondage to a fear of spirits everywhere, in earth and air and sea. To Christianize them would require a distinct and separate mission, as their plain is difficult of access, and the voyage down the coast dangerous. With "very much land to be possessed" in the more enduring cities and settlements in the north, it seemed unwise to expend much of our strength on this unstable and vanishing tribe. The aborigines cannot survive the coming and presence of the dominant race. The repeating-rifle and spear of the mountain savage on the one side, and the unscrupulous greed and destructive vices of the Chinese on the other, are making inroads on this people, who have not the compensating strength and endurance of either the savage or the civilized.

The future of the Lam-si-hoan is not hard to forecast. They have little moral or social recuperative power, and they imbibe nothing of the rejuvenating life-streams of civilization. Theirs is the tragedy of many savage tribes alike in the East and in the West: the first touch of the civilized man is the touch of death. China's civilization in the Ki-lai plain is represented by the soldier and the trader; and in their footsteps follow carnal passion and deadly lust. Already poisonous liquors and corroding licentiousness have begun their havoc, and instead of strength and vigor, physical haggardness and wreckage are added to intellectual degradation and moral poverty.

THE MOUNTAIN SAVAGES

CHAPTER XXVII

SAVAGE LIFE AND CUSTOMS

Of human interest—Personal contact—Trip with Captain Bax—A crafty
chief—Social organization—Houses—Food—Dress—Tattooing—
Musical instruments—Marriage—Morality—Religion—Superstition
—Ascent of Mount Sylvia—Disappointment—On a grave—Hospi-
tality—Christmas with the savages—Destructive influences—
Woman's lot—Missionary work

IT matters little how far removed the civilized may be from
the savage, or how many generations may have come and
gone since our ancestors lived in huts and dressed in skins;
we are all of us interested in the life of those tribes who have
maintained their wild independence, and with much heroic
endurance roam the plains or pierce the jungles, scorning the
sweets of civilization, living only for to-day, and counting a
calamity whatever checks desire or curbs their restless will.
The savage's will "is the wind's will," and there is a fascina-
tion about his reckless dash and careless abandon.

Savage life can be seen in all its lights and shades in the
primeval mountain forests of Formosa. How many centuries
the deer and boar have been hunted among these hills by
swarthy Malays history does not know. A thousand years is
as far back as the annals go, but the island was theirs before
the annals were kept. Save for the encroachments of the
Chinese, circumscribing their territory and furnishing them
with the destructive repeating-rifle, these savages in the mountains are to-day in life and manners what they were ten centu-

ries ago. What I have learned of their customs and beliefs has been through personal contact with them for weeks together in their hamlets and villages. There was constant danger, for no one can tell how or when the savage nature will manifest its savagery; but intercourse with them was always interesting and instructive.

One year after landing I made an extensive trip into savage territory in company with Captain Bax, of H. B. M. ship "Dwarf," who was desirous of seeing the natives in their mountain home. Three days' journey from Tamsui a party of friendly natives, with their chief, got ready to escort us. We were led through many streams, along and over many hills, and halted beside a cool spring at the base of a high mountain-range. After dinner we began to ascend the mountain, but it was steep, rugged, and literally covered with rank vegetation. Those in advance had to cut the creepers and other growths with long knives, and so difficult was the ascent that "the boldest held his breath for a time." Before we reached the top, thirty-five hundred feet high, the chief himself completely collapsed and had to be hauled up with a long rattan. That range was the dividing-line between the Chinese and the savages. To penetrate farther was at our peril, but we had counted the cost and were resolved on taking the risk. After cutting our way over another range we stood on the summit of the last, and our leaders shouted. The answer was returned, and a party from the tribe in the valley below, with guns, spears, bows and arrows, started up in our direction. When half-way down we met them face to face; signs were made, and we were allowed to pass on, they following closely. Tattooed women and naked children came out to see the strangers.

At dark we were in a large valley, where we came upon a group of several hundred savages squatting on the ground together. A halt was called, and as there were no houses or huts to be seen our people started fires, cooked rice, and prepared a shelter for the night. Standing around that glowing fire, shut in by mountain and forest, those savage chiefs, with their wild-eyed braves, heard for the first and perhaps last time the solemn strains of David's Hundredth Psalm. The "people" understood not, but the night wind brought back the echoes telling that mountain and valley understood and answered the call to "sing to the Lord with cheerful voice." The chiefs fixed their eyes on us in silence all the while, and when we lay down they squatted round the fires. It was too cold for us to sleep, and all through the night, like sentinels on duty, those savage eyes kept sleepless watch against anything suspicious on the part of the strangers.

At daybreak we persuaded the chief and his son to take us to see their dwellings. After much hesitation and parleying more than thirty started with us. Through jungle, over windfalls, our clothes torn by thorny shrubs, we pushed our way. A sound was heard, and looking up a large bird was observed perched on a tree. Suddenly all were breathlessly still. The old chief crawled up like a cat, and when under the tree let drive a heavy charge from his Chinese matchlock. The beautiful bird was brought down, put into a bag, and one of the men carried it on his shoulder. Captain Bax and I were beginning to suspect the chief's leading. Presently we came to a clearing, and the chief stepped back and told us that there were Chinese in the huts, and if we would go around and engage them from the open he and his men would attack them from the bush, and they could not escape. The old rascal thought to make us tools for his head-hunting braves. We were indignant, and in no mild terms told him that he was not honorable; that we came far to pay him a visit, and he deceived us. They all listened as the interpreter translated, and anger gleamed from every eye. Then after a little conversation among themselves they seemed mollified; the chief acknowledged he was wrong, and promised to take us to their own

villages. Going in an almost opposite direction we were surprised to come upon a well-beaten path, winding, to be sure,
but good for traveling; and when on the top of a very high
range we were ordered to halt and remain silent. A peculiar
shout was raised and immediately answered from another mountain-top. Going down one range and up another, we saw their
village, with several hundred men, women, and children gazing at us, and half-starved dogs yelping like very devils. Other
terrible noises, wild and hellish, were explained as the shouts
of rejoicing at a feast that was being held over a Chinese head
that had been brought in fresh from the border-land.

We were invited to a seat, and several to whom I had given
quinine for malaria the evening we were in the valley came
forward and claimed me as a friend. We were interested in
the architecture of their huts, and produced note-books and
pencils to make sketches. The savages stared at us for a
while, and when they understood what we were doing they
began chattering angrily among themselves. The young men
darted into the huts and reappeared with long iron-headed
spears. They were wild with rage. Every eye flashed. We
took in the situation and quietly put away our books and pencils. Gradually the excitement subsided and we tried to explain. But no explanation would satisfy. In our ignorance
we had committed a great offense. They have a superstition
that making a photograph or picture extracts the essence of a
thing, and they believed that our innocent sketches would not
only take the essence out of their houses, but could be used
to our advantage and to their hurt. We were afterward assured that had we persisted neither of us would have returned
to tell the tale.

That evening we were again in the valley, and when our
fires were lighted fully five hundred savages from the bush
gathered round. We made some presents, and then by means
of an interpreter I told them of the great Father and of Him

who "died to make us good." Our party sang hymns for an hour or two, and with a prayer that the Holy Spirit would seal something of our message in those dark heathen hearts we lay down to rest. Next day we made our way, through a drenching rain, down slippery paths, out into the cleared land. We had gone farther than white man had ever penetrated before; but on emerging from the bush the captain was prostrated with fever and had to be carried back to Tamsui in a sedan. I kept up until the first night in my own house, when for the first time I felt the dread fever's hands of ice and fire.

There are many different tribes in these mountains, and each tribe has its peculiar features in language, customs, and modes of life; but all that is distinctive of savage life is common to each. They usually live in hamlets or villages built on the top of a mountain or high upland. The largest village I saw had about seven hundred inhabitants; the average population is about one hundred and fifty. Each village has a head man, and each tribe a chief. The greatest brave, the one most gifted to command, is generally chief; and his son, if brave and popular, sometimes succeeds him in office. The chief's authority is absolute, but he has a kind of council, composed of a half-dozen of the older braves, with whom he confers in matters of unusual importance.

Their houses are usually constructed of planks, bamboo, or wickerwork; sometimes of reeds daubed with mud. Their best houses are floored with rattan ropes half an inch thick, but are without division or partition. The parents sleep on the east side, the boys on the west, and the girls on the south. A village consists of a half-dozen such houses; a score makes a large village. The skulls of boar and deer fastened on the walls, shining black with smoke, served for interior decoration; and outside, under the eaves, is an entire row of these ornaments, relieved by an occasional Chinese cranium, some fresh, others old and weather-beaten.

The hunt is the main source of savage food-supply. In the forests game is plentiful, and with guns, spears, bows and arrows, boar, bear, deer, and smaller game—indeed, anything that has life—are secured for food. They are not at all dainty, and eat what they can get, if they cannot get what they want; but as the choicest of morsels they enjoy a piece of raw flesh cut warm from the slain animal before it is dead. A little farming is done, the work generally falling to the women. Three or four acres of ground are sufficient for a village of one hundred, each family having a separate plot. Mountain-rice, maize, taro, a little sweet potato, and pomelos are cultivated, while berries, plums, and a small variety of orange grow wild. A hoe with a short handle is the one implement required.

The dress of the savage is not altogether unpicturesque. A sack of coarse linen, open in front, and with holes for the arms, serves the purposes of a coat, and is often ornamented with bright red or blue threads plucked from a piece of flannel obtained in barter, interwoven about the bottom. Caps are made of rattan, and besmeared with the blood of the deer or boar, and sometimes covered with the skins of animals killed in hunting. Buttons, beads, and brass wire are greatly prized for ornamentation. Women have artistic head-bands of beads, shells, and carnelian. Rows of brass rings are worn on the legs and arms, and armlets of white shell are thought to look well against the reddish brown of a woman's arm. Men and women wear earrings, the woman's style being a stick of bamboo five inches in length and half an inch thick, wound round at intervals with a fine yellow grass; the men are content with ones of a larger size, but shorter. These are stuck through holes made in the ears, and to a foreigner look neither comfortable nor pretty; but custom has laid its hand heavy on these dusky children of the forest, as on the aristocracy of European or American society. However much or little other clothing is worn, every man must have a broad belt of braided rattan, in which he carries a long, crooked, sharp-pointed knife, so useful for cutting tobacco, betel-nut, wood, and in case an animal is to be skinned or a Chinese beheaded. This belt is also very useful when food is scarce; an extra twist or knot is said to greatly mitigate a hungry man's distress.

Tattooing is practised by all the mountain savages, and is done with great care. A well-defined pattern is carefully followed. The blue-black lines on the forehead are short, straight, vertical; those on the cheeks are invariably curved and are regularly arranged. From the ear to the side of the mouth are three curved lines; underneath them a row of diamond-shaped marks; lower down three more curved lines extending from ear to ear below the mouth; below this another row of ornaments; and lower still three curved lines complete the design. No prize-winner on presentation day feels prouder than a savage when standing up to be tattooed.

They have only two musical instruments—one a simple affair made of the hard rind of the bamboo, three inches long, half an inch wide, with a "tongue" cut in the center and a string attached to either end. It is made on the principle of the "jews'-harp," and produces a similar sound. The other is a "nose-flute," made of bamboo, a foot long, blown into with the nose, and played upon with the fingers like a flute.

The savages all marry; old bachelors and old maids are alike unknown. Marriage, however, is a social privilege from which a man is debarred until he has proved his merit as a hunter and has brought in at least one Chinese head; but if the Chinese are unusually careful about their heads, and keep beyond spear-reach of the most daring brave, the chief may grant a special dispensation to one who has won his spurs in a deer-hunt or in a contest with the wild boar. The parents of the girl make arrangements for her, and answer all proper questions. There is no great ceremony, except that the bride is gaily decked with ornaments and articles of many colors

before she is led to the house of her husband, and that dancing, drinking, and wild carousing express the good wishes of
the tribe.

These savages are singularly free from many moral and
social vices common alike among civilized and uncivilized
peoples. Gambling and opium-smoking are very rare; murder, theft, incendiarism, polygamy, and social impurity are almost unknown, except where the baneful influence of Chinese
traders and border-men has corrupted the simplicity of the
savage. Tribes are continually at war with one another, and all
agree in regarding raids on the Chinese as both legitimate and
praiseworthy; but among themselves crime is rare. Should a
brave be convicted of incendiarism or wounding another in a
drunken quarrel he is condemned to procure a certain number
of deer-skins and to give a feast at his own expense for the
tribe.

Whatever of religion these savages possess may be called
nature-worship. They are entirely without any of the notions
or the symbols of Chinese idolatry. They do not bow down
and worship anything seen or unseen, and have no conception
of a supreme personal God. There are feasts, however, that
have a certain religious significance. At the end of harvest
they have a dance and feast expressive of reverence and gratitude to the heavens and the earth. They believe, too, in the
existence and continued influence of innumerable spirits, the
spirits of their ancestors and great braves who have left the
body. The distinction between the soul and the body is marked
by the names given—*ta-ni-sah*, meaning the soul, and *egyp*, the
body. Their notions of the place of the departed spirits are
very vague and general, but the belief in their direful power is
a source of perpetual fear and torture. Food and liquor are
sometimes set for the spirits of the departed, and then consumed with some sort of invocation to the spirits to bless and
prosper. I was present on one occasion when one tribe was

engaged in this ceremony. The right hand was held up with the index-finger extended, and all joined in the invocation: " Na-e-an [Heaven], hang-ni-ngi-sa-i-a-ku [give us hearts of peace, give us long life, give us prosperity]; han-pai-ku [we are about to eat]." At the same time the forefinger was dipped four times in the liquor, and then the following words were added: " Ma-ra-nai [Earth], han-pai-ku [we are about to eat]; ai-mu-na-va-hi [you spirits that have already departed, give us peace]."

Some tribes have ceremonies in connection with the worship of their ancestors three times a year. They regard it a duty to praise and reverence their progenitors for the hardships they encountered and for their skill in killing the boar and deer. In an open space in the village the tribe meets; men and women join hands in a circle around liquor, cakes, millet, and salted fish, placed there for the spirits expected to be present. At times they join hands in a long row, two or three of the leaders waving white-and-red flags at the ends of long bamboo poles. This ceremony invariably takes place at night, and a weird thing it is to watch their half-naked bodies bound forward and backward, with many wild leaps into the air, their flags flying in the lurid torch-light, and all the time the most unearthly yells and shrieks keeping up a sort of pandemonium chant.

They reverence to the utmost degree of superstitious veneration the chirp and movements of little birds. Should any expedition be under consideration—especially hunting, and most of all head-hunting—they will go out and throw sticks up into some tree and disturb the birds. Should the chirp be a certain sound and their flight be in a certain direction, nothing could induce the chief to call out his braves. Their reverence for the little tailor-bird has more than once been the cause of annoyance and inconvenience. On one occasion I planned the ascent of Mount Sylvia, whose peak towers more than eleven thousand feet above the sea. The services of a chief and a dozen braves were secured. The chief's son, who afterward became a Christian, acted as interpreter. Our point of departure was a place we called "Huts." When Captain Bax made his trip this was the farthest inland point then reached. Two of the men went in advance, cutting the prickly creepers; but the first day our clothes were torn and our hands sorely lacerated. The second day, on a high peak, the signal-shout of our guides was answered by several shots in rapid succession, and then another band of savages met us. They surrounded me, scrutinized me from head to foot, then grinned and said, "You have no cue; you must be our kinsman."

After spending the night in their village we crossed another range and followed a dark defile, where, looking over the ledges of rock, an impetuous torrent could be seen dashing over boulders two hundred feet below. In the afternoon we were within the bounds of another tribe. A halt was called; rice-balls were ranged in a circle, a large bamboo of native liquor, with a drinking-cup, in the center. They all sat down, drank, and fired several volleys. Two dozen of the local tribe, with their chief, who had been watching us from concealment all the time, suddenly appeared with their matchlocks ready. Our chief made signs and the guns were lowered. Each one advanced in turn, and putting his hand first on my breast, then on his own, said, "You are our kinsman." Then the members of the two tribes threw their arms around one another's necks, and with their faces together drank to the health of both.

On the morning of the fourth day we were making the ascent of Sylvia. There is excitement and interest in the thought, for Sylvia is the pride of our mountains. Higher and higher we wound and cut and climbed. Far up we reached a little open space among the tangle, and could see that next day would take us to the topmost peak. Below could be seen all the ranges, with their intervening valleys. All around was the wild luxuriance of cypress and camphor, orange, plum, and apple, chestnut, oak, and palm, while the umbrella-like tree-fern rose majestically some thirty feet high, with its spreading fronds fully twenty feet long. Far up in the crotch of the camphor or cypress could be seen the ribbony ferns, and hanging down from the branches orchids varied and beautiful. On one side is a grove of bamboo with sky-blue stems and feathery tops. In the jungle the trees are interlaced by a network of prickly rattan. Standing there on that jutting crag, gazing on that marvelous scene above, around, below, listening to the music of a torrent tumbling from a chasm high overhead, far to the west the waters of the Formosa Channel gleaming like a long line of blue light, and, between, the mountain-ranges, looking as though the dark-green sea stood still, "with all its rounded billows fixed and motionless forever," the effect of it all was overwhelming.

But after that night of ecstasy came the morning of disappointment. With the snow-capped heights of Sylvia almost within reach, the chief announced his decision to return to "Huts." He had been out interviewing the birds, and their flight warned him back. There was nothing for it but to fall into line and retrace our steps. Reluctantly, but with much more rapidity, the descent was made, and we arrived at the village in time for the braves to participate in the devilish jubilation over a head brought in during our absence. One ugly old chief, wild with the excitement of the dance, put his arm around my neck and pressed me to drink with him from his bamboo, mouth to mouth. I refused, stepped back, looked him sternly square in the face, and he was cowed and made apologies. When we left them they were urgent in their invitations to their "black-bearded kinsman" to visit them again.

When in the forests near West Peak, nine thousand feet

high, I strolled about outside a savage village, and was suddenly called to halt by strange and angry shouts. Looking around for an explanation, I saw savages with their chief standing a little way off, their hands on the handles of their long knives. They gesticulated wildly and seemed almost frantic. I then advanced to the chief, put my hand on his shoulder, and immediately the turmoil ceased. The cause of it all was that I had been standing upon an old grave, and, according to their superstitious notions, to touch a grave is sure to bring dire calamity to the tribe. They bury a dead body in a hole several feet deep, the knees drawn up to the breast, and all the weapons of the dead deposited in the grave. It is covered over with twigs and leaves, and then all rush away, not daring to look back or to return to repair the grave.

I was in that region with some of the students for three weeks, unable to return to the cleared land owing to the impassable state of the streams, swollen by continual rains. We had no provisions and were entirely dependent on the savages. But we lacked for nothing. What food they had or could get we shared. They brought us Indian corn and wild honey preserved in bottles made out of the bamboo. They offered us a spirituous liquor made out of mountain-rice, of which they are very fond, and which seems to make them drowsy. Mr. E. C. Baber, the British consul, who was with me on one tour, sampled the liquor and pronounced it " poor stuff."

One year I spent Christmas day with the savages. Koa Kau, another student, and an elder from Sin-tiam accompanied me. We crossed the river at Sin-tiam and were soon within the mountains. Next day, when walking some distance in advance of the others, I came upon a savage woman with a child on her back. She looked afraid at first, but when I spoke she smiled and the child laughed aloud. A little farther on her husband appeared, his hand grasping his knife and a fierce look on his face. The woman spoke to him and then he was friendly. Hearing that I wished to visit their chief, who holds rule over eight villages, they offered to guide me. Through reed-marshes and jungle, up hill and down, over rocks and fallen trees, we made our way. Again and again bird-listening was resorted to, but always with favorable results.

When we reached the chief's village we were taken into his august presence. He received us graciously. The students and myself were to be his guests, while the rest of our party should be given quarters in another house. A bear had been killed that day, and a fresh piece of his flesh was brought in for us; but we were not equal to raw bear's meat not yet cold, and had to decline with thanks. The women gathered some rice, threshed it, tramped it in a large tray to remove the husk, and pounded it in a tub with a wooden stamper four feet long, grasped by the middle, until in a very short time the hulls were off and the rice ready for the pot. The pot was supported by three old knives stuck in the ground as spits. At supper each made rice into a ball for himself with a wooden ladle and his fingers, and reached for some of Bruin's haunches, broiled to suit the taste of a brave.

The chief's house was one large room fully thirty feet long, with a fire blazing at night at either end. Men stood around one fire, women squatted beside the other. There were five beds on poles along the walls. The highest was given to me, and one close by to the students. We had candles made from the heart of the fir-tree, and as one burned out it was replaced by another. On one couch across the room lay the savage mother with her sleeping new-born babe. She was human and had the instincts of a mother; but she was an untutored savage, and, savage-like, she smoked incessantly her long bamboo pipe. The men smoked, told stories, and discussed the chase and an expedition to the border-land to be undertaken soon. The women were busy thread-making on the spinning-jenny; and as they wound the rhea they laughed, twitted one another,

and chatted as their sisters do in Christian countries. Yes,
sisters! for He made them, died for them, and from the glory
bends on them a Brother's eye. We proposed a song—"one
of the songs of Zion." They all looked and listened with evident interest. The aborigines are much more musical than the
Chinese. We sang several hymns, and through the chief's son,
who once visited me at Tamsui, I told them of the far-away
home and of God's love for the world. It was Christmas
night; and away there in a wild place, where no white man
had ever been, and in the company of men and women and
little children who never before heard of his coming, it sent a
thrill to the heart to tell of the Babe of Bethlehem, the Man
of Nazareth and Calvary. I could not help thinking of their
sad state, and of the opportunity and responsibility of the thousands in Christian lands who on that very day took up the
Christmas carol:

> " Hark, the herald angels sing
> Glory to the new-born King."

These tribes are continually changing their headquarters.
When a chief or the head of a family dies they do not care to
remain in that vicinity, but begin anew in some other quarter.
The abandoned site is soon overgrown by shrubs and vines,
and only the absence of immense trees marks the place of their
former habitation. Their mode of clearing the forest-land is
rather novel. Climbing the trees, they lop off the branches
with their knives, then girdle the trunk, and in time the storms
lay the dead trees low. The land is afterward cleared for the
village and rice-fields. Some of the tribes are rapidly diminishing in numbers and losing their independence, and will, in
course of time, be absorbed by the superior race. Natural
increase does not keep pace with the waste. The hard lot
of the savage woman unfits her for maternity, and makes her
progeny less able to endure the hardness of savage life.

One of the sad things about their life is the condition of woman among them. The heaviest burden rests upon her. All day long she toils in the fields, and at night carries home the fruit of her work. Then she goes out into the bush and gathers firewood, returning with a heavy load on her back. Exposure, drudgery, poor food, and all the other ills of her burdened life soon tell on her strength; the strong, healthy, finely developed girl is old before her time, and at an age when her civilized sister is in her prime she is worn, haggard, and utterly repulsive in her decrepit ugliness. Centuries of civilization and the influence of Christianity would equalize the burden of men and women, and teach those idle braves that the weaker sex is not the beast of burden for the lords of the tribe. Whatever new burdens might be imposed by the sharper struggle for existence in a more highly organized and complicated state of society, they could scarcely be more cruel or crushing than those that make a savage woman's life too dreary for pleasure and too unromantic for tragedy.

As yet our missionary work among the savages is little more than skirmishing. Occasional tours to their villages may do something—have, indeed, done something—for their benighted souls. But we do not call that mission work, and at present it seems difficult to do more. No missionary from the West could live long in the mountains, so great is the rainfall, and so ruinous to health. The multiplicity of dialects presents another obstacle. A native may yet be raised up to carry the gospel to his fellows. Till then we hope to do what may be done by such methods as are within our reach. Several of the chapels in the border-land are attended by savages with more or less regularity. We keep in constant touch with them, and under ordinary circumstances have no fear of personal violence ; but all attempts to evangelize them must, for the present generation at least, meet seemingly insuperable obstacles. The blankness of their moral life, the blindness of their spiritual vision, the deadness—not absence—of their receptive faculties, make the effort to move them with the dynamic of truth a seemingly hopeless task. Add to this the extreme hardness of their lot, the keenness of life's struggle, the barrenness of life's outlook, and, most of all, take account of the utterly damning effect of intoxicants introduced by the wily Chinese trader, for which, when once awakened, the savage thirst is insatiable. Facing a conspiracy of such resisting and demoralizing forces, mission work indeed seems hopeless. But the obstacles are only seemingly insuperable; the task is only seemingly hopeless. The gospel has brought light to the savage mind. Men and women have believed and been made free. Their fiercest passions have been tamed, their deadliest lusts curbed and sanctified. Some are still fighting life's winning battle among their native mountains; some have gone to the better world. With confidence I look forward to meeting in the land of the hereafter one and another who first heard of God and heaven around the gleaming night fires in the forests of Formosa.

CHAPTER XXVIII

WITH THE HEAD-HUNTERS

Their ruling passion—Probable origin—Hereditary hatred of Chinese—
Pe-po-hoan a traitor—By nature a hunter—Head-hunter's outfit—
Planning a raid—Attack by daylight—Under cover of night—Return
of the victors—A head-hunting feast—Disposing of the head—A
fight with Chinese—Failure—In Chinese hands—Vengeance—Betrayed by kinsmen—After British " blue-jackets "

HEAD-HUNTING is the ruling passion among the savages in Formosa. This is the one crime of violence laid
to their charge. To this, as to nothing else, they give themselves from earliest youth to decrepit age, following it with an
ardor that never cools and a cruelty that never relents. The
deer and the boar may lose their power to stir the old chief to
enthusiasm, but to his dying day his right hand never loses its
cunning ; and to see his braves return with the spoils of a head-
hunting raid is as life to his bones. The last desire of the
dying is that his sons may prove worthy of their sire and by
stealthy step and certain thrust add to the trophies of the tribe.

Hideous and gruesome as this passion appears to all civilized
peoples, it must not be taken as incompatible with the coexis-
tence of moral qualities not always found, or found but feebly
developed, in other savage or half-civilized races. As has
already been said, in several points of morality these mountain
savages will compare favorably with other and higher races.
Like their nearest of kin, the Hill Dyaks of Borneo, whom they
resemble with significant closeness in most of their distinctive

features of character and in their customs and habits of life, they are truthful and honest to a remarkable degree ; and gross immorality, when found among them, is nearly always traceable to border-land association with the Chinese.

Head-hunting may be traced back to the petty village and tribal wars; and as life has no sacredness in the eyes of the savage, and an enemy has no rights, it became simply a question of mode as to how their enemies should be put to death and some wrongs atoned for. The bringing back of the head was regarded as satisfactory evidence—a kind of medical certificate—that the sentence of the tribe had been carried out. When hostilities became fixed, and certain tribes or races were regarded as unforgivable enemies, a premium was put upon their heads, and the brave who showed most skill was counted worthy of greatest honor and made head man of his village or chief of his tribe. So it may have come about—at all events it has come about—that the hill savages of Formosa look upon the enemy of their tribes as a mark for their spears, and his head as specially designed to ornament their huts.

These aboriginal inhabitants held the island to be theirs by the right of centuries of possession ; and when the Chinese came they were regarded as intruders, who would not respect native rights. The Chinese justified every suspicion, and shrank from nothing that would give them possession of the land. The natives were driven back into the mountains, their liberties curtailed, and their life molested. The Chinese, therefore, became the hated enemy of the savage, and to avenge the wrong of his tribe not only merited applause from men and maidens still living, but won the approval of ancestral braves, whose spirits, watching the fortunes of the tribes, had powers for weal or woe, and would surely punish the family whose sons held back from the work of vengeance.

While the Chinese are hated with the intensest hatred, and their heads prized as trophies of highest price, the savages have no tenderness of feeling for their kindred who have acknowledged Chinese authority. The various tribes of conquered aborigines in the plains are looked upon as traitors, and when opportunity offers they are made to pay the penalty. A Chinese head may be a first prize, but the chance of a Pe-po-hoan is never missed. Indeed, it would almost seem that the treason of those who have yielded to the oppressor inspires a bitterer hate.

The savage is by nature a hunter. He has the instincts, the senses, and the hardy endurance required. He knows the haunts and habits of game. He can wait long and follow far. His foot is soft, his aim sure, and into the chase he throws all the passion of his soul. When the game is human, not animal, there is added zest in the chase, and his vengeful hate suffers not his energies to flag. No sleuth-hound is truer to the scent, no tiger is stealthier of foot. Everything is planned beforehand. For weeks, perhaps months, back of all other thoughts is the prospective raid. From some ambush on the hilltop the movements of the fated victims on the plain are watched. What time the farmers come and go, when the rice will be reaped or the vegetables dug, when the fishermen leave home and when they return, who among the country people go into town, what the defensive strength of a village is, where and when the raid could best be made—all this the scouts know long before the appointed day arrives.

The outfit of a head-hunter is simple. The necessary things are a spear, knife, and bag. The spear is of bamboo, about twenty feet long, with an iron arrow-shaped head eight inches long. This is light, strong, and easily used, and always carried in the hands. The knife is of iron, eighteen inches long, sharp-pointed, and generally crooked, with a one-sided open hardwood sheath. This knife is always in the savage's belt, and the belt is always worn. The bag is of strong twisted rhea-cord, open like a net, carried over the shoulders with

strings tied round the neck, and capable of holding two or
three heads. Every head-hunter has the spear, knife, and bag.
Sometimes bow and arrows are taken, and occasionally a
matchlock gun.

Always on the lookout for Chinese, they will attack them
anywhere and at any time, should the opportunity be favorable. But should a month or two go by without a head being
brought to the village they become restless and unhappy. The
old-time passion begins to burn, and arrangements are made
for a head-hunting expedition. The chief calls his council
braves together, the matter is talked over, and proposals considered. The raid having been settled on and preliminaries
arranged, the hunters then look to their weapons. As many
as fifty sometimes join the expedition; but when they come
near the border territory, where the Chinese may be seen, they
divide into small companies under the guide of the oldest and
bravest.

Sometimes they start out during the day, in which case the
savages go singly. They know where and when their victims
may be found, and rely more on the surprised attack and sudden thrust than on the skill or strength of open combat. With
all his daring the savage is at heart a coward, "bold in ambush, base in open field." He watches from behind a boulder
or bush until his victim is within spear-thrust, when suddenly
and without warning he strikes the blow; or he creeps up behind the unguarded workman and takes him unawares. This
is his method with the rattan and camphor workers in the forest. The rattan industry is very extensively carried on by the
Chinese, and many woodmen are employed. The rattan grows
sometimes to the length of five hundred feet, creeping vine-
like over other plants and above the branches of trees. The
workman cuts the stalk near the root, and, going backward,
pulls it out of the entanglement like a long rope. While he is
so engaged the savage creeps up and thrusts him through with

his long spear. Camphor-working is equally dangerous. The Chinese chip the trunks of the camphor-tree with a short adz, on their knees or bending over all the while. That is the hunter's chance, and many a Chinese head is off before its owner has time to turn around. The farmers are exposed to danger in their fields near the mountains. Often the face of a hill is cleared and planted, while the top and opposite side are still bush. The savages are concealed in the bush, and having observed the coming and going of men and women to the potato-patch, watch their chance, and before the alarm can be given the deed is done. The head-hunter frequently conceals himself beside lonely paths through fields of reeds, tall grass in the plains, or at the mouth of a mountain gorge near the sea. Then he waits the coming of some solitary traveler, and the first warning of danger is the last thrust of the spear. In such ways head-hunting is carried on in the daylight, and in a surprisingly short time the hunter is back again in the security of the forest, with the proof of his skill in the rhea-net on his shoulder. A wild yell gives the signal to his village, and in the plain below friends are beginning to wonder what is keeping husband or father—he never was so late before.

But night is the favorite time for the head-hunter. Then the men go in companies. Their plan is to select a house standing apart and to surround it, making a wide circle, and gradually closing in until at a signal the attack is made. Sometimes one creeps up and sets fire to the dry thatch of the roof, and when the inmates are aroused and rush out they are instantly speared, their heads thrust into the bags, and in a moment not a sound is heard but the crackling of the burning embers. If there is no reason for such haste, the hunters first secure the door, then thrust damp grass smudges through the chinks and openings, smoke the inmates to suffocation, and then secure their heads. This is safe only when a house is in a lonely place, where there is no danger of relief from neighbors.   Failing to find a house to their liking, the hunters will take account of any theatrical performance in town, or other attraction that may be depended on to draw the country people and detain them until a late hour.   Stragglers are never safe on these roads at night.   Or, failing in this, they lie in wait for the farmers and their men, who go to the harvest-field early in the morning and return when the light has failed in the evening.   A man or woman bent over the hoe all day, or trudging in the rice-field, is not always on the alert, and proves an easy mark.   The women and children in the fishing-villages are always afraid for the terrors of the night; and men never know, when they push off in the evening, but that their loved ones will have fallen victims to the cruel savages before they return; for on the mountains behind the village the savage spies are taking note of all.

The heads having been secured, the hunters return with all haste to the village.   When on the peak of the nearest mountain they shout their wild whoop of victory.   The villagers have been waiting, and when that yell is heard a party is sent out to meet the braves and escort them home.   All the village is out of doors.   Old men and women, youths and maidens, the youngest child in the settlement, even the very dogs, all know the meaning of the yell, and go wild with excitement. They are all on the way to welcome home the heroes.   Such shouting, shrieking, and demon-like howls!   The dogs seem as though they were made for nothing but yelping on that one occasion.   The hunters recite their experiences—how they escaped detection, how they did the deed, perhaps what wounds they got in the fray.   Everything is tóld with many gesticulations, and every point is greeted with fresh demonstrations of delight.

In due time the hunting-party reaches the chief's house, and the spoils are exposed to inspection and further jubilation.   If there be more than one head the joy of the village knows no bounds; but one is sufficient to call out all the fiendish noises that men or devils could well desire. The head is placed in the middle room, or, if the crowd be too large, in an open space outside. Beside it is set a vessel with liquor distilled from the mountain-rice; this is for the spirit so rudely surprised out of its body, and in return it is asked to put the hunters in the way of securing other Chinese heads. A circle is formed round the head, all joining hands—old hags with girls of sixteen, boys of ten with men of seventy. An old man carries a hollowed gourd-shell full of liquor, and with a bamboo cup supplies old and young. They all drink, and the liquor, which is mildly intoxicating, adds to the excitement. Round and round the head they circle, dancing a sort of double step, the braves leaping and yelling, the shrill voices of the children mingling with the broken-voiced utterances of their grandmothers, who are the most hideous and excited of all, and over all the old chief urging on his tribe to fresh manifestations of delight and gratitude. All the while a wild bacchanalian song is chanted, the sound of which is like nothing outside the caverns of perdition. No alphabet I know can be so arranged as to represent such sounds. The nearest approach to spelling the song I heard in the village at the foot of Mount Sylvia would be "Hi-yah; hi-yeh; hi-yo-heigh!" That begun low and ending in a high nasal screech, with many reduplications, and punctuated with many fiendish yells, might give some idea of the song of the savage at a head-hunting feast. The meaning of the song is that they are rejoicing now over their enemy, and are grateful for the head brought back by their braves.

This demonstration is kept up all night and until the third day. Should any get dizzy with the dance, or drunk with the liquor, their places are given to others, and they given time to recruit. On the third day the head is finally disposed of. In this the tribes differ. One sets up a tripod of poles in the village, with the head on the top. Others leave it exposed till the flesh drops off. Only rarely is the head boiled and the flesh eaten; but it is common enough to boil the brain to a jelly and eat it with vengeful relish. They offered it to me as a rare treat.

When the flesh has been removed the skull is hung up as a trophy to be prized, sometimes on the wall inside, oftenest outside under the eaves. The brave who can exhibit the longest row of skulls is the envy of the tribe. Every house has this decoration, and the chief's looks like the museum of an anatomy specialist. They are never taken down, and the smoke and rain of years only adds to the ghastliness of the sight. The cue is always hung up on the wall inside. I have more than once, during hours of sleeplessness, counted the skulls and cues in a savage's house and thought of all that passion meant to them and to sorrowing families out in the plains. I cannot say that I dreaded a like fate, or that those ugly evidences of cruelty kept sleep away or made sleep miserable with fearful dreams.

Far inland from Toa-kho-ham there is a Chinese settlement and trading-post, where in 1877 I witnessed a fight between the settlers and a band of two dozen head-hunters. The band had divided into two companies and attacked different points. One company had already secured their prize and were making their escape with three heads. The other party had surrounded the camp in which we were, but the yells of their comrades alarmed us and we rushed out in time to resist attack. A few moments more our stockade would have been burned and the inmates beheaded. The alarm was now sounded and the entire settlement was in hot pursuit. The savages fled beyond the cleared land, reunited their forces, then turned viciously upon their pursuers. A battle ensued. It was a wild and bloody scene. Both sides were armed, but the rapidity with which the savages dropped on their backs, lifted one foot, steadied their leveled matchlocks between their toes, and fired was something marvelous. Leaping, firing, yelling all the while like demons, these bloodthirsty Malayans held their ground for nearly an hour. But the Chinese were no cowards, and at last, fearless of death, dashed forward and drove the savages back into their mountain retreats.

Should the head-hunting expedition end in failure the braves are utterly ashamed, and in some tribes dare not return to their own village for three days. Failure is in any case a disgrace, and they take care to fail but seldom. But should one of their number be caught or killed, then there is wild lamentation in the tribe, and the fatal place is shunned for years.

And woe to the head-hunter that falls into the hands of the Chinese. The mercy he has shown is meted out to him. At Sa-kiet-a-koe, a Chinese city of sixteen thousand inhabitants in the Kap-tsu-lan plain, I witnessed a scene illustrative alike of the character of both races. A month before, at a Chinese house a mile out of the city, where many were assembled at night for idolatrous worship, one came in and reported a mysterious stirring among the stalks of hemp outside. Savages were at once suspected, and the men armed themselves with guns and other weapons and started in pursuit. The savages fled. Five were killed, five escaped to the bush, one sought refuge in a tree; but the dogs traced him, and he was taken prisoner, brought to the city, and imprisoned. He was kept in ignorance of his fate until on the appointed day he was led to the execution ground near the military mandarin's yamen. People crowded about in large numbers. Two executioners arrived, each with a heavy broadsword about two feet in length. Men and boys stood around feeling the weapons and remarking on their worth. The third gun sounded, and in a few minutes twenty soldiers with musty Remington rifles came hurriedly along. Behind them two coolies carried the miserable creature in an open, shattered sedan-chair. A bamboo stick, holding a paper with written characters stating the crime for which he was to die, was stuck through his hair and down his back, inside the cords which bound his hands behind him, and extended two feet above his head. When the chair was dropped the wretch crouched and had to be dragged out. His face was horribly contorted and the very picture of despair and cowardly fear. He crouched for a moment, then fell forward. One blow was struck from behind, then the other executioner advanced and sawed the head off with his large blade. The head was tied to a bamboo pole and carried away to be put up on the west gate. Scores were there on purpose to get parts of the body for food and medicine. Under such circumstances, or if a savage is killed inland, the heart is eaten, flesh taken off in strips, and bones boiled to a jelly and preserved as a specific for malarial fever.

Sometimes the savages are taken by the treachery of their kinsmen, the Pe-po-hoan. One famous old chief was on the top of a mountain with a band of twenty-four braves, when he was beckoned by a party of Pe-po-hoan to approach and drink one another's health. After much hesitation the savages came; but hardly had the liquor been tasted when the crafty design was revealed and the savages attacked. After a desperate hand-to-hand struggle the men escaped, but the chief was taken a prisoner. He was handed over to the Chinese authorities, who gave a reward to his captors. After being imprisoned, beaten, tortured, he was dragged through the streets, and women rushed forward, thrusting long needles into his flesh by way of avenging the death of their husbands, sons, and friends. When the signal was given for him to kneel, with diabolical glee he said he was not ashamed to die, for at his house on the mountains was a row of Chinese heads lacking only six of completing the hundred, every one the prize of his own daring skill. Around him were several Chinese border-men who had adopted the cannibalism of the savages, and these cut away the skull and ate the brains, in the hope that they too would be brave like the chief whom they so greatly feared. The savages do not scruple to take the heads of foreigners, and sometimes those who are unacquainted with the shores have narrow escapes. In 1876 I was invited on board H. B. M. ship "Lapwing" as the guest of Lieutenant Shore, now commander of the Coast Guards of England, and went for a sail down the east coast of the island. At So Bay the great man-of-war stood at anchor, and two dozen of the blue-jackets got leave to go ashore. They were told off under charge of navigating officer Murray, and soon had a fire kindled on the rocks and were out with their drag-net for fish. I accompanied the officer, and was strolling along the beach. Suddenly a Chinese rushed up to me, pointed his finger toward some boulders near the water, and without speaking disappeared. I looked in the direction indicated, and a few yards away saw objects moving toward us. They were the head-hunters, with their eyes on the blue-jackets, creeping stealthily, like so many tigers, until they would be within reach. Without giving any reason I had the fire moved to another spot. This told the savages that they were discovered, and they vanished into the darkness. Had they not been detected they would certainly have succeeded in their designs, and in the night could not have been overtaken. The blue-jackets returned with the fish, broiled them on the hot stones, ate them with relish, and not until their jollification was over and we were safely back on board were they made aware of their danger.

Many other incidents might be told, but the foregoing will illustrate the kind of life the savages live, and will suggest something of the obstacles in the way of all effort to make mild a savage people and "subdue them to the useful and the good."

AT HEADQUARTERS

CHAPTER XXIX

A SKETCH OF TAMSUI

Nearing port—Up the river—The mission buildings—The town—Population—Industries—Hospital

SAILING northward from Hong Kong, through the Formosa Channel, on the left is seen the mainland of China. At Amoy we turn eastward, and, crossing the channel, the vessel steers for the harbor at the port of Tamsui. If it is high tide she glides smoothly over the sand-bar that guards the entrance; if low tide, anchor must be dropped. From the upper deck of our steamer lying at anchor we get a bird's-eye view of Tamsui. Before us, looking eastward, in the background, stretching north and south, and rising tier above tier in stately grandeur, are those massive mountain-ranges left by tremendous volcanic upheavals of past ages, and now clad in perennial verdure. Here and there on their sloping sides are seen patches of tea-plantations. Farther down, and interspersed with trees and grasses, lie the rich green rice terraces. No fences, no straight lines, no precise measurements, but leveled fields of every size and shape, edged with green, and forming a regular descent, each distinct and lower than the other, down through the valleys almost to the sea-shore.

At last out swings the signal. Up comes the anchor, and with leisurely dignity our vessel heads forward into the mouth of the Tamsui River. On the south, at our right as we enter, lies Quan-yin Mountain, seventeen hundred feet high, covered with tall grass, groves of bamboo, banian and fir trees. Nestling at its feet are villages and farm-houses, almost concealed under ancient spreading banians, swaying willows, and prickly screw-pine hedges. There, too, at times buried in several feet of water, lies a mud-bank, where oyster-beds have been arranged. To the left is a low stretch of sea-sand bounded by black volcanic rocks and broken coral, where women and children are gathering oysters and seaweed. There, among the drift of sand, stands "the black beacon," and a little farther on "the white beacon"; then a fishing-village, with boats drawn up on the beach, and rows of nets hanging out to dry. There is a battered Chinese fort, and up the hill just behind it another fort, with modern massive earthworks, concealing guns and soldiers.

Going slowly on, we pass low whitewashed buildings—Chinese customs offices, with their European residents. But here the hill rises abruptly two hundred feet, and on its face stands a tall, red, weather-worn, solid-looking structure, the old Dutch fort, now the British consulate; and there from its height floats the flag of world-wide empire. Beneath its shadow, surrounded by well-kept gardens, is the handsome residence of the British consul. And there, just opposite us, right on the summit of the hill, surrounded by avenues of trees, are those two red, airy, and artistic-looking buildings that we espied far out at sea, and that present a style of architecture different from anything seen in any of the treaty ports of China. They are Oxford College and the Girls' School—the mission buildings of the Presbyterian Church in Canada. Near them, and almost hidden by trees, are two white dwelling-houses occupied by the missionaries. These are one story high, with tiled cottage roofs and thick whitewashed walls, and are called bungalows. Farther on stand two other bungalows—one, a little in the rear, for the customs secretary, and the other, on a line with the mission buildings, occupied by the foreign commissioner of the Chinese imperial customs. From there a Chinese graveyard slopes down to a gully, where a small stream runs and empties itself into the river in front. Right there begins the town of Tamsui, and it extends along the low bank of the river and the face of the hill at the back.

The Chinese do not call the town by the name Tamsui; that is the name of the district in which it stands. They call the town "Ho-be." The consular papers call it "Tamsuy." Foreigners mistook the name of the district for that of the town.

The population of Tamsui is 6148, with 1013 families. Just here it might be explained that the Chinese in North Formosa, in giving the population of a town, invariably include all the villages and surrounding country coming under the jurisdiction of the town magistrate. Thus, in the case of Tamsui, there are four such villages: Sio-pi-teng, with a population of 73; Sin-tsng-a, with a population of 1112; Sio-pat-li-hun, with a population of 1580; Sio-koe-lang-a, with a population of 1320. The whole population of Tamsui, therefore, according to the Chinese method of reckoning, is 10,233.

Tamsui is a busy enough place. Like other towns, its market is crowded with fishermen, farmers, gardeners, and hucksters, noisily disputing over their wares. Rice-shops, opium-dens, Chinese temples, and drug-stores, side by side, claim patronage, and carpenters, blacksmiths, barbers, and chair-coolies ply their trades. But it is, on the whole, rather a smoky, dirty town, not particularly noted for anything but its shipping-trade, and that it is one of the treaty ports where foreigners can hold property. This is really what gives it its importance.

Close by the chief thoroughfare stands the MacKay Hospital. From a sanitary view, no building could be better situated, because the ravine, with its unfailing stream of water, sweeps around three sides of it. All filth and garbage are immediately carried away. To this institution patients come from miles inland, and are treated for various diseases. Just adjoining the hospital are the chapel and the preacher's dwelling-place. Only a few rods away are the steamship company's hongs. To the east stands the North Hill (Tai-tun), thirty-one hundred feet high; and away northeast, with its head toward heaven, stands the highest peak, thirty-six hundred feet above the sea.

CHAPTER XXX

TRAINING A NATIVE MINISTRY

The dominant idea—Reasons for a native ministry—An educated ministry
—First college—Methods of work—The missionary's museum—
"Cui bono?"

MISSION work in North Formosa is dominated by the idea of a native ministry. The purpose is to evangelize the people, to enlighten their darkness by the power of divine truth, and to drive back the mists of error and the black clouds of sin that have through all the past obscured their vision of the City of God. That is the purpose of all foreign mission work. But in the carrying out of that purpose methods must be adopted suitable to the circumstances of the case. What would be reasonable and effective in one field would be absurd and useless in another. What would succeed in Europe or America would fail in Asia. China is not India, and Formosa is not China. The man or the mission that supposes that a good theory must be capable of universal application, and that social forces, hereditary customs, or even climatic influences need not be taken into account, makes a grievous mistake.

All the reasons that led me to lay such emphasis on a native ministry in North Formosa need not now be recited. They had to do with the language, climate, social life of the people, and the capabilities of the natives for Christian service. I was at the first convinced that the hope of the mission lay not

285

in foreign workers, and every year only confirms that opinion. The Lord of the harvest has raised up from among the natives of the island laborers whose services in those white fields will not be fully appreciated until we and they shall, at the harvest-home, come with rejoicing, bringing our sheaves with us.

One reason for a native ministry that will be appreciated by all practical and genuine friends of missions is that it is by far the most economical, both as to men and money. Natives can live in a climate and under conditions where any foreigner would die, and they can be hale and happy where I would tremble with chills and fever. And the cost of a native preacher and his family is so much less, that the contributions of the churches can be made to support a very much larger staff than if foreigners alone were employed. It is much more expensive to live in Formosa than on the mainland, but even with us the expense of a native is only a fraction of what is absolutely required for one accustomed to life in the West. The total cost per month for a preacher and his family is covered by nine dollars and eighty-three cents Mexican money— less than nine dollars in gold. The following table presents the average:

Rice per month	$3.00
Salt vegetables	4.00
Coal or wood	1.50
Carrying water and cleaning rice	.65
Shaving heads	.30
Shoes, stockings, and clothes	.38
Total	$9.83

But having settled on a native ministry, and having among the first converts those fitted and desirous to begin their studies in preparation for the work, the question of their training came early to the front. Let it be clearly understood that the mission stands for a trained ministry. Whatever good an uneducated minister may accomplish in Christian lands, he is next to useless among the heathen. Be it foreign or native, the ministry that will command the respect of the people and will endure must be intelligent as well as zealous. But in order to an educated ministry, great buildings, large libraries, and wealthy endowments, however helpful they may be, are not, at the first, absolutely indispensable. As good work cannot be done without these, but if the work done is genuine, increased facilities will follow. Our first college in North Formosa was not the handsome building that now overlooks the Tamsui River and bears the honored name of Oxford College, but out in the open under the spreading banian-tree, with God's blue sky as our vaulted roof.

Beginning with A Hoa, I invariably had from one to twenty students as my daily companions. We began each day's work with a hymn of praise. When weather permitted we sat under a tree—usually the banian or a cluster of bamboos—and spent the day reading, studying, and examining. In the evening we retired to some sheltered spot, and I explained a passage of Scripture to the students and others gathered with them. Indeed, wherever night overtook us, in all our journeyings, I spoke on a part of God's truth, ever keeping the students in view. They took notes, studied them, and were prepared for review on the following day.

Another favorite resort was on the rocks at Kelung. In the sampan we placed an earthen pot, rice, leek, and celery. Then we rowed ourselves out to the tables and pillars of sandstone by the sea. At noon each one gathered small sticks for a fire with which to cook our food. But we often dispensed with cooking, for each had provided himself with a sharpened nail with which to open the fresh oysters taken off the rocks. Study continued till 5 P.M., after which we coasted in shallow water. Several would plunge in and bring up shells, living coral, seaweed, sea-urchins, for study and examination. Sometimes an hour was given to fishing with hook and line, for the double purpose of supplying us with food and securing specimens for examination.

As chapels were established we remained at each a day, week, or month, studying daily till 4 P.M. All were trained in singing, speaking, and debating. After four we made visitations to converts and heathen in the vicinity. Students were frequently invited to dine with friends, and thus they had golden opportunities for presenting the truth. Every evening a public service was held in the chapel where we were.

A fourth method, and by no means the least profitable part of their training, was on the road in our traveling together. All manner of subjects were then discussed—the gospel, the people, the way to present the truth, and God, the Author of all. It was the daily habit of each one, when on the road, to collect specimens of some kind—plants, flowers, seeds, insects, mud, clay—and then to examine them at the first halting-place.

In all these ways, during the early years, and sometimes even since the college buildings were erected at Tamsui, the students were trained to become efficient workers, fluent speakers, skilful debaters, successful preachers. The college is now the center of our work, but whatever helps to develop the faculties of the students, inform their minds, or chasten their hearts, is pressed into service.

My own study and museum in Tamsui are open to the students, and good use has been made of their resources. After twenty-three years of accumulation the study is well furnished, having books, maps, globes, drawings, microscopes, telescope, kaleidoscope, stereoscope, camera, magnets, galvanic batteries and other chemical apparatus, as well as innumerable specimens illustrative of geology, mineralogy, botany, and zoölogy. What would be otherwise a parlor is in our house a museum. In that room is a vast collection of every conceivable kind of article of use or interest to Chinese, Pe-po-hoan, or savage. There are collections of marine shells, sponges, and corals of various kinds, classified and labeled. All sorts of serpents, worms, and insects are preserved. There are idols enough to stock a temple, ancestral tablets and religious curios, musical instruments, priests' garments, and all the stock in trade of Chinese idolatry, as well as models of implements of agriculture and weapons of war. The various savage tribes in the mountains are well represented. There is one idol ten feet high, different from any other I ever saw, and a complete collection of relics representing every aspect of savage life. Some things are quaint enough, others suggestive of sad thoughts, others gruesome and repulsive, because indicative of ferocity and savage cruelty. Keeping watch and ward over the whole scene are four life-size figures representing four sides of life in Formosa. In one corner is a Tauist priest, arrayed in his official long red robe, with a bell in one hand to arouse the devils possessing any man, and a whip in the other to drive them out. In the next corner is a bare-pated Buddhist priest, robed in drab, one hand holding his sacred scroll, the other counting his string of beads. Opposite to him is a fierce-looking head-hunter from the mountains, his forehead and chin tattooed, his spear at his side, bows and arrows strapped across his shoulders, a long knife at his girdle, and his left hand clutching the cue of some unfortunate victim. In the fourth corner is a savage woman, rudely attired, and working with her "spinning-jenny," as they may be seen in their mountain home.

There may be good people in Christian lands who will read these pages with painful astonishment, horrified that a missionary should spend time collecting and studying such things. I do not attempt to justify my conduct in the eyes of such persons. Had they any conception of what it means to train native-born heathen to become missionaries of the gospel of the Lord Jesus Christ, or could they conceive the reflex influence of all this study on mission work, in humbling the proud graduate, conciliating the haughty mandarin, and attracting the best and brightest of the officials, both native and foreign, they would not so readily write across these paragraphs their ignorant and supercilious " Cui bono ? "

CHAPTER XXXI

OXFORD COLLEGE

The building—Canadian liberality—The grounds—Reflex influence—
College work—Curriculum—Students—An evening in the college
hall—Drill—Addresses—An inspiration

OXFORD COLLEGE stands on a beautiful site about
two hundred feet above the waters of the Tamsui River,
which it overlooks, facing south. The building is seventy-six
feet ·from east· to west, and one hundred and sixteen from
north to south. It is built of small, red, burnt bricks from
Amoy, on the mainland of China. The entire outside was
oiled and painted, as a protection against the heavy rains.
The main hall has four arched windows of glass. A raised
platform extends the entire breadth, with a blackboard of
equal length. There are desk and stool for each student; a
map of the world, astronomical diagrams, and a rack for tunes
on cotton cloth. The college has accommodation for fifty
students, two teachers, and their families. There are two
lecture-rooms, a museum and library, bath-room, and kitchen.
Every room is well ventilated, lighted, and furnished. There
is an open court, around which runs a porch or veranda two
hundred and fifty feet in length.

It was during my first furlough in Canada, in 1880, that the
people of my native county, Oxford, Ontario, at the suggestion of the " Sentinel-Review " newspaper of Woodstock,
undertook to raise funds sufficient for erecti..g a college build-

ing in Formosa. Ministers and other Christian friends approved of the proposal, and it was carried out with enthusiasm and vigor. At an immense farewell meeting held in the Methodist church, Woodstock, on the eve of my return to Formosa, the sum of $6215 was presented to me; and with that money the college building at Tamsui was erected, and, as was fitting, it was called Oxford College. It is with gratitude and pleasure that I recall this and other tokens of regard on the part of my home friends; and when I think of that farewell meeting in 1881 there stand out against the background of loving memory the form and features of Oxford's greatest son, the late Rev. John Ross, of Brucefield, whose life of faith was to me an inspiration, and whose labor of love the Canadian church ought not to forget.

After finishing the building, the next work was to lay out the grounds. In the proper season, trees, shrubs, and seeds were planted. These had to be attended to, lest the ravages of worms and white ants would destroy them all. To-day there is an avenue of evergreen banian from the new public road (named by the foreign community College Road) up to the college door. It is three hundred and sixty feet in length. The trees meet overhead and form a great shelter for the students during exercise hours. There is another avenue, quite similar, between the college and the Girls' School. It is three hundred and seventy feet long, and extends to the wall behind the two buildings. There is also an avenue, though not so long, on each side of the college. The paths are about ten feet wide, and are covered with coral gravel from the sea-shore. A hedge of privet and hawthorn incloses the mission property; it is four feet across the top, several feet high, thirteen hundred and four feet in length, always green, and at times covered with beautiful purple flowers. There are twelve hundred and thirty-six evergreen-trees planted on the grounds as groves, and one hundred and four oleanders between five hundred and fifty-one banian-trees; and when the oleanders are in bloom—and they bloom for months— their lovely flowers contrast beautifully with the dark foliage of the evergreen spreading banian.

My evenings at Tamsui are sometimes spent walking round and round the paths among the trees and groves, exercising, superintending, meditating. The order and beauty are refreshing, and the fine appearance of things is a help to the college. Chinese people and officials visit, wonder, and admire; converts walk around and rejoice. Is such a part of mission work? Yes; most emphatically, yes. I, for one, went among the heathen to try to elevate them by making known to them the character and purposes of God. Our God is a God of order. He loves beauty, and we should see his handiwork in trees, plants, and flowers; moreover, we should endeavor to follow the order which is displayed so visibly throughout the God-created, star-studded universe.

In Oxford College I addressed the students daily from one to five times. They always took copious notes. Subjects were regularly reviewed and the classes constantly drilled. On being questioned as to what lines of thought were most convincing, one who is a literary graduate said, "The fulfilment of prophecy, especially the resurrection of Jesus Christ." Another thought the ten plagues and their critical import would influence many if studied. But twenty out of twenty-five unhesitatingly declared that the reasoning from effect to cause, and particularly from design to designer, would deeply impress the native mind. Thus I have been right all along as to how best to present the eternal truth of Jehovah to Chinese minds.

The Bible is used as our great text-book. Biblical geography and history are studied with special reference to Judea, Egypt, Persia, Greece, Syria, Arabia, Jerusalem, Rome, Babylon, Nineveh, Corinth, Ephesus. Courses of study are fol-

lowed in the Old Testament and in the New Testament. A
study is made of the lives of the great men of the Bible.
Attention is given to the zoölogy, botany, and mineralogy of
Bible times. Nor are the modern sciences neglected. Due
prominence is given to all the important subjects in the curriculum of a Western college. Special attention is given to
the systematic study of the doctrines of God's Word. The
biblical doctrines of God, man, sin, the person and work of
Christ, the church, sacraments, death, judgment, future rewards
and punishments, with an examination of proof-texts and
arguments on all sides, are the subject of much study and exposition.

In the college are freshmen, students of several years'
standing, and helpers who have had considerable experience
in preaching. About a dozen students are Chinese, and the
rest Pe-po-hoan. Perhaps the former surpassed the latter
in mental acumen and unabated diligence; but it must be
admitted that all studied with a commendable spirit, energy,
and zeal. Every hour was turned to good account in the
development of the physical, mental, and moral man. We
devoted hours to church history, biblical theology, zoölogy,
geography, astronomy. Addresses, varying from one to six,
were given every day. The questions of the Shorter Catechism
were all discussed and committed to memory. We met every
night in the college hall for one or two hours, and there women
from the Girls' School sat in the center, surrounded by the
college boys. It would be impossible to estimate the sound,
solid, and far-reaching results accruing from these continuous
nightly meetings; but a sketch of an evening in the college
hall may be of interest.

Promptly at seven o'clock the college bell is rung. Students
file into their places along two sides and the end of the hall.
Women from the Girls' School occupy the center; children
take seats in the front and corner· onlookers gather about the

door. In all, over a hundred busy workers assemble. The illness is serious indeed that will keep any one away at this hour; sometimes a student appears shaking with malarial fever and wrapped in a blanket. The desks are movable, so that all can sit closely together if necessary. On the platform are table, lamps, and generally flowers. Behind it, and in constant use, are blackboard, maps, and a frame containing twenty-four hymn-tunes neatly copied by a student on white cotton. On the table are laid copy-books ready for inspection.

First we sing a hymn, then have a few words of prayer, in which one of the students leads. Children, then women, read and recite in turn and answer questions. All the exercises are enlivened by singing. There are no organs in North Formosa churches, and the truth is, we do not feel in need of them. All the people, old and young, endeavor to take part in the service of praise ; and, whatever may be said of our music, we have never had indifferent, half-hearted singing. Foreigners of many nationalities, who could not understand one word of the language, have enjoyed and heartily commended this part of our worship. Many have been evidently touched as they looked and listened.

Our college drill is varied but orderly. One student takes the platform, pointer in hand, to indicate notes in the tune to be learned ; all in the hall stand and beat time with the right hand. One, with the children, leads off with the first line, and the rest chime in. A second verse may be sung by the women alone, the third by the students, the fourth by the whole band. One row of students may sing the first line, another row the second, the women the third, and so on. No one knows when his turn will come, and so all are kept on the alert. If the sounds are not full and clear, we have a few minutes for cales-thenic exercises, especially such exercises as develop the throat and chest. Then they sing again. Scripture lessons, geography, history, or any subject may be taken up next.

Students take turns in five-minute addresses on the platform. Each is criticized by his fellows, and any fault in the manner, dress, expression, or the matter is pointed out. New-comers tremble, but as months pass by they overcome bad habits, learn to stand fire, and become ready platform speakers. They develop their own natural talents without aping any one, and in time learn to speak in public with a confidence, and yet with a freedom from conceit, that could not be obtained without such persistent training.

In the midst of all I often take twenty or thirty minutes to address all assembled on some biblical or scientific subject. Our drill and worship over, the women retire first, students follow, and all disperse for fresh studies. Sometimes there is a debate, sometimes an exhibition of magic-lantern views, with an address. No two evenings are exactly alike throughout the season. They are most enjoyable meetings. Cramming, dullness, and monotony have no place in Oxford College. Would that mission critics could see for themselves the glistening eyes and the eager faces of little children, strong young men, and gray-haired women in that crowded hall! Would that some echo of those soul-stirring songs of praise—many of them mountain airs—could reach my native land! In the midst of care, sickness, and toil, what an inspiration to hear those converts from heathenism, many of them preparing to carry Christ's blessed evangel into the darkness from which they have been led, ring out on the midnight air "The Lord's my Shepherd," or "A day's march nearer home"!

CHAPTER XXXII

NATIVE WORKERS FOR NATIVE WOMEN

Woman's ministry—Reaching Formosan women—A glimpse at Chinese
social life—Tin-a from birth to marriage—The foreign worker among
native women—" Low-born barbarian "—Meaningless etiquette—
Fever—The native Bible-woman—Her training—At work—The
Girls' School—Curriculum—Students—The plan that succeeds

WHEN Jesus went through every city and village preaching, the Twelve went with him, "and certain women
also." The great Head of the church knew well the need
that existed, and would exist in all future ages, for the special
ministrations of women in the living temple he was erecting.
In North Formosa some of the most zealous and successful
workers, who were one with the little band of students in our
early struggles, and who bravely, and almost single-handed,
stemmed the tide of bitter persecution, were women, of whom
fragrant memories are still cherished by the church there.
With terrible odds against them, some of them lived and died,
clinging to the one living God with a simple confidence, te-
nacity, and determination not easily understood by those who
spend their lives in the walled gardens of Christendom.

How is it possible to convey to Christians in Western lands
any definite conception of the life of a Chinese woman? How
is it possible to present the difficulty of bridging the chasm
that exists between Circassian and Mongolian, or of reaching
women to whom the customs, ways, and ideas of their Western

sisters are altogether incomprehensible, and in many cases ludicrous and absurd? But without some insight into Chinese social life one cannot understand the nature and obstinacy of the difficulties in the way of reaching Formosan women with the gospel, or how those difficulties are to be overcome. Only a glimpse can be given, but to those who care to think a glimpse may be full of meaning.

The Chinese wife who is childless has a sorrowful life and often a miserable death. Those who have no children of their own frequently buy or adopt a child, or the husband may take to his home a second wife. As might be expected, there is even less happiness when a second mistress has been installed. If the first wife be loved by her husband, all the more intense is her grief that no son of hers will ever worship at her husband's tomb. The fact is, barrenness is considered sufficient justification for ill-treating a wife, or casting her out on the cold charities of the world.

When a daughter is born, little notice is taken of the event. If she should be deformed in any way, such as having a harelip, she may be immediately destroyed. If the parents already have girls, and are poor, even though it costs the mother a terrible struggle—for the maternal instinct cannot easily be eradicated—the child must sooner or later be put out of the way. As the struggle for life is hard and keen, the sooner the unwelcome baby girl is sacrificed the better.

But let us follow little Tin-a. If she come into this world in, say, a fairly well-to-do merchant's family, she is destined to grow into womanhood in a respectable circle. But how many strange superstitions are connected with her childhood! When four years old her pink plump toes are bent tightly together under the foot, cramped into position, and firmly bound by strong cotton bandages. The foot is then thrust into a little pointed shoe, the large toe being the prominent part of the foot. This wretched shoe she wears night and day. The mother steels herself against the daughter's screams, for the feet must not be neglected, lest Tin-a's chances for a good marriage be spoiled, and she be doomed to slavery all her days.

For several years she is allowed to play with her brothers about the door. She becomes the plaything of those around her, and is scolded, indulged, and beaten by turns. It is understood that she must be submissive to her brothers, who rule over her; and in due course she must learn to cook rice, wash clothes, and to sew and embroider dresses. She must use every artificial and natural means of rendering herself outwardly as attractive as possible, for she believes that the great end of existence is to be well married. Heart and intellect receive a wretched kind of training, if training it can be called. She is taught some Chinese proverbs and the moral maxims, which pass glibly over the tongue, while her mind is filled with ill-natured gossip, low jests, filthy sayings, and a thousand slavish superstitions.

When about ten years of age she is confined to the house, and no man, save those of her own family, is allowed to converse with her. If strangers enter her father's house she may peep through the cracks from an inner room, but she must on no account permit herself to be seen. Whatever she may be in reality, the parents, who are looking forward to a few hundred dollars at least when she shall leave their home as a bride, represent her as being endowed with numberless virtues; and she herself, at New Year's or on heathen festivals, with the aid of silks, satins, powder, jewels, embroidery, and perfume, must make a fine show. Above all things, she must, with due amount of simpering, profess to be so exceedingly modest that she cannot bear to have men look upon her. This period of close confinement is an anxious one to the parents, because such is the state of society that, should she break through the restraints and be seen alone on the streets, all their labor would be lost, the family would be disgraced, and the girl's chances of marriage ruined forever. One would like to draw the veil over such a state of affairs, but we are facing the fact that the morals in heathen lands are very low. Could we expect them to be higher? Perhaps not, and yet the picture has a brighter side. It is under such conditions that the power of the gospel of Christ is seen. Already its power has been manifested in raising out of such surroundings women and girls who become neat and cleanly in appearance, ladylike in deportment, and lovely in character.

When Tin-a is about fourteen years of age, a go-between, who is generally an aunt or some quick-witted old woman, is secured. This almost indispensable lady, by making many journeys and holding many conversations, arranges with the parents of some young man for a betrothal, which is usually settled in consideration of a sum of money, say from one hundred to three hundred dollars, which is paid over to the father and mother of the expectant bride. The augurs having been consulted, and an auspicious day fixed upon, a feast is prepared at the bridegroom's home. The bride is carried thither in a closely covered sedan-chair, over which a red cloth is thrown. After bowing with him before the ancestral tablets and household gods, and going through many other ceremonies, she belongs henceforth, soul and body, to this man and to his mother, to use or misuse as they see fit. Those of us who love the Chinese most are saddest to confess the cruel bondage that too often faces the Chinese bride.

And now the question comes, How are women in such a state of society, with such social customs, and in such a country as Formosa, to be reached and taught the gospel of Jesus? A foreign lady goes to take up her abode in Tamsui. Rosy-cheeked, healthy, and hopeful, she thinks she can do her own housework while studying the language. In this she proceeds for a few months. But the hot weather comes, and with it fever. The color gone from her face, and strength from her arm, the lady must hand the housework over to a Chinese male cook. She studies faithfully, but the Chinese language is of all things earthly the most intricate and difficult to master. Even if she learn to articulate clearly, she is surprised to find at the end of one year how few ideas she can express. Enthusiastic, perchance, and eager to be at work, she goes out among the Chinese, who crowd about to stare at her. Her dress is not like theirs, and some dispute as to whether she is a man or woman. Presently the cry is taken up, and it follows her everywhere: "Barbarian! low-born barbarian!" The very fact of her being there in a foreign land, far away from relatives, lowers her in their estimation; for however much the heathen in North Formosa have learned during the last twenty years about Western lands, they are so busy earning their rice that they will not take time to study Western ways and customs. The foreign lady, in the simple act of going out on foot into their streets, offends against their ideas of propriety.

She has heard, perhaps, that a little girl, with whose parents she is acquainted, is ill, and with Christian sympathy and desire to help she makes her way to their home, taking some delicacy with her. They may not seem frightened, and, possibly with a great show of welcome, they invite her in. She tries to speak a little to them, tells them of one God, but she feels helpless amid their chatter and questions about dress, hat, buttons, and why foreign ladies bind their waists and not their feet. They urge and entreat her to stay, to drink tea, to come again. In time she will learn that a great deal of this is only part of Chinese etiquette and politeness, empty and meaningless. The truth is that the Chinese are amazed at her utter disregard of the ordinary rules of polite society, that forbid visiting in this way where there is sickness, and forbid any but members of the family entering the sick-room. They scarcely wait till she is out of hearing before they begin to ridicule barbarians in general, and this one in particular. The foreign lady, kind-hearted, sincere, trying to converse in broken Chinese, and really anxious to do good—who could fail to sympathize with her under such circumstances? Time and the leveling power of Christian influence may change these customs; meantime they must be reckoned with, and stolid facts faced with open eyes.

The foreign lady finds she is confined almost entirely to the seaport; for a week or ten days inland means more fever, and the suspension of her work for a time, if not permanently. To go over mountains to join Bible-women working in the Kap-tsu-lan plain is simply out of the question. Apart from the fact that the way is often impassable, the climate is so damp and the region so unwholesome that even native workers dread it. No foreigner has ever spent many days there without suffering, and no medical man who knows the country would dare give his consent to a foreign lady making the attempt. Even with the best of care in the north she may often be prostrated with fever. At the end of the fourth or fifth year of faithful study and effort, compared with the little Chinese woman at her side, she is still almost helpless in teaching. This native Bible-woman is thoroughly familiar with the language and customs of her own people, and has been trained in the Holy Scriptures so that she can quote and explain with aptness and effect, while her foreign sister struggles with the idioms of the language, and is in perpetual danger of violating one of the thousand rules of Chinese society.

Let us now turn to any one of these native Bible-women and see what she is accomplishing. Who is she? What is her history? How does she work? There is A So, a gray-haired widow, one who has reared a family, has grandchildren, and will, therefore, command respect. Some of her sons are married, and she has an influence over their households. At one time she knew not of Jesus, but a chapel was opened near her door. At first she reviled the "foreign devil," but liked to hear the singing through her lattice-window. Then she listened to the preacher, and noticed the students, who seemed so neat, clever, and affable. At last she began to enjoy the services in the building, and more and more was delighted with expositions of the truth. Especially did she love the psalms and hymns, for she found comfort in their consolatory truths. Her idols were thrown away and she publicly declared herself a Christian. By and by Canadian ladies gave a large sum of money, and the Girls' School was erected. Having spent several sessions there, A So was sent to a chapel, where her time was fully occupied in teaching children and young girls, visiting the neighbors, answering their thousand queries regarding the mission, the missionaries, God, and heaven, and in telling them of the truth that she had learned, and of how she came to cast her idols away. She reads, and they are surprised; prays, and they listen; sings, and they are delighted. She finds out their ailments and afflictions, and, in common with the preacher and his wife, she endeavors to comfort them. She knows when and how to appear in a neighbor's dwelling, and how to act in such a way that her visits may be acceptable. She is respected on account of her gray hairs, neat appearance, and woman-like manners, and the heathen women look up to her because, like the preacher's wife, she is better posted in all the affairs of life than they are. She sympathizes with the women, for she has suffered just as they. She knows all about foot-binding. Sickness and death have been in her home, and when the little ones they love are taken away she knows how to sympathize, and with the comfort wherewith she herself was comforted of God in the dark days of her own sorrow she goes in to bereaved mothers, and not in vain talks of the Shepherd and his fold. Every Saturday she visits the houses of new converts, and tells women to be ready at a certain hour the next day, when she will call for them to go to worship. Gradually and almost imperceptibly the women are drawn toward the truth, and they scarcely know how much they have learned to love this devoted Bible-woman till she is transferred to another station. Not a few of these Bible-women are most enthusiastic and efficient workers, and all are of great assistance to the native preachers. Some of them have been the means of bringing whole families to Christ, and more and more is the Master's seal set to the work of these native workers.

As a college was needed to train men for the ministry, so also a large school building was required at some central point where women and girls could spend months at a time, under constant supervision and such influences as would remodel the lives of the older, and direct in the right channels those of the younger. The ladies of the Woman's Foreign Missionary Society of the Presbyterian Church in Canada came forward with hearty enthusiasm and gave the necessary funds for the building. Near the close of 1883 we began the work of construction on the same grounds as Oxford College, and but a few rods away from it. We often worked till midnight with a large gang of men. Students would stand outside and sing hymns to cheer the workmen. In eleven weeks the neat, roomy structure of cut stone was ready to be opened. It is the same size and on the same frontage as Oxford College. The front door leads directly into the hall or assembly-room. On each side of this is a small class-room. Behind the hall is an open court, surrounded by dormitories, and there are kitchen, servants' bedrooms, and storage-rooms. There is no need for comforts such as are to be found in a European or American ladies' college. These would only unfit the women for their own homes, where foreign luxuries are not to be had. A sufficiency of light and ventilation is most important and is amply provided for.

On the whole, only native preachers are employed; therefore running expenses have amounted to but a small fraction of what they would otherwise have been. Two native matrons, a preacher, and his wife live in the building. Much of the teaching—indeed, most of it—has been entirely voluntary. Older ones, or those further advanced, have taught the newcomers and little children. Often it is convenient to have a preacher's wife and children, or his mother, in the Girls' School while he is at college; so that in this home for Christian workers there are gray-haired women and little children, daughters and daughters-in-law, all busy reading, writing, and singing side by side. Teachers from Oxford College can easily carry on the work of the two institutions. The English language is not taught. If desired, a Chinese teacher can teach them to read and write their own characters. Native women can surpass a foreigner in teaching the romanized colloquial; that is, Chinese words spelled with English letters. That is the hope of our women, for it is useless to expect them to acquire the Chinese characters. Each one who learns the romanized colloquial can read her own Bible. There is a girl there who, when seventeen years of age, learned in one month to read the Catechism of the New Testament. Chinese girls and women are not in need of foreign ladies to teach them sewing, dressmaking, and embroidery; they are experts in the art. In other mission fields it is very different.

It is inconvenient, if not impossible, throughout North Formosa to secure girls, Chinese or Pe-po-hoan, to remain in the Girls' School at Tamsui for any great length of time. It is demanding too much in the present state of our work to expect poor little girls to journey from the east coast away from their parents. There is a hard struggle for existence, and the larger girls cannot be spared from the Kap-tsu-lan plain. In considering a sensible and useful plan for the education of the girls in any mission, the daughters of those employed by the mission, and whose interest it is to patronize the institutions of their employers, must not be taken into account. A school managed on those principles, and reaching only those selfishly interested, is not likely to be largely influential. Our object must be to reach the daughters of independent farmers, mechanics, laborers, and merchants. To attain that in China the plans adopted must be large, flexible, and Chinese-like. Recognizing these fundamental facts, the Girls' School was established. Bible-women are there trained for service at every station in the mission. These are "looked out" by the native preachers just as candidates for the ministry are in Christian lands. They are bright Christian women, and come up from the various churches, often bringing with them two or three girls, the daughters of converts there. It is entirely Chinese-like for a mother to intrust her daughter to another woman who will care for her while absent from home. Sometimes the Bible-women bring their own daughters, daughters-in-law, or other relatives. In this way the Girls' School has had as many as eighty during one session.

The women are taught reading, writing, and singing, Bible history and geography, the Scripture catechisms, and also attend addresses in the college during the day and take part in recitations and other exercises in the evening. They are trained in methods of teaching, and in every way equipped for their work. Then they are sent to stations where their gifts will yield the best service. In this way a hundred little communities are reached, and women and girls, Christian and heathen, in the remotest part of the mission are brought into touch with the stronger and healthier life at the center.

I am not speaking for other missions or other missionaries. Neither am I theorizing about work in Formosa. I am simply explaining the plan adopted there, and stating results which are evident and verifiable. After an experience of more than twenty years I may be permitted to say that, in my opinion, only by some such large, flexible, and Chinese-like plan will North Formosa ever be evangelized. The expense of maintaining a large foreign staff is so great, the language and social customs of the people present such formidable obstacles, the climatic conditions are so wasteful of life, making the field, except in and about Tamsui, a hungry devourer of men, and the success which by God's manifest favor has attended the work of those native Bible-women has been so real and abiding, that I have stood and still stand, now as confidently as ever, for the plan that is least expensive, most effective, and that succeeds. In North Formosa that plan is native workers for native women.

CHAPTER XXXIII

MEDICAL WORK AND THE HOSPITAL

Importance of medical missions—Native doctors—A doctor's charges—
Classification of diseases—Diagnosis—Diseases of the seasons—The
medicine-man—Cures for cholera, catarrh, dyspepsia—Malignant
malaria—Treatment by Tauist, Buddhist, sorcerer, doctor—Malarial
poison—Foreign treatment—Dentistry—First attempt—Instruments
—Methods and results—MacKay Hospital—Influence of medical
work on mission

THE importance of medical missons does not any longer
need to be emphasized. It is admitted by all who know
the history of modern missionary work. From the very beginning of our work in Formosa heed was given to the words and
example of the Lord, and by means of the healing art a wide
door for immediate usefulness was opened. No part of my
preparatory training proved more practically helpful than the
medical studies pursued in Toronto and New York. I found
the people suffering from various ailments and diseases, and
the power to relieve their pain and heal their diseases won for
the mission grateful friends and supporters.

But it must not be supposed that there are no doctors in
Formosa. There are large numbers of them, and the practice
of medicine, if it is not scientific, is certainly interesting and
deserving of study. There are no authorized schools of medicine, no examinations, and no degrees. Custom is the only
law, and success the only diploma. By experimenting on
himself or on others a man may come to know something of

308

the medicinal values of certain compounds. Or he may be associated with an older practitioner and learn from experience. Or by studying books on medicine and copying the important parts, he may learn enough of theory to begin practice. One who has himself been a sufferer and tried many remedies has all the knowledge required for prescribing for other people. A clerk in a medicine-shop, by reading and filling prescriptions sent in by doctors, may begin himself to prescribe. Failing in other lines, a man may purchase a stock of recipes and set out as a doctor. To be sure, one must have either knowledge or shrewdness; otherwise he will lose the confidence and patronage of the people, and then his occupation will be gone.

A Chinese doctor's charges would not be regarded as exorbitant by Western physicians or patients. For one call one hundred *cash*—equal to about ten cents—will be expected. The regular practitioner holds a high place in the estimation of the people, and his services are fairly remunerative. The traveling doctor, however, who generally combines sleight-of-hand tricks with the sale of plasters and nostrums, does not enjoy their confidence or respect.

The native doctors classify diseases as either internal or external, and it is but rarely that both classes of disease are treated by the same man. As internal diseases are more mysterious because of their secret operations, those who devote themselves to their cure are counted worthy of greater honor than those whose specialty is external sores and wounds.

Diagnosis is made by feeling the pulse. The doctor seats himself opposite his patient, whose hand rests on a piece of cloth on the table. If the patient be a male, the doctor, using his own right hand, first feels the pulse of the patient's left hand, then that of his right; if the patient be a female, the doctor, using his own left hand, takes first her right and then her left. He places his thumb on the prominent part of the bone of the wrist, and the first three fingers on the pulse. The different states of the pulse are described by five different words. The first means that it is high and full; the second, that it is low or deep and slow; the third, that it is deeper and lower still; the fourth, that it feels as if empty; and the fifth, that all motion is gone and nothing can be felt.

The heart and liver are supposed to produce these different states of pulse. It is believed that the heart has seven openings, through which wind and an evil principle enter, causing these changes in the pulse. Diseases differ according to the seasons of the year. Those of the spring are supposed to be caused by the liver, those of the summer by the heart, those of the autumn by the lungs, and those of the winter by the kidneys.

The doctor invariably writes out his prescription, which is taken to the drug-shop and filled. The druggist weighs out the various ingredients with considerable care, and wraps them together in a paper, inclosing the prescription along with the medicine, and marking the names of the articles on the outside of the package. The masses are kept in ignorance, however, for very familiar substances are given names quite unknown in the language of the common people. Minerals, rocks, and shells are often ground to a powder and roasted. Vegetables, roots, flowers, barks, and seeds are used as infusions.

In matters of surgery the natives acknowledge the superiority of foreign practitioners, but in dealing with internal diseases preëminence is claimed for their own doctors. It is only slowly that their ignorance is exposed and their superstitious notions overthrown. When one thinks of many of their remedies one wonders at the simplicity of patients that makes such prescribing profitable.

For Asiatic cholera many trust to a counter-irritant and external applications. The skin on several parts of the body is pierced with needles, and jerked or pinched between the knuckles of the index and middle fingers until it becomes red. Hair and ginger are sometimes mixed with camellia-oil and rubbed over the body. A specific for catarrh is made out of three ingredients infused in boiling water—a chip cut from a coffin after it has been put into the grave, a piece of the hempen mourning-clothes, and a handful of the earth out of the grave or taken from beside the coffin after it has been lowered. The tartar allowed to collect around the teeth—of which, I can bear testimony, a supply may be easily obtained—is considered a valuable antidote for dog-bite. The sallow countenance and disagreeable flatulence of a dyspeptic may be cured by a diet of dog's flesh, that of a puppy being preferable, and that of a mad dog not to be despised. A common remedy for gastritis is jerking the skin of the neck with the fingers after steeping them in warm water or spirituous liquor. If an infant's skin be of a black or dark color, pieces of a broken frying-pan are ground together with a screeching noise until the child begins to cry. If a man has been exposed to winds or rain, and painful cracks in the skin result, it is supposed that the real cause of the trouble is that the man offended the moon by pointing at her with his middle finger; and to be cured he must face the offended mistress of the night, placing his hands together as in the act of worship, and politely bow, humbly confessing his sin, and asking forgiveness.

It must not be inferred from what has just been said that the Chinese are simple-minded and gullible beyond all others that dwell upon the earth. It does seem incomprehensible, however, that so shrewd a people can be deceived and blinded by such ignorant quackery. And yet is it so very strange? What about the most enlightened nations of Europe in the last century? What about some Western peoples and countries to-day? One does not need to travel far to find those who are willing to be duped.

The most malignant disease, the one most common and

most dreaded by the people, is, as has been suggested, malarial fever. They suppose the disease to be caused by the patient unluckily treading on mock-money put in the street or on the roadside by a priest or sorcerer; or by a conflict between the hot and cold principles in nature; or by two devils, one belonging to the negative principle in nature, fanning the patient, thus causing the chills, and the other belonging to the positive principle, blowing a furnace and producing heat and fever. But to mention the names of these devils would be to incur their displeasure, and so the people never use the name " chills and fever," but call it " devils' fever," " beggar's fever," or some other harmless name.

The treatment for malaria depends upon the adviser. The Tauist priest makes charms out of peach-leaves, green bamboo, and yellow paper, which are tied around a button of the sick one's clothes, or to the cue. Sometimes red thread is tied around the wrist, and kept there for weeks at a time. Or a stamp, like that of Lau-tsze, the founder of Tauism, is pressed on the back. But perhaps most effective of all is for the priest to arouse the devils by ringing a bell or blowing a kind of horn, after which he proceeds to drive them out with a whip.

The Buddhist priest prescribes tea made from the ashes of burnt incense, or he writes such a word as " arsenic" on a puffed cake, which he puts into boiling water and, when cool, gives it to the patient. Failing other remedies, he sends the afflicted to the nearest temple, where he must remain for some time under the table of an idol to escape the attacks of the designing devils.

The sorcerer takes three bamboo sticks about three feet in length, ties red cloth around one end of each, and charms the fever demons away from those possessed. Or he makes a figure like a man out of rice-straw, into which he invites the wicked spirits to enter, and having carried the straw man some distance from the house, he presents to the spirits an offering of mock-money, pork, duck eggs, rice, and vegetables. As effective a remedy as any other used by the sorcerer is the tying of seven hairs plucked out of a black dog around the hand of the fever patient.

The native doctor will talk wisely about the disagreement between the two principles in nature, which nothing but his medicines will overcome. The chief ingredients of his remedies are seeds of plantain, prepared orange-peel, licorice root, root of white peony, *Pterocarpus flavus*, *Sida*, *Panax* (ginseng), *Levisticum*, *Bupleurum*, *Scutellaria*, *Clematis libanotis*, and quince.

I have no more faith in the prescriptions of the native doctors than I have in those of the priests or sorcerers. Indeed, I have known doctors to write out prescriptions for their patients and collect their fees, but for their own use they kept carefully folded in paper from five to twenty grains of quinine.

To this dreaded disease foreigners give such names as sun-pain, intermittent fever, chills and fever, fever and ague, dumb ague, jungle fever, African fever, and I have heard it called Tamsui fever. Its real cause, no doubt, is malarial poison generated by the decomposing of organic matter, and its intensity depends on the constitution, climate, and surroundings of the sufferer. I spent weeks with the savages in the mountains near Mount Sylvia, and found them generally healthy. Pe-po-hoan farmers moved into that neighborhood and began to build their huts and cultivate the land. Within one week the entire settlement was prostrated with fever in its most intense form, and the sufferings of those poor savages were sad to see. Another instance of the poison being generated by the upturning of the decomposed matter in the soil occurred in connection with the building of the Girls' School at Tamsui, where, after digging down several feet for the foundation, the workmen suffered more or less until the building was finished. A singular thing is that one limb or one hand or one side may be affected and may go through all the stages, and the other parts of the body remain as before.

Several methods of treatment are followed. A first attack, in a good constitution, may be overcome by anything that will produce a good sweat; but when the system is saturated with the poison, long-continued and persistent treatment is required. Lemons cut in slices and boiled till all the juice is extracted make not only a refreshing drink, but, if used liberally, an unquestionably good medicine during a fever attack. I have used *Podophyllum* and *Taraxacum* in pill form at first, then frequent doses of quinine, followed, if necessary, by perchlorate of iron. A liquid diet, exercise, and fresh air are always insisted on. My prayer is that some discovery may be made that will do in the case of malaria what vaccination does in the case of smallpox, and that by killing or eradicating this devouring poison life in tropical lands may be made less cruel alike for native and foreigner.

It is not an uncommon thing in Formosa to find half the inhabitants of a town prostrated by malarial fever at once. I have seen households of twenty or thirty with not one able to do any work. In such circumstances the native preachers, living in the midst of the sufferers and knowing their life, are able, by means of foreign medicine, in the use of which they have been trained, to do incalculable service to afflicted humanity, and so to commend the gospel of their Master, who " healed many who were sick of divers diseases."

Dentistry should be mentioned, along with the treatment of fever, as a most important department of medical missionary work in Formosa. Toothache, resulting from severe malaria and from betel-nut chewing, cigar-smoking, and other filthy habits, is the abiding torment of tens of thousands of both Chinese and aborigines. There are numberless superstitions cherished by the people regarding the growth, defects, and treatment of the teeth; and the ways by which they attempt to drive out the black-headed worm, believed to be gnawing inside and causing toothache, are, some of them, amusing, some disgusting, and some, indeed, ingenious.

The methods by which the natives extract teeth are both crude and cruel. Sometimes the offending tooth is pulled with a strong string, or pried out with the blade of a pair of scissors. The traveling doctor uses a pair of pincers or small tongs. It is not to be wondered at that the people all dread the operation, as jaw-breaking, excessive hemorrhage, fainting, and even death frequently result from the barbarous treatment.

My first attempt to extract a tooth was in 1873. On leaving Tek-chham with the students one day we were followed by a dozen soldiers who had been sent to watch our movements. One of their number was suffering intense pain from a decayed tooth; he said, "There is a worm in it." I had no forceps, but after examining it I got a piece of hard wood, shaped it as desired, and with it removed the tooth. It was primitive dentistry, to be sure, but the tooth was out, and the poor soldier wept for joy and was most profuse in his gratitude. Years after, when a number of soldiers were reviling the "barbarian missionary," a tall officer stepped forward and reproved them, saying that I was the teacher who relieved him of the aching tooth.

My first dental instruments were very rude, having been hammered out by a native blacksmith according to my directions. Now I have the very best instruments made in New York. The lance is rarely used, and the key, hook, punch, or screw, never. A chair is not needed, and with a hundred other sufferers waiting their turn any elaborate preparations would be a waste of time. The Chinese have considerable nerve, and endure the pain of an operation wonderfully well.

Our usual custom in touring through the country is to take our stand in an open space, often on the stone steps of a temple, and, after singing a hymn or two, proceed to extract teeth, and then preach the message of the gospel. The sufferer usually stands while the operation is being performed, and the tooth, when removed, is laid on his hand. To keep the tooth would be to awaken suspicions regarding us in the Chinese mind. Several of the students are experts with the forceps, and we have frequently extracted a hundred teeth in less than an hour. I have myself, since 1873, extracted over twenty-one thousand, and the students and preachers have extracted nearly half that number. The people now know that they do not need to suffer the excruciating pain of toothache, and that they need not run any risk in obtaining relief. The priests and other enemies of the mission may persuade people that fever and other diseases have been cured, not by our medicines, but by the intervention of the gods; but the relief from toothache is too unmistakable, and because of this tooth-extracting has been more than anything else effective in breaking down prejudice and opposition.

Patients are treated in all the cities and villages where we may happen to be. Medicines are given, and treatment prescribed for them in their homes. The headquarters of this department, however, like those of all others, are at Tamsui. There is the hospital building, with its wards and necessary equipment. At first I had only one room, but in 1880 a commodious building for hospital purposes was erected at a cost of three thousand dollars, the gift of Mrs. MacKay, of Detroit, in memory of her husband, Captain MacKay, and is now known as the "MacKay Hospital." This has been a great blessing to thousands of people. Referring to the report for 1894, during which time I have been on furlough in Canada, I find that thirty-one hundred and fifty-six new patients and seventy-five hundred and eighty old patients were treated in the year.

Now it is not claimed that all treated were cured, or that all cured became Christians. Large numbers were cured during these twenty-three years, many more were relieved, and the services rendered made them much more kindly disposed toward the mission. Many became converts themselves, and their example told with their relatives and friends. The reflex influence of all this medical work cannot be estimated. The direct results in the conversion of patients cannot be told. We could tell of many interesting cases. Bun Hien, a man of fifty-six years, almost blind, formerly a ringleader of bad characters, was cured of his blindness and converted to God, bringing his children and grandchildren with him. A young woman who took opium to commit suicide was treated, and recovered; and as a result her father-in-law, sixty-two years of age, came to the chapel and believed the gospel, living consistently on to the close of his life. A man named Chiu was badly burned, and a native preacher dressed his wounds successfully, so that they were healed; and Chiu came to the chapel, bringing his seven children, and they all became Christians. But space would fail to tell of Chhi Hok, of Lim O, a gong-beater, of Kho Ban, whose son was healed after being gored by a water-buffalo, of Chhi, a fever patient, of Ku, who was bit by a dog, and Ong, an opium-smoker, of a Confucianist teacher who was a victim of "furious insanity"—space would fail to tell of these and of hundreds of others who by being healed of physical infirmities were led to a knowledge of the Saviour who heals the great trouble of the soul. Many of them were adversaries of the truth, and were brought to consult the foreigner only as a last resort; but out of enemies they became friends. Some of them are now in the presence of their Lord; others are constant in his service in the church on earth.

CHAPTER XXXIV

FOREIGNERS AND THE MISSION

Reported hostility—Sympathetic relations in Formosa—Experiences with
foreigners—Foreign kindness to native preachers—"Barbarian"
rarely heard—Address and presentation from foreign community

IT is a common complaint on the part of missionaries that
foreigners, whether merchants residing in the country or
travelers passing through it, are either indifferent or hostile to
Christian missions. One reads of the haughty contempt,
sometimes ill concealed, of the foreign community for missionaries and their work. One hears of a chasm deep and wide
between the missionaries and the other foreigners in the cities
and port towns of China and Japan. We are told by merchants, officials, and travelers that the missionaries are weak,
narrow-minded, entirely without influence, and that their work
is a failure or a fraud. Missionaries, on the other hand, hint
that the foreign merchants are worldly, the military and naval
officers and men loose livers, the consuls unsympathetic and
unspiritual, and the average traveler a one-eyed, prejudiced,
vagabond globe-trotter, whose presence in the vicinity of a
mission is a distinct calamity.

It is not for me to speak of things as they exist in other
mission fields, although I should be sorry to think of what one
hears regarding the relations of foreigners to mission work as
having any very substantial basis in fact. There may be a
chasm such as has been referred to, and, if so, it has probably

been dug by both parties. But speaking of Formosa, and looking back over the entire history of our mission there, I am bound to say that the most cordial relations have ever existed between the workers in the mission and the resident or transient foreign community. Again and again in the preceding chapters reference has been made to kindnesses shown and services rendered by European and American merchants, and by consuls, commissioners of customs, and physicians. The representatives of the great foreign firms of Tait & Co., Boyd & Co., Douglas, La Praik & Co., as well as others in the employ of the Chinese, have always taken a genuine interest in our work. Consuls and commissioners of customs like Frater, Allen, Hosie, Ayrton, Morse, Hall, Bourne, and Hobson have been my personal friends, and I recall their names with gratitude. More than one trip into savage territory was relieved by the company of one or another of those gentlemen.

Hobson, when commissioner of customs, went with me once, and neither of us will forget our experiences in the mountains. Shivering with cold, we spent the greater part of one day in a hut filled with smoke from the wet firewood, and at night poor Hobson was kept awake, partly, perhaps, by the savage atmosphere of the place, and partly by the noise of a dry deerskin in which I had wrapped myself, and which at every movement cracked like the going off of a pistol. I remember, too, one hot evening when Hobson and Dr. Ringer walked from Tamsui to Pat-li-hun to share with me such a dinner as I had not seen before in a twelvemonth.

Medical men have invariably manifested a desire to assist our work, and have rendered valuable services in many ways. Dr. Ringer not only waited upon me in times of serious illness, but during his residence at the port of Tamsui rendered gratuitous service to the mission, having our hospital under his charge.

Scientists from various countries have visited us at Tamsui, and an hour or two in my museum secured for the mission their sympathy and interest. They saw there what would take them years to discover for themselves, and not infrequently have they been made friends of foreign missions by accompanying us on a tour of the chapels.

One Sabbath in 1873, when at Go-ko-khi, I was surprised by the sudden appearance of a tall stranger, who saluted me by name with an accent that suggested the Stars and Stripes. He was J. B. Steere, an American scientist, now professor in the University of Ann Arbor, Michigan, who was making a tour through the tropics, collecting specimens for the museum of his college. He became our guest at Tamsui, and for a month we had delightful intercourse together. He took great interest in my students, and once during my absence, when he was left in full possession for several days, he undertook to teach the students two tunes. He did not know the language, but he could use a hymn-book in the romanized colloquial. He put the notes of the tunes on the blackboard and drilled the students in singing them, and on my return I was greeted with the One Hundredth and the One Hundred and Twenty-first psalms, sung to tunes that are still favorites, and are called the "botanist's tunes" to this day by those who were in the class then.

So I might go on to tell of ship-captains, officers, and engineers who have in different ways rendered aid to our work in Formosa. High and low have expressed their sympathy, and the foreign residents have gone out of their way to show kindness to the native preachers and converts. British Ambassador O'Connor and British Admiral Salmon visited Oxford College, as did also the commander of a British man-of-war, and, addressing the students, myself interpreting, spoke in the kindliest terms of greeting and good will. I have found foreigners of all nationalities ready to acknowledge their indebtedness to Christianity, and willing to help the mission and

missionaries. The fact that they were not themselves missionaries gave peculiar emphasis to their words, not only in Europe
and America, but also in heathen communities. In return the
students and converts have been taught to treat with respect
and honor all foreigners, and the contemptuous epithet "barbarian," so often cast at foreigners twenty years ago, is rarely
heard in North Formosa to-day.

That the relations existing between the mission and the foreign community are sympathetic and cordial is testified to by
the address, engrossed on silk, and accompanied by a magnificent telescope, presented to me on the eve of my departure
for Canada in 1893. I value this address, even though it
does me honor overmuch, and I have consented to its repro-
duction here because it expresses in unmistakable terms the
interest of the entire foreign population in the work into which
I have put my life.

*"To Rev. G. L. MacKay, D.D., on the eve of his departure from
Formosa.*

"TAMSUI, 17th August, 1893.

"DR. MACKAY: We here assembled felt that we could not
let you depart without wishing you God-speed and a pleasant
voyage home, and expressing our regard for you, and our
estimation of the great work you have so nobly undertaken in
Formosa, and carried on so successfully during the past twenty
years.

"We have not always given expression to our thought, but
we have highly appreciated your great success, and the marvelous progress you have, by God's help, been able to make
in getting at the hearts of the Chinese people around us; a
success which, we think, is without parallel in the history of
Christian missions in China.

"You cannot but regard with much thankfulness and satisfaction the great and noble work you have been engaged upon,

and to which you have devoted your life these many years.
In material blessings alone, resulting from your labors, resides
sufficient cause to make any man proud and happy; and if
there were nothing else to show than the good feelings between natives and foreigners, due to your teaching, that alone
would be sufficient cause for triumph. Those of us who
remember Formosa as it was at the time of your arrival recognize a great alteration for the better in the demeanor of the
natives generally; and we ascribe the improvement in a great
measure to you. Suspicion has given place to confidence, and
the most timid never dream of fearing molestation, let them
roam the country where they will. Who with time to ramble
can forget the neat and wholesome-looking mission chapels
scattered broadcast through the land ? And who can fail to
remember the bright and cheerful welcome received at such
spots as Sin-tiam, when on pleasure bent amid the glorious
scenery of Formosa the Beautiful; the kindly reception and
smiling welcome, the glad readiness to anticipate one's wants,
the keen desire to make our stay at the mission station comfortable, and to give us a bright memory to look back on?
All this is the outcome of your teaching and your influence.

" Besides the admiration and respect we feel for your work,
and the gratitude for the benefit we derive from the good feeling between Chinese and foreigners, which you have done so
much to develop, we also feel that we have even, as a community, a special relationship with Kai Bok-su. You have
been a standing symbol and example to us of faith in the
Unseen, especially at those times when one or another has
passed from among us and from the visible world. You have
been ever ready to sympathize with us and help us, and to
remind us of the great realities, sharing with us, as only such
a man as yourself can, in all our last offices for those who have
gone from us. Had we marriage or other occasions for joy
among us, we feel that you would then equally sympathize

with us and help us. Therefore, individually and as a community, we wish to express our appreciation and our gratitude.

"It only remains to ask you, Dr. MacKay, to accept from the foreign community of North Formosa, and the captains, officers, and engineers of the visiting steamers, a feeble token of our esteem. If our offering should serve to bring nearer to your vision the 'glory which the heavens nightly declare,' and give you delight and relaxation in the bringing, we shall all rejoice.

" L. te Breton,	James Cromarty,
B. P. White,	Isaac Roberts,
Charles Pye,	J. D. Edwards,
Alfred G. Robson,	V. Larsen,
J. R. Wilson,	J. Remusat,
R. Mussen,	H. B. Morse,
Arnold C. Clarke,	W. S. Ayrton,
Harrison W. Lee,	O. E. Bailey,
G. Ball,	G. M. Hinrichs,
F. W. E. Dulberg,	G. Schneider,
William Gauld,	G. Nepean,
William Davis,	W. Cloney,
Fred B. Marshall,	A. F. Gardiner,
F. M. Tait,	A. Butler,
R. H. Obiy,	P. W. Petersen,
M. Jenssen,	A. Schwarzer,
B. C. Matheson,	J. S. Roach,
F. Fenwick,	William Roberts,
E. A. Donaldson,	F. F. Andrew,
Paul Schabert,	E. Hansen,
J. Merlees,	F. Ashton,

F. C. Angear."

CHAPTER XXXV

WITH THE ENGLISH PRESBYTERIANS

North and South—Mutual respect—Founding of their mission—Staff of workers—Visit of Mr. Campbell—Tour with Mr. Ritchie—Stations and statistics—Medical work—Education—A noble history

ALTHOUGH the island of Formosa is not more than two hundred and fifty miles in length, those living in the south are separated from us in the north as far as if the length of a continent lay between us. There is no direct connection by sea, and the overland route is tedious, difficult, and dangerous. The mission in South Formosa, carried on by the Presbyterian Church of England, although reaching northward to a point not far from the most southerly station supplied by our mission in North Formosa, is still so far away that for all practical purposes we are in different countries. Once in years missionaries from Tamsui and from Tai-wan-fu may meet, but it is only as

" Ships that pass in the night and speak each other in passing."

No two missions could possibly be more friendly; and although we have not touched each other except remotely, and although our methods of work differ very materially, we are "one in hope and doctrine, one in charity." They have a larger foreign staff, while we throw greater emphasis on a native ministry; but God has no fixed method by which his servants must work, and each according to his ability and his

circumstances must serve our common Master. The missionaries in South Formosa are indeed brethren beloved. When I
landed in their midst, a stranger and a novice, those then in the
field gave me the heartiest welcome, initiating me into the
work, and then accompanying me on an exploring expedition
through my own chosen field. The story of their work has
been told by one of their number, the Rev. William Campbell,
F.R.G.S., in his "Missionary Success in Formosa." I have by
me only the two most recent reports submitted to the Synod
of the Presbyterian Church of England, upon which I depend
for extracts and statistics.

The work in South Formosa was begun in 1865 by J. L.
Maxwell, M.D., a devoted Christian physician. Writing of
his service in 1870, the convener of the Foreign Mission Committee under whom he labored said: "It is in some respects
almost romantic in its incidents, and very glorying to God in
the large results of the work as compared with the smallness of
the human agency; for it is principally through one missionary, a noble Christian physician, who went out for us in 1865,
Dr. Maxwell, that the work has been carried on." The
founder of the mission is indeed a noble Christian, and since
his retiral from the field he has continued in the service of
foreign missions, being editor of "Medical Missions," published
in London, England.

When I arrived in 1871, Revs. Hugh Ritchie, William
Campbell, and Dr. Dickson were on the field. The present
staff, according to the report for 1894, includes Rev. William
Campbell (1871), Rev. T. Barclay, M.A. (1874), Rev. Dun-
can Ferguson, M.A. (1889), Peter Anderson, L.R.C.S. and
P.Ed. (1878), W. Murray Cairns, M.B., C.M. (1893), Mr.
George Ede (1883), Miss Annie Butler (1885), Miss Joan
Stuart (1885), Miss Barnett (1888). The report records "the
unexpected removal by death of the Rev. William Thow,
which has left a deep wound in the hearts of all the brethren

and of the entire native church. Mr. Thow was a noble missionary, and had got into remarkable touch with the Chinese Christians, from many of whom the most tender, sympathetic communications have been received." It was my privilege to know Mr. Thow, having met with him on the field, and he deserved the words of appreciation that have been spoken by his fellow-workers and his church. Mr. Ritchie and Dr. Gavin Russel have also been called to rest from their labors in Formosa.

The first missionary to visit me at Tamsui was the Rev. William Campbell, who traveled inland with me, preaching the gospel in the towns and villages. Years afterward he visited me a second time, and made a trip through the Kap-tsu-lan plain. He was a delightful companion. One evening at Kelung we agreed to spend ten days without speaking English, beginning on the following morning. We were to set out on a tour in the morning, and before daybreak the call to rise was heard: "Liong tsong khi lai." We were soon making our way along winding paths, talking all the time, but never using an English word. At last my friend turned to me and said, "MacKay, this jabbering in Chinese is ridiculous, and two Scotchmen should have more sense; let us return to our mother tongue."

In 1875 the Rev. Hugh Ritchie came up to Tamsui, and, accompanied by nine of our preachers, I set out with him on a trip that lasted seventy days. We inspected all our work in the north, visiting all our stations, and then journeyed southward, over mountains, across sands, through forest jungle and rocky gorge, until we reached the most northerly stations in the South Formosa mission. We went from station to station, inspecting their entire work. Then we met with the missionaries and native workers in a conference of preachers and office-bearers at Tai-wan-fu, where for several days we took sweet counsel together, myself and the preachers from the north being privileged to take part in the discussions along with the southern brethren. I have visited South Formosa several times since then, and have lost none of my affection for the mission whose missionaries have labored so devotedly and whose converts impress a stranger as being earnest and sincere.

At the close of 1894 the South Formosa mission reported twenty organized congregations, eighteen not yet organized, with twelve hundred and forty-six members on the communion-roll. The work was greatly interfered with by the sickness of several of the most efficient and experienced missionaries. Malarial fever is their foe, as it is ours in the north. Their stations are among Chinese, Pe-po-hoan, and Sek-hoan. In the Tai-wan district there is one station among the Chinese and four among the Pe-po-hoan. In the Tong-soa district are eleven among Chinese and one among Hak-ka Chinese. In the Ka-gi district are five among Chinese and four among Pe-po-hoan. In the Chiang-hoa district is one station among Chinese and five among Sek-hoan. On the east coast are three stations among Pe-po-hoan. There are twenty-six native preachers, none of whom have yet been ordained, and eight students studying with a view to the ministry. Cheering items of news are reported from several churches, and the report says that, "at a general conference of preachers and office-bearers to be held in February, it seemed all but certain some decisions would be reached by the native brethren which would lead to their assuming a greater amount of responsibility in the management of the church's affairs. The brethren are of opinion that the day is not very distant when they will be able to go forward to the ordination of one or two native pastors, which would indeed be a red-letter day in the Formosa mission."

Of the influence of medical work in their mission the Rev. William Campbell writes: "Work in our hospital reaches two classes, the out-patients and those, every Tuesday and Friday, who have medicines dispensed to them. Thus every year a wide door and effectual is opened for seeking to influence thousands of persons—coming, moreover, not from one town or village, but from a region covering many hundreds of square miles." A deeply interesting work for the blind was initiated by Mr. Campbell, and is contributing its quota to the success of the mission, being conducted with every token of blessing.

The missionaries—some of them, at least—are convinced of the importance of throwing more responsibility on the native preachers and teachers, and hence of developing native talent by thorough education. Mr. Campbell writes: " It is a source of much regret to us that the work in our college does not develop as we wish to see, or as the necessities of our field now urgently require. With very little effort about twenty students could be accommodated in the present college buildings; and, taking the usual percentage of loss into account, this number ought to be always at work if we are to make anything like healthful and necessary progress. During 1892 we had the names of only eight regular students on our roll; one a native of Chin-chew, two Hak-ka Chinese, and five children of Pe-po-hoan parents. There is obviously much need for full and sympathetic inquiry into the causes which for years past have been preventing a larger number of Chinese youths from accepting our offers to bring them within reach of college instruction. Chiefly on account of having no Christian teachers, our congregational schools have been few indeed, and it is well known to friends at home that, for want of proper accommoda-dation, Mr. Ede's middle school had to be given up in the autumn of 1890. The few years' work of this latter institution convinced us all of its exceeding importance and value at the present stage of our mission. It was only necessary that it should have gone on a number of years longer in order to furnish young men for the college, for managing local schools, the hospital, and almost any other department of Christian effort."

The mission in the south was founded under trying conditions, but it has done a great work and has a noble history. There are worthy names on its roll of service. It has been a light in a dark place, a witness for God and truth, a bringer of good tidings to thousands. The methods adopted differ from ours, but the spirit is the spirit of the gospel of Jesus, and I rejoice with the brethren there in every success achieved, and hail with supreme delight any "forward movement" for the ingathering of souls and the upbuilding of the City of God in South Formosa.

CHAPTER XXXVI

RETROSPECT AND PROSPECT

Survey—Foreign medical assistants—Rev. J. B. Fraser—Rev. K. F. Junor
—Rev. John Jamieson—Rev. Wm. Gauld—Mr. Gauld and the native
preachers—Statistics for 1894—Mr. Gauld's report—Chapels—Native
preachers—Self-support—The changed relations—" Eben-ezer "

STANDING on the prominence of the present, one is disposed to look backward over the past and forward into the future. Twenty-four years ago, in the autumn of 1871, I first left my native land, young and inexperienced, the first foreign missionary sent out by my church. I went out not knowing whither, for my field of labor had not been chosen. But the God who "shapes our ends" led the way, and early in 1872, lifting my eyes to the green-clad mountains that stand round about Tamsui, clearer than human voice ever spoke to the outward ear, I heard the voice of God whisper to my listening spirit, " This is the land." In the autumn of 1881, at the close of my first furlough, I set out a second time, not alone now, and not unknowing, for Formosa, the land of my labors, the native home of my wife, had been written upon my heart. And now for the third time, in the autumn of 1895, at the close of my second furlough, I am setting out again, this time with my wife and our three children, and Koa Kau, my Chinese student-companion. Farewells have all been said, and trusting the guidance of Him who knows the way and never leads astray, we go out in the glad confidence that in Formosa we have work to be done and a witness to be borne for Jesus our Saviour and King.

There are many things about missionary experiences in North Formosa that are still untold. Looking back over the years, I see one helper after another entering into our life and taking part with us in our work. Mention has already been made of Dr. Ringer, the resident physician to the foreign community, who from the beginning until 1880 gave such valuable service in connection with the hospital and medical work, taking upon himself the chief responsibility of that department. Dr. Johansen followed him, and for six years, until 1886, during which there were trying and troublous times, he laid the mission under obligation. Then came Dr. Rennie, and from 1886 till 1892 he was chief officer of the hospital and medical work. Since then Dr. F. C. Angear has had charge and oversight of this important department, and, like his predecessors, has given generously of his time and rendered most efficient service to the mission.

In 1875 we were joined by the Rev. J. B. Fraser, M.D., and wife. Dr. Fraser, son of the late Rev. W. Fraser, D.D., for many years one of the clerks of the General Assembly of the Presbyterian Church in Canada, had two years' experience in medical practice, and, after graduating in theology, was ordained and designated by the Presbytery of Toronto in September, 1874, and sent out by the Foreign Mission Committee to have charge more especially of the medical work. After a faithful service of nearly three years his home was broken up by the death of his wife, in October, 1877, and he was compelled to return to Canada with his children. He is now minister in Leith, Ontario, and is an active and useful member of the Foreign Mission Committee.

The year following, in the summer of 1878, the Rev. Kenneth F. Junor arrived at Tamsui, having been commissioned by the Canadian church, and he continued in the service until

1882. For a considerable part of the time, during my first furlough in 1880–81, he was the only foreign missionary in the field, and, with the native preachers, had oversight of the entire mission, which at that date had twenty chapels, each with a native preacher, and in all over three hundred members in full communion with the church. Mr. Junor's health broke down, and in November, 1882, he returned to Canada. He is now engaged in important city mission work in New York.

In 1883 the Rev. John Jamieson and his wife arrived and entered upon their work, which was carried on against great odds until 1891, when Mr. Jamieson, after repeated and prolonged periods of physical weakness, was called away by death, and his wife returned to Canada.

In May, 1892, the Rev. William Gauld, having completed his college training, was appointed to Formosa by the Foreign Mission Committee, and in September of the same year he and Mrs. Gauld arrived in Tamsui. They were most heartily welcomed by the workers in the field, and with commendable ability and zeal began the study of the language, people, and methods of work. During my present visit to Canada Mr. Gauld has been the only foreign missionary in the mission, and through all the times of disturbance and unrest consequent upon the recent war and the long-continued resistance of the islanders to Japanese rule, the affairs of the mission have been managed with great discretion and success. The Foreign Mission Committee was enabled to report that " Mr. Gauld has entered upon the work in Formosa with such sympathy and judgment as encourages us to expect gratifying results. The committee was somewhat alarmed lest Dr. MacKay's return home so soon after Mr. Gauld's arrival would lay upon him a responsibility he might not be able to bear. These fears have been disappointed."

A Hoa, Sun-a, and Thien Leng were associated with Mr. Gauld in conducting the mission, and their experience and judgment were to be depended upon. Of A Hoa Mr. Gauld wrote at the close of 1893: "Though constantly in consultation, there has never been the slightest approach to friction between us, and the longer and better I know him the more I can love him, trust in his honesty, and respect his judgment. In cases of difficulty that have arisen he has invariably been deputed to visit the locality in which the disturbance took place. On his return his smiling face, no less than his words, invariably announced his success in restoring harmony. Yet this man receives only $20 (silver) or $11.43 (gold) per month from the mission for his services."

In the report submitted to the General Assembly of 1895 the statistics of the mission showed: 2 foreign ordained missionaries; 2 native ordained missionaries; 60 unordained native preachers; 24 native Bible-women; 1738 native communicants (male 1027, female 711) in good and regular standing in the church; 2633 baptized members; 60 dispensaries at chapels; 10,736 treatments at the hospital; $2375.74 contributed by natives for mission purposes; $264.10 contributed by natives for the hospital; $269 contributed by foreign community for the hospital.

In his report for the same year Mr. Gauld says: "Oxford College is still closed, pending Dr. MacKay's return. It has been one of the most useful institutions in connection with the mission, and we doubt not will continue to exercise its influence for good in days to come.

"During 1894 the Girls' School was kept open for a short time. After the commencement of the war it was deemed unwise to keep the girls so far away from their parents, and accordingly they were sent home.

"The longer our experience the more do we value the native ministry as an important factor of the work. The majority of our native agents are doing excellent work, and the two native ordained pastors are superior men. When I last visited Pastor

Tan He's congregation at Sin-tiam—a country town, or rather village—worship was held on Saturday evening, when about seventy were present. On the Lord's day there were present in the morning about one hundred and seventy, in the afternoon about one hundred and twenty, and in the evening about seventy. Of course many of the country-people returned to their homes, not remaining for the evening service. What a delight to address such attentive audiences! At week-night services, besides singing and prayer, an attempt is made to teach the people to read. In this young church there is certainly a variety of gifts. To know Tan He is to love him. He is not so good a superintendent as Pastor Giam Chheng Hoa, but in his own sphere is a most useful man, cheerful, orderly, cleanly, and true, a faithful pastor, a good preacher, a sympathizing friend. He has now for many years been exercising a Christian influence upon his countrymen, and still continues, by God's grace, the same blessed work. Pastor Giam Chheng Hoa is a remarkable man. Well taught in the doctrines of the gospel, he preaches them with faithfulness and power. By nature he has very high executive ability, which has been improved by twenty years of experience. He knows his own people, from the governor of the island to the ragged opium-smoking beggar, and has influence with them all. His services in the mission are invaluable, and we trust we shall be permitted for many years to enjoy the benefits of his influence and counsel. Other preachers and Bible-women are doing their work in their own way, and to good purpose. We long for the time when we shall have a native church supporting a native ministry without foreign aid, and also helping the needy in other parts of this poor sin-cursed world. It is a cause for thankfulness that, while the death-rate here was very high during the past year, not one of our mission staff, foreign or native, was called away from the work in which all are so much needed.

"We long for a rapid increase of true believers, and we desire, even more earnestly, that those received into the church may be true to Christ, steadfast in the faith, showing clearly by their lives that they daily live with him."

In preceding chapters reference has been made to many points where mission work is being carried on and where chapels have been erected. The location of each chapel is indicated on one of the maps, which gives the names of the sixty points occupied by the mission. The complete list is as follows:

1. Tam-sui.	21. Ta-ma-ian.	41. Poeh-oug-sia.
2. Pat-li-hun.	22. Hoan-sia-thau.	42. Aug-chha-na.
3. Go-ko-khi.	23. Ki-lip-pan.	43. Thiau-sang-pi.
4. Chiu-nih.	24. Ka-le-oan.	44. Teng-phoa-po-o.
5. Lun-a-teng.	25. Pho-lo-sin-a-oan.	45. Tang-koe-soa.
6. Toa-tiu-tia.	26. Lau-lau-a.	46. Teng-siang-khoe.
7. Bang-kah.	27. Lam-hong-o.	47. He-is-a.
8. Sin-tsng.	28. Sai-tham-toe.	48. Pak-tau.
9. Sia-au.	29. Chin-tsu-li-kan.	49. Pat-chiau-ua.
10. Sa-kak-eng.	30. Pi-thau.	50. Pang-kio.
11. Tho-a-hng.	31. Ta-na-bi.	51. Toa-kho-ham.
12. Ang-mng-kang.	32. Sau-hut.	52. Pi-teng.
13. Tek-chham.	33. Tang-mng-thun	53. Lam-kham.
14. Tiong-kang.	34. Sin-a-han.	54. Tiong-lek.
15. Au-lang.	35. Bu-loan.	55. Toa-o-khau.
16. Sin-tiam.	36. Ki-bu-lan.	56. Pak-mng-khau.
17. Sek-khau.	37. Ki-lip-tan.	57. Gek-bai.
18. Tsui-tng-kha.	38. Toa-tek-ui.	58. Tho-gu.
19. Koe-lang.	39. Thau-sia.	59. Sin-kang.
20. Sin-sia.	40. Sa-kiat-a-koe.	60. Ba-nih.

At each of these chapels a native preacher is stationed, and in many cases there is associated with the preacher a native trained Bible-woman. The students of Oxford College give valuable services, assisting the preachers at various stations, preaching the gospel, and teaching the people from house to house. Irregular and occasional services are held at many points where there is no chapel or organized congregation. In this way the mission is gradually extending, and its growth is substantial and healthy.

Several of the preachers are engaged in the superintendence of the mission and in the educational work at Tamsui. The following native preachers, trained and equipped for their work, are in charge of chapels:

1. Tan He.	21. Tan Kui.	41. Tsui Eng.
2. Tan Leng.	22. Eng Jong.	42. Chheng He.
3. Go Ek Ju.	23. Ang An.	43. Chhun Bok.
4. Tan Theng.	24. Thong Su.	44. Tiu Thiam.
5. Chhoa Seng.	25. Jim Sui.	45. Bio Sien.
6. Lim Giet.	26. A Hai.	46. Eng Seng.
7. Tsun Sim.	27. Pat Po.	47. Chhong Lim.
8. Siau Tien.	28. Jit Sin.	48. Teng Chiu.
9. Li Kui.	29. Chin Giok.	49. Beng Tsu.
10. Lau Chheng.	30. Ki Siong.	50. Tek Beng.
11. Tan Ho.	31. Pa Kin.	51. Tu Iau.
12. Tan Ban.	32. Hok Eng.	52. Li Iau.
13. Keh Tsu.	33. In Lien.	53. Tsan Un.
14. Tan Eng.	34. Hong Lien.	54. Tan Sam.
15. Eng Goan.	35. Kai Loah.	55. Li Sun.
16. Tan Siah.	36. Sam Ki.	56. Eng Chhung.
17. A Lok.	37. Keng Tien.	57. Tsui Seng.
18. Iap Tsun.	38. A Seng.	58. Kho Goan.
19. Thien Sang.	39. Gong A.	59. Lim Ban.
20. Lau Tsai.	40. Tong San.	60. Bun Seng.

The all-important question of self-support is constantly kept before our minds, and the native Christians in North Formosa are taught to give of their means for the maintenance of ordinances and for the extension of the church. A self-supporting mission is our ideal. But what is meant by self-support? What I understand by a self-supporting mission is one in which all the work is carried on and all the agents supported by those in the mission itself. The church in North Formosa will be self-supporting when its college, school, hospital, chapels, and all other departments, with all laborers, whether native or foreign, will be supported by the members and adherents of the native church. We are as yet a long way from that position, but we are on the way, and are moving in that direction. Four of our congregations are now entirely self-supporting; and last year the contributions from the natives themselves amounted to $2639.84. There is a great work to be done, not in Formosa alone, or China, but throughout the entire foreign mission field, before help from the churches in Europe and America can be dispensed with. The statistics of native contributions call for patience on the part of ministers and churches in the home field. It is too much to expect the heathen, either at home or abroad, to pay for his own conversion. Converts must be taught self-reliance and self-denial, but it sometimes happens in heathen countries that to accept Christianity is to invite oppression, boycotting, and robbery. In many native congregations there is not one member who, even according to native standards, has " a competent portion of the good things of this life." But out of their poverty I have seen them give willingly for the support of gospel ordinances.

Another problem facing the mission in North Formosa is the coming of the Japanese. We have no fear. The King of kings is greater than emperor or mikado. He will rule and overrule all things. We do not speculate. We do not prearrange. The Japanese question must be faced, as all others have been faced, with plans flexible enough to suit the changed circumstances, and faith strong enough to hear the voice of God across the storm. There will be difficulties, dangers, and trials before things are adjusted, but Formosa is given to Jesus, and the purposes of God shall be fulfilled.

Why should we fear? Surely we can say, " Hitherto hath the Lord helped us." I look back to the first days, and recall the early persecutions and perils, of which the reader will never know. I remember the proclamations issued and posted up on trees and temples, charging me with unimaginable crimes, and forbidding the people to hold converse with me. In 1879 I was burned in effigy at an idolatrous feast. Again and again have I been threatened, insulted, and mobbed. But "the things which happened unto me have fallen out rather unto the furtherance of the gospel," and now the church of Jesus Christ is a real factor and a positive power in the moral and spiritual life of North Formosa.

After what has been told, will it be said that missions are a failure? With more than two thousand confessed followers of Jesus Christ now in the churches of North Formosa, who were born, most of them, in the darkness of heathenism, and with the social and moral life of the people impregnated with Christian ideas, am I to be told by some unread and untraveled critic that mission money is wasted, that missionary success is mere sentiment, and that converts do not stand? I profess to know something about foreign mission work, having studied it at first-hand on the ground, and having examined it at the distance of half the globe's circumference. I profess to know something of the character of the Chinese, heathen and Christian, and something of men in other lands than China. And I am prepared to affirm that for integrity and endurance, for unswerving loyalty to Christ, and untiring fidelity in his service, there are to-day in the mission churches of North Formosa hundreds who would do credit to any community or to any congregation in Christendom. I have seen them under fire, and know what they can face. I have looked when the fight was over, and know that it was good. I have watched them as they lay down to die, and calmly, triumphantly, as any soldier-saint or martyr-hero, they "burned upward each to his point of bliss." Tell me not that they will fall away. Four hundred of them have been counted worthy and have entered into His presence, the first-fruits of the harvests now ripening in the white fields of North Formosa.

But the half has not been told.   These chapters are but a fragment.   Not to-day or to-morrow can the story be written. The real story is not finished; it has only begun.   There are chapters to be added from the yet unread pages of the book of God.   Formosa is rooted in God's purpose as surely as Orion or the Pleiades.   That purpose " will ripen fast, unfolding every hour."   To help on its fulfilment this snatch from the history of the past is broken off and sent out to the churches at home, while we go out again to far Formosa, stretching forward to the things which are before.   We are not afraid.   Our confidence is in the eternal God.   Oh, may Jesus, our exalted Redeemer-King, keep us all, and all his church, here and yonder, true and faithful till he come.   May we live in the light of certain victory.   The kingdom of the world shall yet become the kingdom of our Lord and of his Christ.   The isles shall wait for his law.

INDEX

Aberdeen (Scotland), Free Church College at, 21.

Aboriginal tradition, 94.

Aborigines, Chinese contempt for, 102; conquered at Formosa, 205; and the dominant race, 248; savage, 251.

Address to author from foreign community at Tamsui, 321.

Agincourt Island, 184.

Agricultural course, Tamsui mission, the, 209.

Among the Chinese, 101.

Ancestors, worship of, 131, 259.

Angear, Dr. F. C., 331.

Animal life of Formosa, 76.

Asiatic cholera, 43; native treatment of, 310.

Author, the, 3; his parentage, 14; home life at Zorra, Canada, 15; Christian upbringing, 16; early drawn to mission work, 16; preparatory studies at Toronto, 18; graduation, and first missionary duties, 19; theological studies at Edinburgh, 20; great Scottish preachers, 21; called to work in foreign fields, 23; tour among the Canadian churches, 24; ordination, 26; departure for " Far Formosa," 27; crossing the Pacific, 29; at Yokohama, 30; masters eight tones of Formosan dialect, 31; takes passage for Tamsui, 32; arrival at scene of labors, 33; spying out the land, 34; experience of Formosan inns, 35; visits

English Presbyterian Mission at Toa-sia, 36; moves into his home at Tamsui, 38; first attack of fever, 44; difficulties in acquiring the language, 136; acquires facility in spoken dialect from herdboys, 137; tour with A Hoa, 145; records of missionary tours, 174; experiences during the French blockade, 189; suffers from acute meningitis, 195; missionary labors among the Pe-po-hoan, 217; makes a trip down the east coast, 226; threatened by savages, 240; visits the Lam-si-hoan, 241; departure on a visit to Canada (1893), 170, 321; address and presentation of foreign community to, 321; retrospect and prospect of author's work, 330; persecutions and perils things of the past, 337.

Baber, E. C., British consul at Tamsui, tour with, 262.

" Bamboo," the, punishment of, 107.

Banditti, subduing, 160.

Bang-kah, 45; population of, 113; how taken, 164; hatred to foreigners at, 164; hostilities to missionaries at, 165; great change of demeanor toward, 170; author honored at, 171.

Baptism of converts, 148.

" Barbarian " as an epithet addressed to Europeans, 136, 146, 238, 301, 321.

341

From Far Formosa

著　　　者	Geo. L. Mackay
發 行 人	魏　德　文
發 行 所	南天書局有限公司
地　　　址	台北市羅斯福路 3 段 283 巷 14 弄 14 號
	☎(02) 2362-0190　Fax:(02) 2362-3834
郵　　　撥	01080538（南天書局帳戶）
網　　　址	http://www.smcbook.com.tw
電子郵件	e-mail:weitw@smcbook.com.tw
國際書號	ISBN 957-638-072-3
版　　　次	2002 年 3 月台一版 3 刷
印 刷 者	國順印刷有限公司